THE LOST TREASURE OF
COCOS ISLAND

BY RALPH HANCOCK:

Puerto Rico: A Success Story
Blondes, Brunettes and Bullets
Laughter Is a Wonderful Thing
The Comemoral
The Forest Lawn Story
Baja California
Douglas Fairbanks: The Fourth Musketeer
Exploring American Neighbors
Fabulous Boulevard
The Magic Land: Mexico
The Rainbow Republics: Central America
Opportunities in Latin America
Our Southern Neighbors
Let's Look at Latin America
America's Southern Neighbors
Mexico and Central America
Caribbean Correspondent
Latin America

BY JULIAN A. WESTON:

The Cactus Eaters

THE
LOST TREASURE
OF
COCOS ISLAND

by
RALPH HANCOCK
and
JULIAN A. WESTON

THOMAS NELSON & SONS
NEW YORK

Edinburgh   Toronto

For all our friends
y amigos Ticos,
adventurers, *aficionados,*
a la isla del Coco.

PREFACE

IN the voluminous true histories and legendary accounts of buried treasures, no other place on earth can match Cocos Island, off the coast of Central America, for romance, adventure and the size of its hoard. It is the one treasure island in which the public has maintained constant interest ever since the first treasure was buried on it. Not a year goes by without a new and "infallible" chart coming to light that shows the hiding place of *the* Cocos Island treasure. Not a year passes without a new treasure-hunting expedition landing on the island. Since the last big treasure was buried there nearly one hundred and forty years ago, more than that number of expeditions have gone to the island to search for it.

Today, for every expedition that is known to visit Cocos, with government approval, at least a dozen go unheralded and unsung. They sneak over to the island, stay a few days or a few weeks searching for treasure, and then they sneak away again. From Europe and America in recent years have come several expeditions richly financed and generously outfitted. Some of these were headed by such names as Sir Malcolm Campbell, Count Felix von Luckner, and others. In between, and frequently at the same time, smaller and more surreptitious expeditions have landed on the island, spent a few days digging and testing their clues, and faded away into the mists that often surround the island.

The most authentic sources place the estimated value of the treasures on Cocos Island at $100,000,000. There are others who say that at least that much money has been spent in attempts to locate the treasure. But it is still there, we think, for the treasure remains undiscovered.

Dozens of stories and articles, both fiction and fact, have been written about the Cocos treasures, their origin and burial, and newspapers have been filled with accounts of expeditions. But no one has attempted to tell the whole story, the true story of Cocos Island. Few have really known it.

What were the facts relating to the burial of the treasures? What is the inside story of the principal expeditions? Have they been legitimate treasure hunts or elaborate stock promotion rackets? Are the treasures still there?

Only two men knew the whole story of Cocos Island and had the skill and objectivity to sift fact from fiction. These two men, both newspaper correspondents long resident in Central America were Julian A. Weston and the undersigned.

I first met Weston in Guatemala or Nicaragua in my early days as a news correspondent covering Central America. By the late 1930's we had become very good friends and collaborators (we were never competitors) on many a news story, and Weston supplied much of the material that went into some of my first short stories about the Latin Americas. I was able to reciprocate to some extent later when I became director of publicity for TACA (*Transportes Aereos Centro-Americanos*, the big jungle-hopping airline that blankets Central America) by providing certain courtesies within the power of my office.

Throughout this period and in the years since I left Central America to devote full time to writing books, we kept up a running interest in Cocos Island and I think it has been generally agreed that no two people in the world knew more than we did about the island and its lore. Indeed, Weston's proximity and access to the island, and his friendship with succeeding political regimes in Costa Rica, gave him many opportunities to collect data, original documents, maps, clippings, letters, photographs, personal narratives, etc., not vouchsafed any other person. I scanned the American newspapers and magazines for articles and stories about Cocos Island and its expeditions. These I clipped and added to Weston's collection.

We frequently discussed the possibilities of putting this vast storehouse of materials to some profitable use and Weston even attempted once to produce a book manuscript. He asked me to help him on this project, but my own career in writing had not then reached the stage where I felt I could devote the necessary time to it.

But my inclinations in the matter underwent considerable change when Weston died without realizing anything much from his long years of interest in the Cocos subject, and when all his material was turned over to me by his heirs, I determined to make it available in *The Lost Treasure of Cocos Island*.

At a special memorial luncheon to Julian Weston held two years ago at the International Luncheon Club of Costa Rica, José Figueres F., President of Costa Rica, suggested that some bay or cove or stream on Cocos Island be given the name of Julian Weston. The suggestion was unanimously accepted by the three hundred people present and the Government engineers immediately set about deciding what physical feature of the island could be given Julian's name. In March of last year the President issued a proclamation naming one of the bays on the north side of the island "Weston Bay." New maps were drawn and these, along with the proclamation, were published in all the Costa Rican newspapers.

This is a fitting memorial to a first-class newspaperman, and though this book is in no sense intended as another

9

monument, certain standards are obligatory. Since Cocos is the treasure island to top all treasure islands, its story should top all treasure stories. How well we have labored toward that goal, only you may judge.

RALPH HANCOCK

Palm Springs, California

ILLUSTRATIONS

FOLLOWING PAGE 128

Cocos Island. The northeast approach.

Wafer Bay.

Chatham Bay.

The sign supposedly made by John Keating in 1846 to indicate the position of the treasure.

August Gissler as he looked when he was Governor of Cocos Island.

"The Bird is Gone"—the sign cut from an old palm on Cocos Island by August Gissler.

The *Veracity* at Puntarenas.

Members of the *Veracity* expedition.

Captured British treasure hunters of the *Queen of Scots* expedition in court at Puntarenas.

Pete Bergmans at Wafer Bay.

President Roosevelt on Cocos Island.

A carved boulder on Cocos Island bearing dates of visits to the island over a hundred years ago.

11

James Forbes of Riverside, California, the promoter of several treasure-hunting expeditions to Cocos Island.

The *Spindrift* in the harbor at Puntarenas.

The yacht *Stranger*.

An old wreck on the beach at Cocos Island.

THE LOST TREASURE OF
COCOS ISLAND

THE LOST TREASURE OF

C O C O S   I S L A N D

1.

THE principal Cocos Island treasure originated in Lima, Peru. That much is known and easily documented. Its size, its approximate value, its physical dimensions are also easily substantiated, for old records exist in Peru, faded and brittle with age but legible and accessible still.

We have seen these records, handled them with reverence because of their age, with amazement because of the facts they disclose: The Lima treasure when it was taken from Peru was variously valued at from 12 to 60 million dollars.

That was nearly 140 years ago. We would not presume to appraise it in today's market, for the gold and silver and jewels that are inventoried would have two values—the modern, highly inflated dollar value of all these items and the esthetic value of fine antiques.

The accumulation of the treasure, the history of its collection and acquisition, are part of the revolutionary history of Peru. But the story of the treasure from the time it was taken from the hands of government agents and church officials and deposited on Cocos Island, 1350 miles away, is devious and occasionally obscure. For obvious reasons, no two accounts are ever exactly alike, but here, too, we have had access to all the established versions and no one studying all of them can fail to see a strange similarity. The basic and important facts are not dissimilar. It is as though one were looking at photographs of the same scene taken from different vantage points by different photographers.

We shall not burden our story here with all the versions of the origin of the treasure and the adventures that befell it en route to Cocos Island. Nor shall we pretend to prescience and espouse a singular account. Indeed, in view of the close similarity of data that exists, it should be a greater service to attempt some combination wherein all the known facts could be accumulated into one fairly accurate sequence of events.

Thus, as far as existing documents can be relied upon, the Lima treasure is a historical treasure, by which we mean that it actually existed at one time. Furthermore, the available evidence indicates that the Lima treasure was buried on Cocos Island, and, so far as we can determine, it has never come to light. Therefore, we must presume that the treasure still lies where it was originally hidden and that one of these days it will be unearthed.

Since this assumption has long been popular knowledge one can easily imagine the frantic and intensive search that has continued through the years—indeed, that continues—for this is the stuff and the stimulus of adventure. It has quickened the hearts and stirred the hopes of a multitude of fortune seekers. It has prompted the expenditure of considerable money—a sizeable treasure in itself—and cost the lives of countless men.

Our task shall be to squeeze as much of this as possible between the covers of one book.

We must begin with a little history, by no means new to many people, but which is the foundation for much that follows.

For two centuries the history of Peru was virtually the history of Spanish South America. The Viceroy, installed at Lima, ruled not only the Vice-Royalty of Peru, comprising the present territories of Bolivia and Peru, but also held authority over almost all the other Spanish governors of the continent.

It was also the Viceroy's duty to transmit to Spain the royal share (tax) of the precious metals mined in Peru and its subject territories. The fabulous silver mines of Potosí in present day Bolivia were by no means the only source of wealth. Gold had been mined on the remote slopes of the Andes since the days of the Incas. Emeralds (the finest in the world have always come from Colombia) were cut in intricate designs with great skill by Inca craftsmen. The first treasure taken to Spain by the conquistadors included emeralds. And the annual transmission to Spain of this vast hoard had always been fraught with danger and considerable risk for it was the bait that made pirates of many otherwise honest seamen. "Avarice," said Juvenal, "increases with the increasing pile of gold," and the Lima annuity was probably at its peak in the years immediately preceding the wars for independence.

Revolution was in the air over the entire Western Hemisphere in those days. First the 13 English colonies in North America united and threw off the yoke of Old World rule. Their success was undoubtedly the example that encouraged countries in the rest of the Hemisphere. Simón Bolívar, liberator of the whole northern part of South America, once admitted that much of his inspiration came from conversations with American patriots whom he visited in the youthful United States. Certainly the first attempt towards

17

independence was a filibustering expedition organized in the United States by Bolívar's mentor, Francisco de Miranda. It failed, but from that date (1806) on, revolutionary movements flared up throughout South America, and until independence in 1824, Peru was the stronghold of Spanish authority.

However, in 1820, a rebel army under the leadership of the victorious José de San Martín and a fleet under the able command of Admiral Thomas Lord Cochrane began an invasion from Chile. A year later San Martín entered Lima and proclaimed himself Protector of Peru.

Some accounts of the Lima treasure have it that it was Simón Bolívar who invaded Peru and captured Lima, but this does not jibe with recorded history. It was not until 1822 that San Martín and Bolívar met in secret conference in Guayaquil and Bolívar emerged supreme commander. The war continued for a couple of years more, during which Lima was for a time reoccupied by the royalists, and it was not until the battle of Ayacucho in 1824 that Spanish domination in South America was ended forever.

The young rebel republics had a tough time defeating the might of Spain on land but at sea they unquestionably had the upper hand, thanks to Admiral Cochrane, tenth Earl of Dundonald. This bold adventurer and soldier of fortune had accepted in 1817 the command of the Chilean navy and in the years 1819 to 1823 carried out a series of daring and brilliant campaigns which swept the Spanish flag from the Pacific Ocean.

With the sea routes to Spain endangered and eventually closed, the Viceroy in Lima had been, for a number of years, unable to remit the King's annual share. Bullion accumulated in the Lima mint and, according to the most reliable records, some of it had been piling up for 11 years before San Martín invaded Peru.

However, despite San Martín's success in Chile, the Viceroy did not take seriously the rebel invasion of Peru. He and the inhabitants of Lima never for a moment imagined that the rebel general would capture the seat of the Vice-Royalty. Here was concentrated the might of Spain in the Western Hemisphere. The conflicts in the outlying territories of Chile and Venezuela and Colombia were fringe fires that, he believed confidently, would eventually be snuffed out.

With the advantage of retrospect we can label such fantasy pure foolishness, especially since the Viceroy did not become concerned until he suddenly learned that San Martín and his victorious army were within 50 miles of the capital.

One of the Viceroy's first thoughts was for the safety of the vast hoard of gold and silver in his keeping and for which the King held him accountable. A similar thought struck the ecclesiastic officials whose wealthy church treasuries were also in Lima. At that time every church in the city—and there were some 60-odd—possessed immeasurable riches in the form of gold and silver utensils and the impedimenta of church service, images, decorations and reserves of gold coin. If the invading armies should enter Lima, as seemed about to happen, San Martín and his men would have little compunction about helping themselves to the King's gold, or, perhaps, the Church's either.

Now, suddenly, there began a frantic scurrying about throughout Lima and a series of midnight conferences between the Viceroy and the clerics. What to do? Any attempt to hide the treasures on the spot or in the environs of Lima would be foolhardy. Somebody would almost certainly betray their whereabouts to the invaders. The Viceroy and the clerics in secret council could see only one possible way out of their difficulties and that was to take the chance of shipping their combined wealth out of the country.

With this plan in mind, the first step was to get all the treasure down to Callao, the seaport for Lima, which was only seven miles away. The mint and its storehouse of gold and silver were emptied; the churches were stripped of their solid gold and silver accoutrements; even the heavily laid on gold leaf on the church cupolas was removed to preserve it and give an air of poverty to the buildings.

Transfer of the treasure was successfully accomplished. The chests and rawhide bags, several oxcart loads of them, were deposited in the heavily guarded fort at Callao. There the treasure waited while the Viceroy and his *compadres* figured out the next move.

As luck would have it, at anchor in the harbor lay the British merchantman *Mary Dear* of Bristol (one untrustworthy account gives her name as *Mary Dier*; but neither name was registered with the Admiralty, for good reason). She was commanded by one Captain Thompson, a Scot. Her presence suggested to the Spanish authorities a plan whereby they might yet save the stored treasure from the onrushing rebels. Captain Thompson was approached and this canny gentleman readily agreed to the Viceroy's proposition.

The plan was that all the treasure should be placed aboard the *Mary Dear* and Captain Thompson should immediately put out to sea and cruise around out of the danger zone for a couple of months or until he received word that the danger had passed. At that time he could either return to Callao and discharge the treasure or else deliver it up to the Spanish authorities in Panama. Captain Thompson was known and trusted by the Peruvians. He had been trading along this coast for the past three years. He agreed to charter his ship for the required purpose on very favorable terms and he had no objection to their sending along half a dozen trusted men, including a couple of priests, to keep an eye on the fabulous cargo in the ship's hold.

Everything worked smoothly and the *Mary Dear* quickly put to sea with the treasure and the Peruvian agents. The value of the hoard put aboard the *Mary Dear* that night in August, 1821, has been variously estimated at between $12,000,000 and $60,000,000. The wide range in these figures may be blamed in part on the historians who first saw the original inventories, for one of them reported the total in British pounds. Subsequent writers changed these into dollars and got the higher figure. The most valuable item, aside from the readily negotiable gold and silver bullion, is said to have been a solid gold, gem-encrusted, life-sized image of the Virgin Mary. It may well have weighed over a ton, as contemporary accounts state.

All this might sound very much like fiction were it not for the fact that the contemporary records are confirmed by an entry in Admiral Cochrane's diary, dated August 19th, 1821, as follows: "The Spaniards today relieved and reinforced the fortress of Callao, and cooly walked off unmolested with plate and money to the amount of many millions of pounds—in fact, the whole wealth of Lima which was deposited in the fort for safe keeping." *

What the gallant admiral did not know, apparently, was that said plate and money had been taken out of the fort and placed aboard the *Mary Dear*. And it was this ship, flying the flag of the admiral's own country, that slipped out of the port of Callao and made away with the treasure.

One highly fictionalized version of this escapade says that the *Mary Dear* slipped her moorings at night and put to sea without the Peruvian guards. But this never happened. Everything went according to plan and when the British

* See Appendix I. (Authors' note: Since many of the footnotes contained in this work are documentation and, therefore, necessarily long, we have, for convenience and to facilitate the story line, included them at the end of the book.)

barque put to sea, all of the guards agreed upon were aboard and in their places.

The *Mary Dear* had hardly cleared the harbor lights before her "avarice-increased" crew was thinking like gold-crazed pirates. And her hitherto honest British captain seems to have been as much a party to the plot as anyone. Before morning they had turned upon the guards and the two priests, cut their throats and dumped their bodies into the shark-infested sea.

Immediately then they were faced with the question of what to do with the treasure. To take the ship southwards and around the Horn to England was much too risky. There were insufficient provisions aboard for such a long trip, and with Admiral Cochrane's rebel sloops patrolling the coast it would be impossible to escape detection should they attempt to put in anywhere for supplies.

To touch at any Central American or Mexican port would have meant falling into the hands of Spaniards too, for those coasts were still in royalist hands.

There was some discussion about sailing westward, through the Polynesian islands and around Africa to England, but these were long and unfamiliar waters, largely unexplored, and there was considerable doubt that they could reach any of the islands before their supplies gave out. In the end it was agreed that the treasure should be hidden as soon as possible and Captain Thompson had a ready solution.

Cocos Island, he said, was a nice, sizable, uninhabited island, lying several hundred miles off the Central American mainland, where the treasure could be hidden without fear of interference. Then, a year or two later, after the inevitable hue and cry had died down, the captain could reunite his men at some prearranged rendezvous, and they could return to Cocos and recover the treasure with fair chances of getting it home to England.

The men agreed to this plan and so Thompson set the course for this speck of an island lying some 550 miles west of Panama.

Cocos Island has not changed much since that day nearly 140 years ago. It was then, and remains today, a hilly, jungle covered island with an irregular coastline deeply indented by three picturesque bays on its north side. Into one of these bays the *Mary Dear* sailed and dropped anchor and proceeded to disgorge her valuable cargo. The ship's longboat, laden to the last inch, had to make eleven trips from ship to shore to transfer all the booty to the island. There it was hidden in one spot, a place selected after much consideration, by the captain and the mate. Only a small amount of coins was retained and shared out among the crew.

It was soon after this that the *Mary Dear*, probably attempting to scrounge enough supplies from some small coastal village to carry her around the Horn, was picked up by a fast Spanish man-of-war. Some accounts say the ship was out of Panama, but it was most likely part of the Spanish royalist fleet that had escaped annihilation by Cochrane's squadron. In any case, the commander of the Spanish ship knew of the deal which the Viceroy had made with Thompson. Naturally, he wanted to know what had happened to the treasure which had been entrusted to him at Callao. Since no satisfactory answer was forthcoming, the *Mary Dear* and her crew were taken prisoner and conducted to Panama. There Captain Thompson and his crew were immediately put on trial for murder and piracy on the high seas.

The result of the short trial was no surprise to anyone. Everyone, from Captain Thompson down, was summarily sentenced to be hung. And forthwith the hanging party got under way, beginning with the lowest member of the crew and working up, so to speak, to the mate and the Captain.

23

By the time the last member of the crew had been dispatched, Captain Thompson and the mate were offering to make a deal with their captors. If their lives should be spared, they said, and if they could be assured of their freedom, they would lead the Spaniards to the spot where they had buried the stolen treasure. There were Peruvians among the executioners and they were particularly anxious to recover the treasure. At their urging, the bargain was made. Besides, everyone knew it was probably the only way whereby the treasure could ever be found and recovered.

It is interesting to note how fictioneers, seizing upon legend rather than known facts, have distorted the story from this point on. One account, for instance, has Thompson and the mate taking their captors on a wild goose chase to the Galapagos Islands, whence they escape to a British whaling ship and eventually reach home safely. There is no excuse for this sort of prevarication. After all, 140 years is not a long time. At least the trial and subsequent escape of Captain Thompson and the mate occurred within the period of recorded history.

What actually happened was this: Thompson and the mate and an expedition under the command of Peruvian royalists went to Cocos Island to recover the treasure. The captain and the mate, discussing the bargain they had made with their captors, agreed it would be folly to try to mislead them insofar as the general geographic location was concerned. The time and the distance involved in getting the treasure to the Galapagos and sailing back to the point where the *Mary Dear* was captured ruled out that location. And it was pretty obvious that no landfall had been made on the mainland of South or Central America. Besides, several of the sailors had confessed the details of their crime before they were hung.

When the expedition arrived at Cocos and anchored in

Chatham Bay, the two prisoners were taken ashore in the ship's boat with half a dozen armed guards and the Peruvian officials. Then, while pretending to take bearings and make certain measurements, both the captain and the mate suddenly disappeared into the thick tropic jungle which grows right down to the water's edge. The guards fired their muskets at random into the bush and the ship remained at anchor for several days while an intensive search was made. But anyone who has been to Cocos Island or who has seen such a jungle as that which covers this island will understand how utterly impossible it would be to find two men determined to hide themselves in it.

Eventually the ship and its disappointed *expedicionarios* returned to Panama and we have not been able to establish whether any additional search was ever made for the escaped captain and mate of the *Mary Dear*.

For several months the self-marooned men remained on the island, living on coconuts, birds' eggs, fish and small game. Finally, sometime in 1822, they were rescued by a British whaler which called at the island for fresh water.

To explain their presence on the island, Thompson and his companion told the captain of the whaler that they had been shipwrecked on the island. It was a logical answer and no further questions were asked.

During their stay on the island Captain Thompson and the mate had verified the fact that the treasure was still safely hidden there, but they wisely refrained from taking even a handful away with them when they were rescued because they did not want the whalermen to suspect the real reason for their being on the island.

The whaler put in at Puntarenas, on the Costa Rican coast, a few days later and here, according to most accepted versions of the story, the mate contracted yellow fever and died. At any rate in all the stories and legends about the Cocos

Island treasure, the mate fades from the scene at this point and from here on they deal only with Captain Thompson. The unidentified mate of the *Mary Dear,* whose name is never once mentioned, definitely disappears and the story line is carried by Captain Thompson as the first link in a chain of events and adventures that continues to this day.

But there is more to the Cocos Island story than that, and more characters in this fabulous fable than even Dumas could dream up. And one of the most important of them was the mate of the *Mary Dear.*

THE LOST TREASURE OF

COCOS ISLAND

2.

WITH communication what it is today, it is fairly easy to become known for some special field of endeavor. And the field of treasure hunting, being one of the more specialized, offers a quick road to fame—as a hunter, if not as a finder. In our case, since we have confined our interests to one small segment of the field, we have been known for our enthusiasm for anything that pertained to Cocos Island. Hardly a week has passed in the past 30 years when we have not acquired some new bit of evidence, some new light on the many mysteries surrounding the treasures on Cocos Island. Much of this we got by digging into old records, at widely scattered places. Some came to us as voluntary offering from other *aficionados*. And that is how we learned the story of the Mate of the *Mary Dear*.

We shall have to vouch for its authenticity, since the actual records, as you shall presently see, cannot be offered in proof because they constitute perhaps the most valuable possession in our files. Take our word for it, this information, heretofore undisclosed, came into our hands labeled "authentic." We have checked it in every possible way and find it reliable, unadulterated, virgin material, of which not a word has been altered since it was first written down over a hundred years ago.

Every story about the Lima treasure and the *Mary Dear* has told about "Captain Thompson and the mate." Captain Thompson and the mate did this; Captain Thompson and the mate did that; Captain Thompson and the mate were the only ones to escape with the secret of the Cocos Island treasure. It seemed reasonable to suppose that everything that was done, was done at Captain Thompson's instigation, and that the unnamed mate simply tagged along carrying out his captain's orders.

Hence the mate's name seemed to be of little importance to the story so long as investigators could find out what the captain did. That was a grave error in research. Instead of "Captain Thompson and the mate," they should have said, "The mate and Captain Thompson," for the very good reason that after the *Mary Dear* left Callao on her last, eventful voyage, loaded with the Lima treasure, it was the mate who gave the orders and the captain who merely carried them out—to save his own skin.

In an attempt to find the source of the several maps and directions for locating the Lima treasure, we eventually traced them backward to two definite origins. This gave us the first tip that the captain of the *Mary Dear* was not the only one who had started a chain of events with his knowledge of the treasure. From there on it was merely a case of patient search and constant vigilance. We knew what we were looking for and when we found it we easily recognized it as the important missing piece of our jig-saw puzzle.

With the information at hand, it is fairly easy to look back over the intervening years and reconstruct a reasonably accurate picture of what really happened on the *Mary Dear* after she left Callao.

The *Mary Dear* carried a crew of fifteen: Captain Thompson, the mate, the quartermaster, the boatswain, the carpenter (who happened also to be the sailmaker), the cook, and nine deck hands. There had been one more when they left Bristol, but he was lost overboard while sounding off Tierra del Fuego. Thompson was a middle-aged, bluff, easygoing, hearty son of the sea, part owner of the vessel he commanded (a common thing in those days), whose only object in life was to get as much profit out of his ship as he legitimately could by picking up whatever trade was to be had.

The mate, however, is not to be described so easily. He was, in a word, an enigma, with something of a Jekyll and Hyde character. The records show that he was born in Scotland, of a respectable Edinburgh family. His father was sufficiently well off to finance his education as a doctor, but this profession, apparently, never appealed to him. He undertook his studies at the university not so much to please his father as to escape the restraints of life at home. Thus upon the completion of his studies and at a time when young men with his education would be entering upon the first years of medical practice, he went to sea. He had, in fact, studied navigation in his spare time and this, added to his natural intelligence and some practical experience before the mast, finally won him an officer's berth as mate on the good ship later renamed the *Mary Dear* when she sailed from Bristol, England, bound for the west coast of South America.

This was the mate of the treasure-laden *Mary Dear* when she left Callao on that fateful day in August, 1821. He was a young man of superior intelligence and better education than his captain, a man definitely willing to trade a normal

29

life for an unusual one, who would exchange a staid profession for adventure and consider not the risk.

Our attempt to reconstruct the events which occurred on the *Mary Dear*, as she sailed westward into the Pacific from Callao, was not so easy as looking up records in old churches and British shipping files. After nearly 140 years it is rather like looking at a distant scene through the wrong end of a telescope, with the focus a little fuzzy to boot. Still, we can see something. We can see Captain Thompson pacing the deck of his ship as he considers the extraordinary obligation he has assumed. He wonders whether he has done the right thing in accepting responsibility for the enormous treasure put aboard his ship for safekeeping. The Peruvian guards are on the alert for any sign of treachery on the part of the crew. They have split into watches and in the first few hours aboard they take frequent peeps into the hold to assure themselves that the treasure is safe.

If any members of the crew have any ideas of stealing some of the treasure, they keep such thoughts to themselves in the presence of the captain and the heavily armed guards. There is one, however, who has the cunning to formulate a daring plan and the ruthless ambition to execute it. He is the mate. He knows full well that the conscientious captain would not listen to any such villainous scheme but he has no trouble at all persuading the crew.

Furtively the mate visits the fo'c'sle and calls the crew around him. In hoarse whispers he harangues them:

"Millions in the hold, stolen by the Spaniards from the Indians! So what's wrong with stealing it from the Spaniards?" This is reasoning they can understand. "Follow me, my lads," he says, "and we'll be rich." To a man, they are with him.

"But what about the skipper?" one of them asks.

"The captain must come in with us or else," says the mate,

dragging a finger across his throat. Mutiny and murder, apparently, are factors hardly worth considering.

Near midnight of the following night, when half of the guards are asleep, the mate and three of the crew go forward to the captain's cabin. There are no unnecessary preliminaries. The mate puts the point of his knife against the captain's throat. "Skipper," he says. "We're taking the cargo. The crew is with me. Will you go along or would you rather have a few inches of this?"

With a slit throat as his alternative, the captain goes along. The mate takes his pistols and leaves Thompson captain of the ship in name only. From that moment on the real commander of the ship is the mate.

The next quarter hour aboard the *Mary Dear* is filled with terror and soaked with blood. The mate and his motley crew steal up on the standing guards and cut their throats before they have a chance to call out. The guards and the priests asleep below never wake up. They are killed in their sleep and their bodies follow the others over the side of the ship.

"Easy, wasn't it?" boasts the mate. "Dead men tell no tales. We're fixed for life." And while all hands turn to to swab the deck and erase the evidence, the mate sets the course northward. With the entire coast of South America under blockade or on the alert there is no place where they could put in for supplies for the long trip home around the Horn. Lonely, isolated Cocos Island is his immediate objective. It is part of the plan which the mate figured out when the treasure was put aboard. Only a man of his intelligence could have considered all the factors involved and worked out such a grandiose plan. This, in general, is the way he reasoned:

The treasure must be buried as soon as possible. Any point on the mainland of South America is out of the question. The Galapagos Islands nearest and due west would be the next logical place but that site too is discarded because it is the place the Peruvians would expect them to hide the treasure. Tiny Cocos, lonely and beyond the normal sphere of Peruvian influence, is the best place.

The treasure must be buried in a place where it may be easily recovered within a year or two, not a hundred years hence. Therefore, it need not be buried too deeply.

They do not want to be surprised while burying it, nor while disinterring it later on. Therefore, it must be buried as close to the shore as possible, in an accessible, yet well concealed spot.

The stuff is heavy; therefore, they cannot waste time carrying it far inland.

Gold will continue to sink if buried in sand. Therefore, it must be placed on a solid floor.

The place must be easily identifiable so that any changes in the landscape will not affect the relocating of the treasure.

And, finally, all the treasure must be buried now, because if they should be picked up and questioned by a man-of-war, there must be no telltale evidence aboard. The question of returning to recover the treasure can be left until later. The loot is "hot," and the immediate problem is to get rid of it.

Once they had arrived at Cocos the mate's reasoning boiled down to the specific "Where to hide the treasure?" Wafer Bay is quickly discarded. It does not provide a safe anchorage. Chatham Bay must be the place. The anchorage here is more secure. The mate and some of the men go ashore. The tide is high, but they spend an hour or two exploring the rocky shore and after awhile the tide goes out. At low tide the mate sees a rock which peeps above the water. At hightide it is not visible. He takes a sight, lining up this rock with a point on the east end of the bay. He then makes his way along his sighting line until he finds himself in line with a prominent point on the nearby rocky pile known as Nuez Island. This lines up with the west tip of the bay. There is evidence of a shelf of bedrock at this point. It is covered with a few feet of sand, on the top of which lies a field of boulders and jagged rocks. If the gold should sink, it can only sink a few feet until it rests on the rocky shelf.

Under the mate's instructions, the hands clear away some of the small boulders and dig a big hole. Bare chests and brawny arms drip with sweat in the heat of the tropic sun. The longboat is sent back to the *Mary Dear* and soon the entire crew is engaged in hoisting the treasure overboard and transferring it to the beach. Eleven times the big longboat has to make the trip between ship and shore. The stuff is dumped alongside the hole.

But low tide lasts only a short while. When the tide rolls in again they have to suspend operations until the next ebb. No matter. It would require a good many tides to wash away that heavy stuff.

At the next low tide the job is completed. Everything is lowered into the hole and cedar planks and heavy canvas are placed on top of the chests and rawhide bundles containing the treasure. The hole is filled in. And then, to make everything doubly secure, block and tackle are brought over from the ship and with their aid a big square boulder weighing several tons is dragged across the beach and placed on top of the cache. And so that this particular boulder may be properly identified later, the design of a ship's anchor is deeply cut into it with a chisel.

In the light of pitch torches now the mate and crew stand back and survey their handiwork as the tide rolls in again. They rest and when the tide recedes again they nod their heads in satisfaction. The tide has leveled out the ruffled sand and completely effaced all signs of their work. Only the design of the anchor remains, but boulders all over the place have been carved with strange designs and the names of ships and men long dead. No casual visitor to that lonely beach would ever suspect that beneath that gigantic boulder and just below the highwater mark lay a great fortune in gold and jewels.

The mate rechecks his bearings. They are so simple that he could carry them in his head. Then, to make doubly sure, he takes the ship's compass ashore, sets it on top of the boulder, and reads off the magnetic bearings from his landmarks. By a curious coincidence, the compass readings—so many degrees east of north, so many degrees west of north—are in round numbers easy to remember without the necessity of having to consign them to paper.*

The mate looks over the scene once more. Everything seems to be perfect, but the mate is not satisfied. To *seem* perfect is not enough, it has to *be* perfect. Suddenly he realizes that it has not rained for several days and this island is known for its frequent showers even in the dry season and almost a continual downpour during the rainy season. From the creek that discharges into Chatham Bay there comes a mere trickle of fresh water to lose itself on the beach. The spot where the treasure has just been buried is right alongside this trickle of water. That, in itself, is of no importance, but the mate can easily imagine what happens to the stream when the heavy rains come. The trickle will be a raging torrent. It will tear across the beach at every low tide and scoop out a deep channel in the sand. If this should happen, the rushing water might dislodge the treasure and scatter it far and wide. It is, indeed, a remote chance, but it has to be avoided.

The mate traces the rocky bed of the creek back into the

* Our research eventually turned up these original bearings but for obvious reasons we cannot give them here. Nor can we divulge the end results of our calculations which allow for 140 years of compass variation and the natural changes suffered by the landmarks.

forest. Not many yards inland it makes a big right-angled bend and then runs parallel to the shore for some distance before it makes another turn to meander back into the foothills. The mate sends the longboat back to the ship with instructions to bring ashore several kegs of gunpowder. The powder is expertly placed under the boulders and rocks at various points and then, after the noise and smoke of explosion dies away, the mate again surveys the landscape. Finally the job is perfect. They have succeeded in diverting the course of the stream so that from now on it will make its exit across the beach at a point some distance from the original spot. Never again will there be danger of a washout at the place where the treasure is buried.

Meanwhile, Captain Thompson has taken little or no part in all these operations. He has moped aboard his ship, a sullen and unwilling witness to the villainies and the whole nefarious enterprise. He understands quite well that he is in the business up to his neck, but perhaps he hopes to soothe his conscience by not actually putting a hand to the wheel, so to speak.

Finally the business is done. Cocos Island was left behind and the *Mary Dear* was again on the open sea, heading southward on the first leg of the long run home via the Polynesian islands, the East Indies and around the Cape of Good Hope. But, as we have already reported, she didn't get far.

Eventually Captain Thompson showed up in Newfoundland, as we shall recount in more detail later, but it was not until 1844, some 20 years after the hiding of the Lima loot, that he took any steps to try to recover it. Could it be that all this time his conscience was bothering him? Could it be that the same scruples which made him refuse to put a hand to the actual stealing and burial of the treasure (but made of him merely an acquiescent accomplice solely to save his own skin) prevented him from returning to Cocos to recover the treasure? There are certain obvious surmises, which we shall explain later, but this man's conscience is something no one has ever been able to explore with any accuracy.

And what of the hitherto untraced mate? Did he really die in Puntarenas as has been generally accepted by all investigators of the Cocos Island treasure legend? Or did he, too, like Captain Thompson, live to tell his story of the burial of the treasure? This was the real enigma, the core of thirty years' research on the subject. There were so many "authentic" Cocos Island treasure maps in existence we were tempted more than once to cast aside the entire project until we began to see two distinct patterns of similarity and one day finally realized that all these maps were derived from two original sources instead of one as everyone before us had assumed. By the simple though tedious procedure of tracing each pattern backwards to its source we eventually uncovered the most fantastic character of all the villains who strut their moments on our little stage: the one and only other man who could have known anything about the Lima treasure on Cocos Island—the mate of the *Mary Dear*.

THE LOST TREASURE OF

C
O
C
O
S

I
S
L
A
N
D

3.

THE experienced treasure hunter is a skeptic. He has re-
searched and read and dived and dug enough to know that
there is always some element of doubt in every treasure tale.
Only the inexperienced, the naïve amateur, the arm chair
explorer reads the "true" treasure story and swallows the line,
reel and rod. The most pathetic are those who want to believe
so badly they will accept any scrap of old parchment with
a few lines and indistinct cuneiform characters on it for an
authentic treasure map when with the application of only
a smattering of scientific knowledge they might easily prove
it a fake. The psychologists have a name for these gullible
ones and among treasure hunters and pseudo treasure hunters they must surely outnumber the serious professionals
and studious amateurs three to one; else why is the proportion of fiction and fact respectively in this same ratio?

Certainly with respect to the Cocos Island treasures, this
is true.

Once we had established the fact that there were two separate chains of evidence (for the Lima treasure), originating in two different sources—Captain Thompson and the mate of the *Mary Dear* (and resigned to the necessity of telling two stories of one treasure), our only problem was the obvious one of sifting the few grains of fact from the bushels of chaff. This wasn't easy in the case of one story— the Thompson sequence—because of the voluminous versions extant. In the other story our task was simplified by the fact that we were plowing virgin ground; no one had yet cluttered it up with exaggerations of fact and fictionalized fancies.

If all the versions (all Thompson) so far written about the Lima treasure on Cocos Island were printed in one book, you couldn't carry it. And if all the stories about all the treasures hidden on Cocos were published and the profits put in one bag, it would make another sizable treasure. We make no pretense of having heard or read them all, since we boast no facilities of language beyond English, Spanish and a smattering of the Scandinavian, but a careful winnowing of those available to us leaves this handful of facts.

Captain Thompson disappeared from the scene for a few years as we said and there is no true record of his actions or whereabouts during this period. This is an assumption based upon the fact that no two stories about him at this time are in agreement. It is not until 1844 that we find him arriving in Newfoundland on board a ship from Nova Scotia. On the ship, Thompson, lonely, impecunious and mysterious, was befriended by a good natured sailor named John Keating, who took him into his own home and treated him like a brother.

And now again the various versions go wandering off in all directions. One account is that one day Thompson was visited by a stranger and immediately afterwards he left Newfoundland hurriedly, going to London, whither he was followed by Keating. Another version is that Thompson died and that on his deathbed he revealed to Keating the secret of the Cocos Island treasure and also delivered to him a detailed chart and instructions for finding the hidden hoard.

Yet another account has Captain Thompson confiding his secret to his new friend, Keating, long before he died, and persuading Keating to do something about organizing an expedition to Cocos Island to recover the treasure. One account describes John Keating as an illiterate, uneducated sort of individual, and it is somewhat hard to believe that Captain Thompson would have confided his secret to a man of this type. However, whatever happened next, one thing is certain, and that is that Captain Thompson, if indeed it were really he, did not personally go back to Cocos Island. If ever he revisited Cocos after interring the treasure there, then he must have done so some time between 1821 and the time of his arrival in Newfoundland more than 20 years later.

Is it possible that Captain Thompson spent 20 years without once revisiting Cocos Island? Practically all investigators overlook this important point. Nevertheless, it seems unlikely that Thompson did at any time go back to Cocos because there is no record of his ever having had a surplus of money.

Anyhow, whether before or after Thompson died, the next scene in the story discloses Keating in communication with one Boag, or Bogue, who is variously described as a shipowner, a sea captain, and/or a capitalist of St. John's, Newfoundland. Together they organized an expedition to Cocos Island (probably in 1844) on the strength of Keating's possession of Thompson's chart. One account states that they were to split the treasure three ways with Thompson who

39

remained at home because he did not feel equal to the long voyage around the Horn to Cocos, and that, in any case, he had full confidence that Bogue and Keating would be able to locate the treasure with the aid of the chart. In any event, Thompson drops from the story at this point.

In 1846 Keating and Bogue sailed for Cocos Island in the brigantine *Edgecombe,* captained by one Gould or Gault. On the way to Cocos, Gould got wind of the real object of the voyage and demanded to be cut in on the swag. He got his crew to back him and Keating and Bogue were put under lock and key in order to force them to agree to give everybody on board a share of the treasure.

One version says that Keating and Bogue escaped and stole away in the captain's gig while the ship lay at anchor in Chatham Bay and kept out of sight until the *Edgecombe* sailed away. The two men then located the treasure without difficulty. It was in a large cave and Keating later claimed to have seen inside the cavern several large chests full of gold coins, gold and silver ingots, bejewelled swords, boxes full of jewels, and a massive, solid gold image of the Virgin Mary.

The two men loaded their boat with food and water and as much treasure as they could conveniently carry on their persons, hoisted a sail and set out for the mainland. A couple of weeks later Keating arrived at Puntarenas alone. Bogue had disappeared. Keating later explained that Bogue had been taken sick and died and had to be buried at sea.

Another version has it that when the *Edgecombe* arrived in Chatham Bay, Keating and Bogue insisted on going ashore alone. They rowed over to the beach and disappeared into the bush. Late that night Keating ferried himself back to the ship. He was alone. He explained Bogue's disappearance by saying that he had fallen overboard between the beach and the ship and was so weighted down with the gold in his pockets that he had sunk like a stone.

This was the crew's first inkling, according to this version, that Keating's expedition was to search for buried treasure and they immediately demanded that all share alike. Keating did not relish this idea so he escaped at night in one of the ship's boats and eventually managed to reach the mainland. The *Edgecombe* never returned to Newfoundland because she went down with all hands while rounding the Horn.

Some versions have all this happening on a first and only visit that Keating and Bogue made to Cocos Island. Other accounts tell how they both succeeded in getting away with some of the treasure on their first visit and that Bogue did not disappear in the circumstances just related until a second visit that they both made to the island a couple of years later.

One story says that Captain Gould threatened to have Keating charged with murdering his partner, Bogue, and that Keating had to pay heavily for Gould's silence.

Whether after a first and only trip to Cocos, or a second trip later on, we next hear of Keating being back in Newfoundland (or Nova Scotia) where, after lying low for a while, he is said to have suddenly disposed of some old Spanish gold coins, obtained from nobody knew where, for a sum variously stated to run all the way from $7,000 to $110,000.

Yet another version would have Keating making a second trip to Cocos, alone, and still later on, a third trip, both in the schooner *Red Gauntlet*. On his third trip, he is said to have brought back $110,000 with him. One account says the amount was only $6,500.

If you're a little confused at this point imagine our dilemma for, search as we did, we were unable to uncover a single scrap of factual evidence on which these stories could have been based. But John Keating was an old man and approaching death in 1880 and from this point on there are newspaper accounts, public records and authentic, dated and signed letters which substantiate the story which we call the Thompson-Keating sequence.

A Nova Scotia newspaper, the *Herald* of North Sidney, carried this notice on December 1, 1880: "This is to certify that I have given to Thomas Hackett all the papers and all the information that I ever possessed necessary to find the treasure buried on Cocos Island, and that Richard Young nor anyone else has any information that will help them to find the said treasure." The advertisement was signed "John Keating."

Richard Young was a son-in-law who tried unsuccessfully to cash in on Keating's treasure information, as we shall see. Captain Thomas Hackett never made use of the information either. He died of yellow fever in Havana, en route to Cocos, and his papers eventually came into the hands of his brother, Captain Fred M. Hackett of Vancouver.

When Keating died in 1882, he left behind him a flourishing fishing business in St. John's and he was generally considered to be a rich man. Under his will, Keating left copies of his charts of Cocos Island to his widow, his second wife, who was much younger that he. A few years later Mrs. Keating married an old friend of Keating's named Brennan.

Some years later, Mrs. Brennan, again a widow, having satisfied herself as to the value of the documents bequeathed to her by John Keating, organized an expedition to Cocos to search for the treasure. Her partner and the commander of this expedition was Captain Fred Hackett, owner of the only other set of Keating documents. Mrs. Brennan, though by now 65 and grey haired, was described to us by one who met

42

her as being "vivacious, healthy-looking, and a fine example of a woman in her prime." She accompanied the expedition which arrived at Cocos Island in the schooner *Aurora* in 1897.*

At this time a German named August Gissler had already been living on the island for several years and it was from him that we have the details of this expedition.

Mrs. Brennan and Hackett failed to find the clues to the treasure cave indicated by Keating on his charts. These, according to one set now in our possession, were two large stones marked with a "K" and an arrow pointing towards a hollow tree. They abandoned the search without finding anything more exciting than a twisted iron bar. Before leaving the island, however, they made a deal with August Gissler and turned over to him all their charts and papers on the understanding that he would continue the search for the treasure—according to the indications on Keating's charts—on a percentage basis.

Captain Hackett visited Cocos Island again in 1902, presumably to find out whether Gissler had made any progress in the meantime. But Gissler was absent in San Francisco at the time and Hackett's trip was again in vain. Captain Hackett is said to have made one more fruitless expedition to Cocos Island but neither Gissler's memory nor any other account could establish for us a definite date. However, his son, Thomas Hackett (named for his uncle), did make a visit to the island in 1910, sailing from Vancouver.

Though we cannot prove that John Keating made only two sets of charts (one he gave to Thomas Hackett and one to his wife), we doubt the authenticity of half a dozen others which have come to light in the last 60 years. Although many

* There is a detailed account of this expedition in the newspaper *El Imparcial* of San José, Costa Rica, published October 21, 1897.

of these have been accompanied by letters and other documents signed by Keating, and one even purporting to be in the handwriting of Captain Thompson but unsigned, none bore dates.

There is one story, however, which should be told here, since it forms the basis of an important expedition described later. This is the story to the effect that in 1867 John Keating met a seaman named Fitzgerald who acted as a servant to him until Keating died. Fitzgerald subsequently claimed that Keating had given him a map and certain written clues for finding the Cocos treasure. Then, in 1870, Fitzgerald was befriended by Admiral Curzon Howe, who is said to have saved Fitzgerald's life or similar service and when, in 1894, Fitzgerald was on his deathbed, he sent all his Cocos Island documents to the admiral in token of his gratitude for the kindness shown to him by the admiral for a quarter of a century.

Curzon Howe kept the documents at his bank and when he died they passed to his son who eventually gave them to Sir Malcolm Campbell, who, having satisfied himself as to their authenticity, made them the basis of his treasure hunting expedition to Cocos Island in 1926.

These, then, are the principals of the Thompson-Keating sequence in the story of the Lima treasure buried on Cocos Island in 1821. Nearly every expedition for the next 125 years claimed to possess a plan or a chart or documents purporting to have been at some time or other in the possession of Thompson, Keating, Bogue, Gould, Hackett or Fitzgerald and handed down through their friends and descendants. If the charts and documents are not claimed to be originals, then they are usually declared to be "authentic" copies.

One chart which came to light in Costa Rica in 1899 was said to have been left by the unnamed mate of the *Mary*

Dear who had died in Puntarenas 77 years previously. This chart had been passed on from person to person until it finally reached the hands of one Francisco María Jimenez. It is still in the Jimenez family in San José and though it is part of the other sequence which began with the villainous mate, we mention it here to include it among the other doubtful sources.

If all these documents, charts, and maps were laid side by side they would blanket the island. It is surprising how many otherwise normal people have devoted time, energy and money in the pursuit of them. Just let a treasure hunter hear that a Cocos Island chart bearing the name of Thompson, Keating, et al., has been found in the back of an old book which has not been opened for half a century or more and he will go half way around the world to acquire it or a copy, or to persuade the owner to participate in an expedition to Cocos.

On one occasion, August Gissler, the Cocos Island hermit, heard that the son-in-law of John Keating, the Richard Young mentioned above, was living in Boston. Gissler immediately dropped everything and rushed to Boston where he found his man in a hospital. As Gissler surmised, Young had certain letters and other papers which formerly had belonged to Keating, including one which gave a detailed account of the finding of the treasure at the time he went to Cocos with Bogue.

Gissler bought all the documents (so he told us, though he later explained, as do we, that he got partners to help him and he put up his I.O.U. contingent upon his discovery of the treasure). He went back to his island to put them to the test, but he found that the indications (purportedly) given by Keating were much too vague to be useful.

Some years later, this same Richard Young from whom

45

Gissler had obtained the documents passed on his information or a duplicate set to a man named Desborough, a Californian, who, in 1909, also visited Cocos. Desborough afterwards claimed to have located the treasure cache but failed to remove any of the loot owing to the roof's caving in. Becoming aware of treachery among his crew, Desborough decided not to have them excavate the treasure. Instead, he returned to the United States with the idea of organizing a properly financed and trustworthy expedition under the protection of the Costa Rican government, but before he could do this he died.

Desborough had also claimed to have visited Cocos secretly in 1880 but said he was unable to do any excavating at that time owing to the presence of the Costa Rican prison guards who were in charge of the penitentiary on the island at that time. He did, however, so he claimed, verify the location of the treasure cache, which permitted him to find it without difficulty on his second visit in 1909.*

Desborough bequested his Cocos Island charts to an American archaeologist named Cutler who also died, very shortly afterwards, and left his information to his widow. From his widow the information passed to a Miss Genevieve Davis who, on the strength of the Desborough data, organized an unsuccessful expedition from California to Cocos in 1912.

It is a curious fact, and the reader will inevitably note it for himself as he follows our devious route, but almost every story of the finding of the Cocos Island treasure, from the time of Keating and Bogue in 1846 right down to Bergmans and Bellamy (see page 259), almost a hundred years later, has a common central theme and it is only in the minor details that there is any variation.

The story always tells how two men visited Cocos Island, intentionally, accidentally or by being shipwrecked; how they

* See Appendix II.

stumbled across the treasure in a cave; how one of the two men died, either before or after leaving the island; how the survivor eventually managed to get back to civilization, taking with him a "small portion" of the treasure to "prove" his story; and how he spent the rest of his life trying to get back to the island, whether by himself or by persuading a rich backer to fit out an expedition.

Looking over the "evidence," is there anyone who can really prove beyond the shadow of a doubt that the mysterious Thompson who showed up in Newfoundland in 1844 was the same Captain Thompson who commanded the *Mary Dear* in 1821 over 20 long years before?

Might it not be possible that the Thompson of 1844 was the first man to realize that there was money to be made out of credulous treasure seekers by selling them "authentic" charts showing where the Cocos treasure was buried, and that out of a chance, legitimate visit to the island, during which he had memorized the landscape, he successfully built up the legend which is universally accepted as gospel truth today?

Many ardent Cocos Island treasure hunters will call this suggestion sheer heresy on our part. But we were prepared (and ordered) to maintain some degree of objectivity in our study of Cocos and its treasures and in all fairness this is a statement of our own impressions in the matter of the so-called Thompson sequence. Indeed, we doubt if the real Captain Thompson ever disclosed the fact that he had anything to do with the theft and burial of the Lima loot. Even if he carried the act on his conscience for 20 years, it was not in character for him to decide in the end to tell the story to Keating in such detail.

And once we had uncovered the story of the mate of the *Mary Dear* and the definite information on location and the burial operation, we came to the conclusion that if Keating

47

did know of a treasure on Cocos it wasn't the Lima treasure.

Anyway, there were other stories, at least other legends, of other fabulous treasures buried on Cocos Island, and any one of these could have been the one discovered by Keating & Co. *if* it was discovered.

THE LOST TREASURE OF

C
O
C
O
S

I
S
L
A
N
D

4.

THE search for truth can become a tedious if not a totally frustrating experience. After confirming certain facts relative to the Lima treasure, its historical record, its theft and the principal characters involved, and its subsequent burial on Cocos Island, we found the story branching off into dozens of tangents and these in turn splitting up into others. Once we tried to make up a chart like a family tree but the thing ran off both sides of the paper before we got through the first quarter century. Thus any attempt to record here all the stories and legends that have sprouted and blossomed in this fertile tropical soil would only lead to confusion.

However, the Lima treasure is probably not the only hoard buried on Cocos and in order to arrive at some reason for including accounts of certain expeditions, we should give a brief summary of the other treasure stories relating to Cocos Island. Not only has the Lima treasure established a whole tree of expeditions to the island, but there have been

49

a great many sprouts whose roots were in half a dozen other legendary treasures supposedly buried on Cocos.

Indeed, we are inclined to think that the Thompson-Keating sequence, which we have just discussed, had its origin in one of these other treasures rather than the Lima treasure. You will recall that much of the information which Keating was supposed to have pertained to a treasure buried in a cave. We are convinced that the Lima treasure was buried near shore, certainly at no great distance back from mean-tide mark and thus not remotely close to terrain where one might expect to find a cave. Once we had established this fact to our satisfaction it cast the first doubt on Keating's story and thus the authenticity of his "Captain Thompson" which we mentioned. If his Thompson was captain of the notorious *Mary Dear*, then he knew exactly where the treasure was buried for he most certainly must have watched from the deck of his ship as the eleven longboat loads were transferred to shore and buried there within his sight.

We can raise a lot of argument with this kind of reasoning, for the owners of "authentic" Thompson-Keating charts and clues to the Lima treasure buried on Cocos Island outnumber all others about five to one. Nevertheless, we are convinced that Keating's Captain Thompson was not the commander of the *Mary Dear*, and if he did give Keating information about a Cocos Island treasure that information was based on legends other than or in addition to the Lima treasure.

What were these other legends? After the most thorough investigation only one or two proved to have any foundation in fact. Names, especially of ships, are fairly easy to trace. Even when a name was changed, as in the case of the *Mary Dear*, usually there is some record to show that it was changed if not a complete record of the ship's origin. Men, on the other hand, not only changed their names but their

personalities, and frequently were known only by their nick-
names. Thus many of the most important characters that
"brandished sword and pointed pistol with fell intent" during the heyday of piracy in the Pacific are not only shady
but so shadowy they are almost invisible. Take, for instance,
one of the most famous, a Captain Benito Bonito, the notorious "Bonito of the Bloody Sword," who operated in these
waters sometime around 1818–1820.

Captain Bonito existed at one time—of that we are convinced—but of his exploits at sea and his raids along the
Pacific Coast of Central and South America, only fragmen-
tary evidence remains. He is said by some to have been an
associate of Captain Thompson of the *Mary Dear* (which we
doubt), and we have established the fact that he buried
treasure on Cocos Island only a few years before the infamous *Mary Dear* touched there. It is highly probable, however, that at least one member of the crew of the *Mary Dear*
had once served under Captain Bonito for there is evidence
that someone aboard knew the exact location and the major
physical features of the island. It is our belief also that
Bonito made several trips to Cocos to bury treasure and, in
fact, used the island as his base of operations while he ravaged shipping in the Pacific.

The name Benito Bonito (probably a *nom de pirate* for
we have evidence that he was known also as Dom Pedro,
don Pedro and Benítez) was first known about 1814 when
he was the captain of a small Spanish privateer. Two years
later he became master of a Portuguese trader by murdering
the captain and this seems to have launched his role as a
pirate. He captured an English slaver, the *Lightning*, which
he encountered off the coast of Cuba, and renamed her the
Relampago (Spanish for lightning). He proceeded to kill
off any members of the crew who were opposed to serving
under him. Two whose lives were spared and who later

51

figure in legends of their own were a Frenchman named Chapelle and an Englishman or Scotsman named Thompson. There is plenty of conjecture attempting to link this Thompson with the Captain Thompson of the *Mary Dear,* but we "hae our doots."

The *Relampago* operated for a few years in the West Indies and several islands there today are pointed out as Captain Bonito's "headquarters" or as burial sites for some of the loot he took from Atlantic shipping. He must have established a rip-roaring reputation for two British frigates and a sloop of war were sent after him. He escaped around the Horn and for the next several years he ravaged shipping and pillaged the coastal towns of the Pacific. When things got a little hot for him off the South American coast he moved northward and in 1819 he found out that a rich cargo of gold was being taken from Mexico City to Acapulco for transport to Manila. The treasure was being brought down by mule train, escorted by government troops. Bonito and his cutthroats slipped ashore, waylaid the train and captured the treasure. It was one of the most audacious exploits in this pirate's bloody career and it netted a treasure worth some eleven million dollars—all of which was buried on Cocos Island.

Though he is credited with the flat sword enforcement of discipline, mutiny eventually broke out among his motley crew and to this is credited his final demise in 1821 in the West Indies. His was a short life and a bloody one, but in the few short years he operated in the Pacific he buried several large fortunes on Cocos Island. Once on the island, in an attempt to quell his mutinous crew, he divided up one of the great hauls and each man got a large leather sack filled with coins; officers Thompson and Chapelle each got several chests. Each man for himself then scurried off into the jungle and hid his fortune. Inevitably, all these separate hoards became the origins of countless charts and added materially to the number of legends about Cocos Island. You can understand why when we have uncovered still another Cocos tale in the course of our research and are in doubt about its origin, we simply file it in the pigeonhole marked "Bonito," and let it go at that.

Besides "Bonito" and "Lima" we have one other category for original Cocos Island treasure-trove. This, because it is highly documented by contemporary diaries and firsthand accounts, is the oldest but still the most authentic data available to the studious researcher. We file it under the name of Edward Davis, buccaneer.

Edward Davis made pirating a profitable career for nearly 20 years, from 1683 to 1702. He came up through the ranks in that field, having served with Captain John Cooke as quartermaster when the latter was pirating in the West Indies and later in the Pacific. He rounded Cape Horn with Cooke in the famous *Batchelor's Delight* in February, 1684. Among his companions, all well schooled in the trade, were William Dampier and Dr. Lionel Wafer whose journals of this and other expeditions were best-sellers in their day and priceless source material for modern writers, from Daniel Defoe (their contemporary) to the present collaboration.*

Cruising northward the *Batchelor's Delight* stopped at Juan Fernandez (Crusoe's island) and then the Galapagos. Later they put in at Drake's Island (La Plata, now a possession of Ecuador). They remembered that it was here a century before that Sir Francis Drake had casually thrown overboard several tons of silver taken along this coast to lighten his ship. The crew of the *Batchelor's Delight* spent a day fishing for the treasure—without success.

* William Dampier (1652–1715) piloted the expedition which rescued Alexander Selkirk, the prototype of Robinson Crusoe (1709). Dampier Head, a promontory on the south coast of Cocos Island, is named for him. Wafer Bay and Lionel Head were named for Dr. Lionel Wafer (1660–1705).

But the New World colonies of Spain were producing as much wealth in 1684 as they were in the days of the red-bearded captain of the *Golden Hind,* and it was easier to get than fishing for cast-offs on the bottom of the sea. By the time the *Batchelor's Delight* reached Cocos Island it had a rich cargo in the hold and a new captain. Captain Cooke had died and Edward Davis was now in command of the expedition.

Under Davis the enterprise prospered. He was a quiet, capable man, businesslike in all his dealings and a born leader of men. He probably never considered himself a pirate, certainly not a criminal. He did his duty as a patriotic Englishman and his raids on the ships and towns of his country's enemy were all in the day's work.

Davis and his men made Cocos Island their headquarters and raided the coast of New Spain from Baja California to Guayaquil. From time to time the *Batchelor's Delight* was joined by the ships of other freebooters—the famous *Cygnet* under Captain Swan and the *Nicholas* under Captain Eaton—and an occasional French buccaneer. All these made stops at Cocos Island to bury the plunder of their raids. And when one considers the tons of silver ingots, the chests stuffed with jewels and pieces-of-eight, and the leathern bags filled with gold that must have been buried all over the island, the marvel is that so little of it has ever been found.

It is recorded that the *Batchelor's Delight* intercepted several cargoes bound from Lima (Callao) to Panama en route to Spain, and these were put away on Cocos in one last visit before Davis sailed around the Horn and returned to Jamaica. Here he "surrendered to his Majesty's mercy," sort of confessed his sins, as it were, accepted the amnesty offered to all pirates by the grateful King James II, and retired to a life of ease and comfort in Virginia while he

54

waited for a chance to return to Cocos Island to recover his treasure. He started out in a little ship called the *Blessing*, but old temptations were his undoing. En route through the Caribbean he detoured for a little pirating along the coast of Central America, made a fruitless attack on old Porto Bello, and mysteriously disappeared from the pages of history.

In a sort of pirates' museum in England there was for some years on exhibit an old silver mounted pistol engraved with this legend: "CAPTn AVERY HIS BARKER." When last we heard of it, it had a printed tag attached which said it was dug up on Cocos Island in July, 1927. It is the one bit of factual evidence that links this notorious pirate with our island, but there are many legends about his Cocos caches too.

Only one man, to our knowledge, mined the Cocos Island treasure hoard and thereby gained fame and fortune. Robert Louis Stevenson was fascinated with the story of Cocos Island. According to him, he discussed it by the hour with Peg Leg Benton in Harry White's Bar on the waterfront of San Francisco. Peg Leg was a fine cutthroat fellow, with a swivel eye and one leg, who had seen both blood and gold on Cocos Island and he was not at all reticent about discussing it with the young writer.

THE LOST TREASURE OF

5.

C
O
C
O
S

I
S
L
A
N
D

Cocos Island is a scrap of tropical jungle afloat in the Pacific, off the coast but out of sight of the mainland of Central America. Except for the temporary sojourn of occasional treasure hunters, one short period when the island was a penal colony, and a few years when August Gissler was its "Governor" and "colonizer," Cocos has always been uninhabited. And historians have been a little careless about its early records, for no one knows who saw it first.

The first map on which Cocos is shown is that compiled by Nicholas Desliens, in 1541. Since this was a dozen years after other islands in the area were discovered by explorers putting out from Panama, one may conclude that Cocos was as fortuitously found, probably sometime around 1535. But the island has always had an elusive quality, as the most recent visitor will tell you. Surrounded by strong and tricky currents, concerning which much still remains to be known, and frequently veiled by such heavy mists and rainstorms that a ship may pass within a few miles without glimpsing a trace

56

of land, the very existence of Cocos Island has more than once been flatly denied. Then, too, in the days when navigation was more an art than an exact science, the precise position of Cocos was difficult to establish. Long after its discovery it was located, at the caprice of the geographers, now south of the Equator, now north, moving from side to side, on some maps completely ignored, and on others enlarged 20 times beyond its proportion in relation to mainland areas.

In 1600 the Dutch circumnavigator, Oliver de Noort, tried to find Cocos and failed, and in 1615 another Dutchman, George Van Spilberg, wishing to replenish his supplies with coconuts and water at the island, missed it because his charts showed it south of the Equator. Dampier had a similar experience aboard the *Batchelor's Delight* in 1684, so the careful and accurate accounts with which he conscientiously covers the rest of his eventful trip are here left to heresay:

"The Island Cocos is so named by the Spaniards," he quotes, "because there are abundance of Coco-nut Trees growing on it. They are not only in one or two places but grow in great Groves, all round the Island by the Sea. This is an uninhabited Island, it is 7 or 8 leagues round, and pretty high in the middle. . . ."

The *Batchelor's Delight* eventually stumbled on to Cocos later that same year, but after Dampier had left the ship to go with Capitain Swan in the *Cygnet* to the East Indies.

The approach to Cocos Island should be made from Puntarenas, the Pacific port serving the little Central American republic of Costa Rica. There are a number of very good reasons for this: Cocos Island belongs to Costa Rica and you cannot legally set foot on it without permission from the government of Costa Rica; and since Puntarenas is the nearest port of entry, it, therefore, is the official gateway to the island.

Cocos Island lies about 325 miles west-south-west of Puntarenas and about 550 miles due west of Panama City and Balboa. No other island lies between it and the nearest mainland. It is small—about three miles wide by four long and less than 20 square miles of about 12,000 acres in all— so, unless you are a pretty good navigator, Puntarenas is a good jumping-off point. On the other hand, if your instruments are dependable and you know how to use them, Cocos Island lies in latitude 5° 32' 57" North, longitude 87° 2' 10" West, in the Pacific Ocean. It is approximately halfway between San Francisco and Valparaiso. Still, as we said, we have known old hands to come within three miles of the island and miss it entirely. And we know of one small sloop carrying an expedition from Los Angeles that wandered in the vicinity of the island for a week and never did sight it.

Those who know Cocos Island do not laugh at such a mishap. Indeed, few people have ever seen the island completely in the clear. It rains on the island almost continuously for nine months of the year and intermittently for the other three. A local wit once told us there were only two seasons on Cocos—a rainy season and a wet season. Even when it is not totally obscured by heavy rainfall, the island may be blanketed by fog. And there have been visitors who would swear that it was not fog at all but pure steam generated on the island, for its temperatures range from warm to hot and sultry throughout most of the year.

Cocos is a tropical island in every meaning of the word, so it is a pretty tough proposition for the casual visitor. Mountainous, with peaks in the interior rising to 2,800 feet, it appears from a distance to stand up-ended. A *tico* (Costa Rican) poet friend of ours once said it "stands knee-deep in the Pacific." It rises almost vertically out of the sea, with sheer and forbidding cliffs rising two or three hundred feet on three sides. Except for two small rocky beaches at

Chatham Bay and Wafer Bay, there is no adequate landing place even for small boats.

The island is covered with a dense tropical forest with a thick undergrowth of vines, bushes, tree ferns, and thorny brambles. These cling to the steep slopes of the mountains and fill the deep ravines. The rains keep the island as saturated as a sponge, and the squashy yellow clay and dripping vegetation seldom seem to become even approximately dry. Wherever one goes the way is barred by vegetation through which a way may be forced only by the diligent use of a machete. The only passable paths are up the center of the rocky brooks which leap and swirl down from the high interior. A few of these streams reach the sea after spreading fanwise in broad shallows across the bays, but others spurt from the tops of cliffs to fall in long white ribbons to the wave-washed rocks far below. One of the most spectacular of these spills directly into the ocean from the top of a high cliff west of Wafer Bay. The waterfalls of Cocos are, in fact, an outstanding feature of the island. They are mentioned frequently in the earliest recorded descriptions of Cocos Island.

Lionel Wafer, "Chyrugeon," serving under Captain Davis on the *Batchelor's Delight*, in 1684, described the "Island Cocos" as ". . . thick set with Coco-nut Trees, which flourish here very finely, it being a rich and fruitful soil. They grow also on the skirts of the Hilly Ground in the middle of the Isle, and scattering in spots upon the sides of it, very pleasantly. But that which contributes most to the Pleasure of the Place is, that a great many Springs of clear and sweet Water rising to the top of the Hill, are there gathered as in a deep large Bason or Pond, the Top subsiding inwards quite round; and the Water having by this means no Channel whereby to flow along, as in a Brook or River, it overflows the Verge of its Bason in several Places, and runs trickling down in many pretty Streams. In some places of its overflowing, the rocky Sides of the Hill being more than perpendicular, and hanging over the Plain beneath, the water pours down in a Cataract, as out of a Bucket, so as to leave a Space dry under the Spout, and form a kind of Arch of Water; which together with the advantage of the Prospect, the near adjoining Coco-nut Trees, and the freshness which the falling Water gives the Air in this hot Climate, makes it a very charming Place, and delightful to several of the Senses at once."

The first fairly accurate chart of the island was that published in 1838 by Sir Edward Belcher of the British Royal Navy. The next was a U.S. Government map of the island published in 1898. The one and only official Costa Rican government survey of Cocos Island was made by a British ex-naval officer, Captain R. McCartney Passmore, in 1895. He said then that its outlines had never been accurately delineated, and that the highest point was 2,250 feet above the sea. "The interior is broken up into numerous fertile valleys," he reported, "and there is probably not a square kilometre of level ground in the island. Chatham Bay, which is best, has anchorage for large ships and wood and water are good and abundant . . . but, even at high tide, the surf makes landing difficult. Wafer Bay, which is separated from it by a 700 foot high ridge of land, has anchorage in 25 fathoms of water. A heavy surf also beats round the rocky margin of this bay, and a danger, not noted on the Admiralty charts, exists to the west of Cape Dampier. It is a small rock, visible only at low tide, and around it the water is very deep. The rock lies right in the track of passing vessels and is a real danger, especially at night. There are numerous bogs, and I believe the interior of the island has never been explored. There are signs of mineral wealth, and it is reported that gold has been found. The island had two colonists, in 1894, part of the emigrants sent there under a contract with the Costa Rican government, to establish an agricultural colony. It is, however, suspected that the real object of the impresario is to hunt for the immense treasures of gold bars, said to be buried, in three separate parcels, in as many places, by the pirate Bonito, or by the captain of an English brig. . . ."

A proper survey would be a difficult and expensive undertaking in such terrain and so much of the island is still relatively unexplored.

Several small rocky islets jut out of the sea around Cocos and these are the homes of countless thousands of sea birds, mostly boobies (red-foot and the rarer green-foot), pure white terns, frigate birds and gulls. (On a few old maps the island is named Cocos Frigate or Boobies Island, and in one account it is called Red-leg Boobie Island.) There are less than half a dozen species of land birds on Cocos besides the occasional migrants, and of these the ones most usually seen by the visitor are a species of insular cuckoo, the olive-green Cocos flycatcher, and an island finch, anomalous little birds with slender curved beaks, the males black, the females mottled with olive and buff as though permanently saturated by the everlasting rain.

There are no snakes on the island but it is overrun with rats, a large mangy breed that must once have jumped ship. Domestic cats have gone wild here too and one would think that they should have brought about a balance of nature in the years they have been known to inhabit the island but the rats are more in evidence. On almost every tree one may see little Anolis lizards, scampering up and down the bark, and in flecks of sunlight expanding their relatively enormous bright yellow throat wattles as they charm their mates or intimidate their rivals.

Writers in the past have dwelt at length on the scarcity

of insect life on the island but any safari inland will disclose an astonishing abundance. Moths large and small, including at least two species of beautiful, pink-spotted sphinx, several kinds of butterflies, large winged grasshoppers with extraordinarily long antennae, cicadas, wasps, wood roaches, dragonflies, mosquitoes and ants—especially ants! More than one expedition has been written off as a casualty of the Cocos Island ants, as we shall later recount. They swarm over the trees and bushes and every bit of ground and anyone making his way through the forest gets covered with them. Not only do they bite, but they infect the puncture with formic acid causing an intense irritation that lasts for hours.

It was the plentiful supply of fresh water on Cocos that made the island a favorite place of call for the oldtime whaling ships. No one knows how many old buccaneers and pirates, whalemen from New Bedford, Nantucket and Salem, merchant ships, three and four-decker men-o-war, wooden-walled frigates, brigantines and schooners, and modern steamers and launches have called here and landed, or missed it in the fogs, or gone away cursing it, or blessed its sweet waters and "coco-nut" milk. Some of the earliest visitors left domestic pigs ashore.

Captain Colnett put in at Cocos on the *Rattler* in the summer of 1793, on a voyage which had for its purpose the extension of the sperm whale fisheries, and the investigation of anchorages which would be useful to the whaling fleets. The good Captain left us a long, accurate account of his visit to Cocos, much of which has to do with helpful suggestions for future visitors. He suffered the usual difficulties with the island rain, and concludes: "We were much wearied, during the four days we passed off this island, and prepared to quit it. We therefore took on board, two thousand coconuts; and, in return, left on shore, in the North Bay, a boar and sow, with a male and female goat. In the other bay, we sowed garden seeds of every kind, for the benefit and comfort of those who might come after us."

The hogs have multiplied and evolved into a lean, wild species that offers fair sport for the guns of occasional treasure hunters, as well as good eating. The goats gorged themselves on the luxurious vegetation and died. Many deer roam the island and these also provide excellent shooting.

The streams are alive with large crayfish and the waters around the island abound in an extraordinary variety of fish. They range in size from colorful little creatures an inch long to giant mantas and sharks. There are tuna, bonito, mackerel, jewfish, sailfish, swordfish, and red snapper in unusual quantities. Shrimp, crabs, oysters and other crustaceans and mollusks are found in all the island's coastal waters.

For the last 200 years, almost every ship that visited Cocos had on board at least one energetic individual who took the time and trouble to carve his ship's name and sometimes the date of her visit on one of the big boulders scattered over the beach in Chatham Bay or Wafer Bay.* Here, in a veritable guests' book in stone, is the living legend of Cocos Island. With every headland and inlet named for some brigand of the sea, a stroll among these rocks is guaranteed to inspire some fascinating dreams of the days when pirates bent their calloused knees to drink the island's "sweete watter" and dribbled doubloons from the pockets of their ragged bloomers.

Strewn over both beaches also are the remains of many a fruitless treasure hunt, the end result of high hope and no little expense. Rusted iron rods, bent and twisted odds and ends of machinery, shovels, picks, crowbars, and ragged sheets of corrugated roofing tell their own sad tales of disillusion and disappointment. This is the famous island of

* See Appendix III.

63

mystery, where more pirate treasure is supposed to have been buried than anywhere else in the world, and where, as we shall show, more lives have been lost and where more people have spent more time and more money in search of it than in all the other treasure islands put together.

THE LOST TREASURE OF

6.

C
O
C
O
S

I
S
L
A
N
D

THE main theme and most important story we have to tell
about Cocos is not so much the story of the various treasures
supposed to have been buried on the island, as it is the story
of man's search for nebulous values. The extremes to which
men have gone in their quest for Cocos wealth is more fantastic than any record (true or legendary) of the existence
and location of such wealth. Since these records are the basis
for all treasure hunting expeditions on Cocos, we have had
to mention them even though they seem legion (we could fill
another volume with Cocos legends), but this is not the
whole story nor even the half of it. Nor do we have room
for smugness, for who knows what our reactions would have
been had we been faced with the same set of circumstances
that brought on the gullibility of others. No, our theme concerns not only these motivations, but especially their capri-
cious end results.

Thus, on second thought, that family tree of Cocos Island
treasures which we once tried to draw might be a good gim-

mick to help our readers avoid confusion. Indeed, with so many threads to handle we should be in danger of making a hopeless tangle instead of a smooth fabric were it not for the fact that our demand for truth has greatly simplified the story.

We shall proceed with confidence, therefore, to tackle the most involved sequence of the Cocos story for herein lies the outstanding example of man's hunt for hidden wealth.

Of the hundreds who have come to Cocos to dig in its unyielding soil, or pace off some clue to the place where "X marks the spot," few remained for any length of time. The inclemency of the tropical climate, the constant battle with island insects, the rigors of malnutrition, and above all the fight against loneliness, have driven more than one treasure hunter to seek his fortune in less forbidding environments. Only one man in all the history of Cocos Island had the vision, the fortitude and the physical stamina to stay with the quest. August Gissler spent a lifetime searching for the treasure he believed was buried on Cocos Island.

August Gissler was not an ordinary man. From a news story about him that appeared in the *New York Times* in 1907 we read that "Captain Gissler is a man of 47 years, and a breathing replica of Michael Angelo's heroic statue of Moses. His reddish beard reaches to his waist, his hair is luxuriant on a splendidly poised head, his eyes are as clear and searching as an eagle's, his nose is classic, his voice is profoundly mellow, fitting the man to perfection. His height is 6 feet 3 inches. He is built like a wedge, as a man should be, with massive shoulders, firm hips, and an almost imperceptible embonpoint. His hand is as big as the hand of Providence, and so hard that his clinched fist is used as a spike maul." *

* For Gissler's description of the island see the complete text of this *Times* story in Appendix IV.

August Gissler acquired his fortitude and physical stamina by inheritance—he was born in Germany—but he came by his dream of Cocos Island wealth by a more devious route. This is August Gissler's story, told for the first time in his own words:*

In the month of November 1880, I made the acquaintance of two gentlemen, the second mate and the steward of the German barque *Highflyer*. I was then in London, where I had left an American full-rigged ship. Having previously been before the mast in several vessels, I thought that a spell on shore would prove more beneficial than another voyage across the Atlantic in the dead of winter. Through frequent meetings with these two men a friendship developed between us. They invited me to join their vessel, which was bound for Honolulu around the Horn, and I accepted the offer.

The day after my arrival on board we hove up anchor. A tugboat took us out of the Thames, and the sails were set; but strong contrary winds forced us to anchor again in the Downs, where we lay for two days. At last, helped by a favorable wind we set a course down channel, and 20 days after leaving London we anchored in the roadstead of San Miguel, one of the Azores islands. We lay there four or five days embarking some 450 emigrants bound for the Sandwich Islands.

Several of the barque's crew had bought Portuguese grammars and from these we learned brief sentences, by means of which we endeavored to converse with the Portuguese passengers. This proved at first a rather arduous matter, but gradually many of us came to understand the most fluent of them. Most of the emigres had been shipped under contract to labor for five years on the sugar plantations of the Hawaiian Islands. However, several young Portuguese had paid their own passage, among whom was a young man by the name of Manoel Cabral, who appeared to be of better extraction than the rest of his countrymen. He could speak a few broken English sentences, and he appeared to know Spanish as well as his own language.

* Gissler's diaries, letters, an original manuscript of his Cocos adventures, and other personal material came into our possession and form the basis from which his story is written.

The long voyage from San Miguel to Cape Horn was without incident, but soon after passing Staten Island at the entrance to the Straits, they ran into heavy weather, followed by severe gales. The Cape Horn passage was accompanied by the usual hardships. Almost nightly the watch below was called on deck to shorten sail or repair some damage of the storm. Several seamen were injured by heavy seas that frequently washed over the barque, throwing the men down and tossing them across the deck. It was a miracle indeed that no one was washed overboard.

The man most severely injured was the engineer who tended the water condenser. "We had 45 tanks of water in the hold when we left London," Gissler recorded, "but after leaving San Miguel we relied on condensed water. Unfortunately during these heavy gales around Cape Horn, the engineer was unable to produce condensed water, and after he was injured we found ourselves short of water."

In London, Gissler had told the second mate that he knew something about machinery. The mate now remembered this and so informed the captain who immediately sent for Gissler.

I went aft and learned from the captain that the engineer would probably be unable to attend to his work for several weeks, and being short of water it was urgent that somebody should endeavor to work the condensing apparatus.

"Now, my boy," the captain said, "let us see what you can do. I want to know in a short time whether you can manage the job. Otherwise, I shall change our course and put in somewhere for water."

I went forward and started a fire in the boiler. When enough steam had been raised I opened the valve for the condensing machinery and waited anxiously for the result. There was a test faucet on the condenser, and as soon as it began to flow, I tasted the water. To my consternation it was a good deal more salty than the water in the ocean. While I was pondering the possible cause

of this the captain came to the door and said: "You have it running, but how is the water?"

"Salt? How is that?" the captain asked. "Let me take it."

The captain sipped a few drops and spat in disgust. "This is
worse than ever," he said. "What do you think is the matter?"

The only reason I could imagine, I told him, was that by standing idle so long salt had accumulated in the boiler and the condenser. I added that they should be cleaned out and then perhaps
the water would run fresh and sweet.

"I don't know," said the captain, "whether after all it would
not be better to alter our course. How long do you think it would
take to clean out the salt?"

"Three days," I said.

"Too long," answered the captain. "It must be done in two
days, even if you have to work all night. If you do it in that time
I'll make it up to you."

With that I said, "I'll try, sir," and at once began to rake out
the fire.

After the pressure was reduced I blew out the steam, and as
soon as the boiler had cooled sufficiently I opened the man-hole
and cleaned out the salt. I worked steadily all day, the whole
night through and most of the next day.

When the job was finished and we were ready to start operating again, I discovered we had no feed pump and the sailors
were ordered to draw water over the side to fill the boiler.

This task, of course, was not performed without much grumbling on the part of the men, one of whom said to me: "You're
a dandy. Why don't you give it up? Let the skipper run in to the
Chile coast and buy his water, so we might have a chance to go
ashore. Now we have to draw water for your damned boiler and
it's no use in the end anyhow."

Despite the growls and recriminations from the sailors the
boiler was soon filled. Gissler started the fire and an hour or
so later he tried the test faucet. The first flow was dark and
unpalatable, but in a few minutes the condensed water began
to run sweet and fresh. The mate had come forward to watch
the operation and at the first evidence of success he ran aft
and informed the captain who himself came forward with a

bottle of rum and a pound of tobacco and the news that he had ordered the steward to give young Gissler a bottle of rum daily as long as he should run the condensing machine.

According to the prevailing rule on emigrant ships the crew and the passengers had a certain allowance of water given them daily. This was ample for all needs as long as the ship was in cool climates, but when she entered the tropical zone everyone wanted extra rations. Gissler, by working overtime, was able to supply all needs. In addition, since he had no taste for rum, his water room became a daily port of call for every sailor aboard. His daily allowance of rum passed from hand to hand and probably earned for him more friends than his water.

Among the Portuguese passengers, too, he was well liked and Manoel Cabral volunteered to help him fill the endless line of water bottles that came to his door every day. Working together they soon became friends. As Gissler recorded it: "After performing his task, Manoel would stand by the engine room, watching, and as I had by that time mastered a good many sentences in Portuguese and Cabral had greatly improved his English, we grew accustomed to holding long conversations together."

For the sake of the rum, the sailors continued to be pleasant and helpful. They fetched the coal from the forepeak for Gissler's boiler and were always ready to help when the young engineer needed them. One day an old salt named Jack, with whom Gissler had had some words during the repair of the condenser, came in and said: "Now, Sonny, I've had many a drink out of your rum bottle, but I see by your looks that you don't like me as well as you did before when we were together before the mast."

"You're right," Gissler answered. "Only recollect what you said when you had to draw water for the boiler and judge for yourself."

70

Whereupon old Jack burst out in an uproarious laugh and slapped him on the back. "Haw!" he shouted. "It wasn't the drawing of the water that made me and the rest down on you. We would have been well pleased if the captain had been compelled to put into some Chilean port for his water, so we could have had a fling ashore. But you fixed the contraption and that spoiled our fun. So it is no more than fair that you should let us have a pull out of your bottle. Let's say no more about it, sonny. Here's to you!"

With that he took another long swig, wiped his bristly mouth with the back of his hand and rolled off down the deck. His laugh was still to be heard when Cabral remarked: "That fellow looks like a pirate."

"A pirate?" Gissler asked. "I don't think old Jack has courage enough for that. Anyway, pirate days are over. What made you think old Jack looks like one?"

"Old Jack fits the description my grandfather gave me. He knew pirates. He saw a lot of them. My grandfather was a sailor and he sailed this very same ocean."

"No doubt if your grandfather was a sailor and he sailed the Pacific, he must have seen a pirate or two. Those were the days when they roamed these waters."

"Yes," agreed Manoel, but his eyes had a far-away look. "Do you know a place called Guayaquil?" he asked.

"Yes," said Gissler, "that's in Ecuador. Do you want to go there?"

"No," said the young Portuguese. "I want to reach a small island about four days' sail from Guayaquil." Then, looking straight at Gissler, he added, "Maybe you can help me."

"What island is it?" asked Gissler, only mildly curious.

"On a chart I have in my cabin, it is called 'La Palma,' " said Cabral.

Although young Gissler had not sailed the Pacific before, he had a good general knowledge of these coasts and the is-

71

lands offshore. He could not recall having seen or heard of La Palma on any of the charts he knew.

Days passed and the friendship between these two quite different young men grew and developed into something strong and fine. And eventually Manoel Cabral, the young Portuguese, confided in August Gissler, the young German seaman, the reason for his voyage. It was a tale of strange mystery and full of import for the German.

THE LOST TREASURE OF

7.

AMONG the old papers and ancient documents which the young Portuguese, Manoel Cabral, showed August Gissler aboard the ship *Highflyer* during her voyage around the Horn in 1880–81 was a long letter written by Manoel's grandfather. The letter was in effect an autobiography, and since it was a most extraordinary document Gissler asked and received permission to copy it virtually word for word. We do not have space to quote the entire work here, but in rewriting and condensing it to fit within our present limitations we did check names, dates and as much of the action as possible and are convinced that the original document in Cabral's hands was not only true in every detail but it shed new light on the Cocos Island treasures.

Our use of it here will show the original motivation for Gissler's enduring interest in treasure hunting. A stolid, practical young man by inheritance and nationality, August Gissler was the antithesis of the typical treasure hunter. He dealt in facts and figures; he believed in things he could see—

73

dreams and fantasies and wild imaginings were never part of his make-up. The papers Cabral showed him had to be authentic; the story they told had to be logical. They were. Furthermore, they were the most extraordinary papers Gissler ever read, for they were the original, unpublished documents of a real pirate. Rarely has anyone had such an opportunity and so it is not difficult to understand their impact on young Gissler.

This is the story of how Manoel Cabral came to possess his grandfather's documents as he told it to August Gissler off the coast of South America one day in January, 1881:

My grandfather landed in Fayal from an American whaler. He was paid off there and decided to stay on shore. Soon after that he was married, and a little later he and my grandmother moved to the island of San Miguel where my grandmother owned a small farm bequeathed to her by a relative. It may have been her dowry.

A boy was born but he died in infancy. Later a girl, my mother, was born. There were no other children. My mother was married to my father, Pedro Cabral in 1838. I was born in 1859. I never knew my grandmother for she died when I was quite young or maybe before I was born, but I remember well that my grandfather lived until the year 1870.

Many times as a boy I went out with my grandfather in a small boat. He always said that I should be a sailor and learn to handle a ship and many other things. I was then too young to understand. Once he said it would be necessary for me to learn Spanish and also English. My father did not like my grandfather and now that I know all the circumstances, I am fully convinced that he was afraid of him.

Our farm was about an hour's walk from the village. Every Sunday my father, mother and I would go to church but I never saw my grandfather there. One day my mother took me to the village and said I should have to go to the priest to learn, and this I did regularly for some years. My grandfather often accompanied me within sight of the priest's house, but he never

74

entered it. His apparent dislike of the church was the cause of much perplexity on my part. One day I had a fight with a boy whom I soundly thrashed. He ran home crying, and the next day his mother went to see the priest and said, "Father, the little pirate beat my boy. The cursed old pirate never comes to church; why don't you turn the little one out?"

The priest went out with the woman and I could not hear his answer.

That afternoon the priest came home with me and had a long conversation with my father and mother. While this was going on, I besought my grandfather and asked him whether he was a pirate, repeating all that the woman had said. He did not answer me.

In the evening, while I lay awake in bed, I heard some high words passing between my father and grandfather. At last mother said: "Father is right; the boy must go to a regular school in town."

For a week then I did not go to school. My grandfather had gone to San Miguel on business of some kind, and when he returned, he said to my mother:

"Antonina, everything is arranged. On Monday we shall take the boy to town. Never mind what that fool of a husband of yours has to say."

The following Monday the three of us sailed for San Miguel in grandfather's boat and upon arrival there I was conducted to a boarding school kept by priests. There were many boys at the school. All of us had to sleep and eat in the house and go to school mornings and afternoons. Discipline was very strict but every three months we were given two weeks vacation. And these vacations were my happiest times. Every day my grandfather would take me in his boat and teach me some of the things he knew. He also had a fine gun and he taught me how to shoot.

One day, when I was nearly eleven years old, a messenger came to the school to tell me I was wanted at home. Upon reaching home my mother informed me that grandfather was very ill and wished to see me before he died. I was led into the old man's room and upon catching sight of me he called out, "Manoel!" I rushed to his side, barely able to hold back the tears.

"My boy," he said, "promise me to do what your mother will tell you." I promised, trying manfully to control my voice. To my mother he said: "Antonina, your husband is a fool. Keep this boy at school till he is 17. Then give him those papers. He is your only hope."

My grandfather turned again to me and I could see his voice was faltering. "You may go now, my boy, for I have something more to say to your mother."

I went out and looked for my father. I found him in the orange grove picking fruit. I helped him pack the oranges into crates and I recall that he explained that they were to be sent to San Miguel, whence they would be shipped to Liverpool.

I was preoccupied with thoughts of my grandfather and I asked my father if he thought the old man would die. He remained silent for a few moments, then he looked at me and said: "Probably." That was all. A few days later grandfather died. He was buried the next day which was a Saturday. On Monday I was sent back to school, though before leaving the house I asked mother what it was grandfather wished me to do. "When you are 17," she said, "you shall know all."

For another six years I remained at the priests' school and throughout that time the thought of what my mother would tell me was constantly on my mind. Eventually when I became 17 years old, I returned home for good.

I began immediately to question my mother, but notwithstanding my importunities, a whole week passed before she would say anything to relieve my anxiety. But one day, when father had gone to town on business, she called me into the room where grandfather had died and she gave me these papers. I have read and reread them time and again, and now I shall show them to you. What you cannot understand I will explain the best I can.

Manoel thereupon produced a bundle of papers sewn up in an oil cloth, which upon examination Gissler found to be a manuscript of goodly size, closely written in Portuguese. The reading and interpretation of this took several days, but the young German sailor managed to transcribe it in his diary almost word for word as the narrative unfolded. It is not often that one comes across such pure and unadulterated source material as this so it is with considerable pleasure that we share it here. This, then, is the autobiography of the grandfather of Manoel Cabral as he wrote it down about a hundred years ago:

Our family lived on the island of Flores. My father was a fisherman. We caught fish, dried it and sold it to buyers who called regularly at the island. One morning in the year 1812, father was not feeling well enough to go out. He told me to take charge of our boat and go out and do the day's fishing. A few men who had no boat of their own used to go out with us and work on shares; that is to say, the fish caught were divided, so much for the boat and so much for the crew.

On the morning that I speak of, five boys went out in the boat with me. We were not very lucky in catching fish close in shore, so we stood farther out to sea, helped by a fair wind. We had at last taken a fairly good catch and were preparing to return home when a squall struck us suddenly and broke our mast. Unable to reach land in our crippled condition, the wind being dead against us, we drifted all that night and the next morning we hardly could see land. However, we caught sight of a ship sailing toward us, and although we were in distress there was something in the appearance of that ship that, somehow, brought us more foreboding than comfort.

Since the French had taken possession of Portugal, the Azores Islands had often been visited by a privateer, or letter of marque, named *Le Renard*. Imagine our terror, then, when the ship came closer, we saw that we had fallen in with the *Renard*. She hove to and signaled to us to come alongside. We brought to and were ordered on board. Our fish were then hoisted aboard the privateer and our boat cut adrift.

Through an interpreter we were informed that we should have to join the crew and help work the ship as they were short handed. Whatever our feelings were in the matter, we had no choice for we were in their power; but we were all determined to jump ship at the first opportunity.

We were assigned various jobs on deck and a few days later the man who did duty as interpreter ordered us to carry a big

77

kettle of soup from the galley to the fore hatch. There the hatch was taken off and the kettle lowered into the hold. Later we were ordered to go down into the hold and fetch the kettle back. Down in the hold we saw more than 20 men, two of whom were bound to a stanchion. One of these was a handsome young fellow who said something to me in what I took to be French. I answered in Portuguese that I did not understand him; then to my surprise he asked me in my own tongue whether I was a Portuguese. I told him that I belonged to the island of Flores and that six of us had been picked up by the ship and forced to join the crew.

"Six," he said, "and 25 here make 31." He could not say more to me then because we were ordered to bring the kettle back on deck.

The next day the soup kettle was again lowered into the hold and shortly afterwards two of us had to go down and fetch it back as before. The young man at the stanchion called me to his side and said:

"I am a Portuguese like you and a prisoner like you and all the rest here. Can you find out for me how many men are in the ship? I mean men that are able to fight. Don't betray me."

I told him I would do all I could to help him.

"Good," he said. "But you must be very careful. Now go up with your kettle."

When I came on deck that time I found everybody looking aft. Wondering what was attracting their attention, I stood on a coil of hawser to look and saw the captain gesticulating and shouting at the mate. I, of course, could not understand what was said, nor did I see what was causing the commotion, but remembering what I had promised to do I took advantage of this opportunity to count how many men were on deck. There appeared to be 42 in all, including the captain and the mate. I slipped down to the 'tween deck but I saw no one there and I concluded that even including the cook and one or two others, there could not be more than 45 or 46 men aboard.

All of that afternoon I noticed that the sailors never ceased to argue with each other. There seemed to be a great deal of dissension among them.

The next day the soup kettle was again lowered into the fore hold and once more I was ordered to fetch it up. Walking straight up to the stanchion I informed the prisoner of what I had witnessed the day before.

"That is good," he said. "Now mind carefully what I tell you. I hope you and your five companions will help us carry out our plans. Six of our men down here will join the crew. We were all asked to do so when we were caught and when we all refused they imprisoned us in this stinking hold. But now six of our fellows will say they have changed their minds and will join the crew if they are allowed. And amongst the six will be that short, stout fellow who is lying under the hatchway. Do you see him? He speaks French and will easily find out what is the matter on deck. He will give you a message for me and I shall send him his orders through you. Do everything he tells you to do. Now, quick, go up with your kettle."

That afternoon I saw the interpreter go down to the fore hold. A little later six prisoners came up on deck and were put to work, being assigned to the mate's watch, while my five companions and myself were in the starboard watch.

For the next four days nothing unusual occurred, but on the fifth day, just before I went below to fetch the kettle, the short, stout fellow thrust a piece of paper in my hand and whispered, "For him, and watch sharply, mate, that nobody but he sees this."

I pocketed the paper without a word, and later, when I went for the kettle, I succeeded in slipping it to the young man in the stanchion. That afternoon again the interpreter went below and later eight more prisoners were brought on deck and turned to for duty; but these, however, were divided, four men on each watch. The next day as I was about to go for the kettle, the stout fellow passed me and whispered:

"Bring me his answer and be careful to remember exactly what he says for your freedom as well as ours depends on it."

Down in the hold I immediately made for the stanchion. "The word is 'yes,'" said the prisoner. "That is all you have to say to him on deck; but to you I will add that you and your five friends must do exactly what he will tell you to do and all will be well. Now, go with your kettle. The answer is 'yes.'"

Coming up on deck, I brought the kettle to the galley and there I found the mate, the stout fellow and the cook whispering together.

"What did he say?" asked the stout fellow.

"The word is 'yes,'" I repeated.

"Good," exclaimed the mate. "Now, cook, you have to fix up a nice supper for tonight."

The cook nodded his head. I went out, followed by the mate and the short fellow who told me to go forward with him ". . . to fetch firewood for the cook."

Down in the quiet darkness of the forepeak, while we gathered pieces of firewood, the stout one explained quickly the plan for taking over the ship and what my job would be. I was to release all the prisoners on signal and rouse my friends and we all were to perform prearranged duties. The whole plan depended on quiet and absolute obedience to orders.

That night at eight bells, instead of turning in, I went forward as instructed. The night was dark but by now I was thoroughly familiar with the ship and I groped my way to the small hatch leading into the forepeak. Once below I made my way to the small door connecting the forepeak with the hold where the prisoners were. I waited there for the better part of an hour when at last I saw a lantern being lowered to me. That was my signal to open the door and free the prisoners.

In a few moments we were all assembled on deck and the short fellow handed a pistol to the tall young man whom I had just cut loose from the stanchion. "Now is your turn, Dom Pedro. Take five men and go aft to the wheel. You will find the mate on the poop waiting for your orders. We will handle the rest."

It was all over in a few minutes. The mate, who had had some disagreement with the captain, was in the conspiracy as were ten of his renegade Frenchmen. With their cooperation the rest of the French crew were locked up in the 'tween deck quarters while the captain had been nicely drugged by the cook.

When I came on deck the next morning Dom Pedro was in command of the *Renard*, the French mate was second in command and the stout one, whom we were now calling Miguel, was his assistant. Miguel could speak French and Portuguese with equal ability.

The ship was trimmed, a course set, and a few days later we sighted land. This proved to be the island of Madeira. Here in a small isolated cove, the French captain and the part of the crew that chose to side with him were landed and the *Renard* stood out to sea again.

At noon that day all hands were called on deck and our new captain, Dom Pedro, informed us in a brief speech that he had been a second lieutenant in a Portuguese man-of-war, operating off the coast of Brazil, when they had captured a French barque. He with 25 men were put on board as a prize crew to bring the barque into Rio de Janeiro, but a few days later they were re-taken by this French privateer which in turn had made them prisoners. Now, since he did not care to return to Rio, or to Portugal, he had agreed with Cadouse, the French mate, to go privateering on their own account and take as many ships, French or otherwise, as possible. The cargoes of any ships taken would be sold, he said, and each member of the crew would receive his share in money as soon as it was paid.

My Azores companions and I agreed that we did not like the outlook, for we wanted to return to our families, but we had no choice but to follow the young captain and his motley crew. And, in all honesty, after awhile we became accustomed to the situation and so turned pirates with the rest.

8.

From this point on, the narrative written down by the old pirate, the grandfather of Manoel Cabral, was fairly easy for us to check. The names and much of the action which the old man described are pretty well known to a great many authorities on the subject and the reader will see many connecting links between his story and some of the greatest exploits in the days of pirates and privateers. Here, too, is the part that eventually changed the course of life for a young German sailor named August Gissler.

For several years we sailed in the *Renard* and all hands "prospered." One day we captured a brig. As she was both a larger and a better sailer in general than our vessel, Dom Pedro and most of the Portuguese betook themselves to the brig, while Cadouse became captain of the *Renard*. Later, the brig was renamed the *Relampago*.

Up to this time we had never ventured to attack large vessels, confining our raids to smaller craft and an occasional sortie ashore. But from then on we captured any ship we caught sight of. We had agents in many ports who sold the stuff we landed and who gave us information regarding the movements of good prizes. Every three months our two ships would anchor in the bay of a small island where the spoils were distributed amongst the crew. For several days then a part of the crew was given shore leave while the rest remained on board to overhaul the ship, make repairs and paint. Those on leave would take a boat and sail to another island some ten miles distant, where they spent their money and enjoyed the fruits of their toil. As soon as all had had their spell ashore and all their money was gone, anchors were hoisted and we put to sea again.

Our ships were known from St. Augustine to Para, throughout the Caribbean Sea and the Gulf of Mexico. But in time we were chased so often by men-of-war that it became too dangerous for us to go on a long cruise. It was decided then that Cadouse and the *Renard* should remain on the Mexican coast while we in the *Relampago* should sail into the Pacific. Both ships were thoroughly overhauled in our island retreat and then we went our separate ways.

It was a long voyage down the coast and around the Horn but after three months of sailing we reached the coast of Chile. We were short of water and provisions by this time so we ran into a small creek where we found fresh water. We took all our barrels ashore and filled them and then rafted them back to the ship. Meanwhile, with our largest boat we sailed up the coast a way in quest of a village where we could obtain some provisions.

We found a village but provisions were scarce. However, we learned from the people there that we could obtain all we needed in Concepcion, about 20 leagues north, they said. We returned to our ship, therefore, and informed the captain of what we had heard. We hove up anchor and proceded north along the coast and when we thought we were about abreast of Concepcion the brig was hove to, the large boat launched again, and I with others was detailed to man it and sail in to Concepcion.

After two hours of sailing we sighted a small town and headed straight for it. Upon gaining the shore we found that the place was called Talcahuano and that Concepcion was farther inland. Leaving men to guard the boat, two of us proceeded to the village where we bought some provisions though we could not procure any great quantity.

Upon our return to the boat, the men informed me that a priest had asked whether this was the boat to take him and his companions to the ship going to Spain. The men said they did not know, but said they would send me to see them as soon as I returned. I thought at once that this might be a good chance for profit, as priests seldom returned to Spain without considerable valuables. Anyway, I thought, it would do no harm to see what they wanted and report to the captain.

Leaving my companions at the boat, I went ashore again to hunt for the priests. Someone directed me to their house where, upon knocking, I was admitted to a small plain room. In it were four priests. One of them said: "Why doesn't your ship come into the bay and take us on board? We have been waiting a week."

"It is calm outside," I replied, "and the captain told me to sail in with the boat to buy a few provisions and inquire from you whether you were ready and have not too much luggage for us to take in the boat."

"One boat cannot take all," answered the priest, "as you can see for yourself." He indicated a pile of boxes and crates that filled one side of the room. "In that corner are the provisions we were told to bring along, and here is our luggage. You could not get it all in your boat."

I tried to lift some of the luggage and found it very heavy, though not bulky, and I thought at once it would be worth while to bring their things on board, so I said:

"It would require two boats to bring the provisions and the luggage and you four also, so I will sail back and inform the captain that he must come in with the ship, even if we should have to wait a week for the wind."

This appeared to disconcert the priests and the spokesman quickly answered: "We will not wait any longer. The country is in revolution and we do not know what may happen before the ship can come in. Therefore, we must leave in boats as soon as possible and it must be done in darkness. I will give you a letter for your captain to that effect."

He went at once to another room and returned in a moment with the letter. I took it and returned to the boat and by mid-afternoon we pulled alongside the brig. I went at once to the captain's cabin and gave him the letter.

84

"A letter for you, captain," I said.

"A letter, and from whom? We don't know anybody on this side."

"The letter is not intended for you, but you had better read it, and what you don't understand I may be able to explain," I said.

Dom Pedro, the captain, looked puzzled, but he opened the letter and read it. Afterwards I explained what had taken place on shore. The captain looked at me with a curious sidelong glance and all at once burst out into an uproarious laugh.

"By Santa Maria," he howled, "I knew you were a smart boy the time you cut me loose in the *Renard,* but I never thought you could play a trick like this. What do you think we should do, sail in and anchor or send the boats?"

"We must not sail in, captain," I said. "They expect a ship to take them off. We do not know what that ship is, whether she has been here before, or whether they know the captain. It is not advisable to write either, for if they know the captain's handwriting they might become suspicious and not come aboard. On the other hand they are afraid of the people there and that is the reason why they told me to come after dark to fetch them."

"You are right," agreed the captain. "Go on deck, pick enough men for three boats, and be ready at two bells. Then come to my cabin and I shall give you further orders."

I went on deck immediately and told the cook to have supper ready for 18 men. Then I selected my crews and overhauled the gear for the boats. In each boat we concealed a quantity of cutlasses and pistols. At five o'clock we were ready and I went to the captain for final instructions.

"I cannot give you any specific order," said the captain. "You must be guided by circumstances as they arise. Keep cool. Don't be hasty. First make them believe that none of the men in the boat like the job of fetching passengers off at night. The men must do a little grumbling while carrying the luggage to the boats. Land first with your boat alone. Take only one man with you to the priests, and tell them that as there is no wind I had to send the three boats for them. If they have no men to convey the stuff into the boats you will have to do it yourself, but leave three men in each boat, even while you are loading. Don't beach the boats; keep them afloat all the time in case you should have to pull out in a hurry. I shall go on deck with you now and talk to the men."

"Men," said the captain when we came on deck, "all of you will obey orders from Manoel until you are back on board. No one must leave his boat without instructions. We are on a strange coast and among strange people, so you must be careful. I shall keep as near as possible to the entrance of the bay and have our usual signals burning, but if another ship should turn up, keep out of the way. That is all, now get under way."

Just before dark we came in sight of the houses of the village and I took bearings by compass N by E. We then lowered the sails and waited until it grew darker when we hoisted sails again and steered on our course, all boats in one line. From time to time I hove the lead and when soundings showed only a fathom of water we lowered the sails again. Then I took out a thin line and had it passed to the next boat and the next, telling them if I wanted them to come in I would pull the line. My lead boat was run close to shore where I landed with one man and ordered the boat to pull out a little way and wait.

The streets of the village were quite dark and we found great difficulty in locating the priests' house. I knocked on the door and someone inside asked: "Did you come for us?"

"By the captain's order we came with three boats," I answered, "and he told me to inquire whether you wanted to embark in the boats as otherwise he would try to come in with the ship as soon as he had wind enough."

"We are ready to go in the boats as soon as you can manage it," said the priest, unbolting the door.

"Have you anyone to carry these things down to the boats?" I asked.

"We have nobody," the priest answered, "but we will pay you and your men for carrying them."

"All right," I said, "my companion and I can take some now and come back with more men."

We each picked up a bundle of provisions. When we reached the beach I hailed the first boat and pulled the line of the others. Nine of us went to the house again, leaving three men in each boat as the captain instructed. We had to make three trips before we had everything placed aboard, the men grumbling without coaching, but at last we helped the priests aboard and pulled away. As soon as we felt a breeze we set sails and toward morning came alongside the *Relampago*. Ready hands helped hoist everything aboard and then I went to report to the captain. I said that everything was on board, the provisions, the luggage and the four priests.

"You fool!" exclaimed the captain. "What made you bring the priests? Didn't you have sense enough to leave them behind?"

"We could not take the luggage without them or without risking a row," I protested.

"Bad business," said the captain. "We cannot very well throw them overboard. I must think about this a moment. Meanwhile, take them into the small cabin. Four bunks are in there, so tell them to turn in and that I shall see them later this morning. When you have them safe in the cabin, lock the door and come back."

I went into the cabin and lit the lamp. Returning on deck I told the priests to follow me. I pointed out the four bunks and told them to get some rest, that the captain would see them but went out immediately and locked the door.

"Are they locked in?" asked the captain, when I had returned to his cabin. I nodded. "Now," he said, "come on deck and we two will overhaul the provisions. Their luggage must be brought into my cabin as everybody need not know what is in it."

The provisions were overhauled on deck and taken forward to the storeroom. The captain and I then examined the luggage in his cabin. There were several bundles of gold church vessels, a large quantity of crucifixes inlaid with precious stones, several heavy boxes of great value and four large bags of doubloons. The captain put everything away in his lockers and then said:

"Take anything you can find, old iron, ballast stones or chains and wrap it up in their luggage again as near as possible to resemble the original shape and at daybreak you must take the priests back again to the village. I shall tell them that it is all a mistake and that they have come to the wrong ship."

At daybreak the captain sent a man to each top to take a good look around and they reported nothing in sight. He then went to the small cabin and returned with the four priests. I do not know what he told them, but when he saw me he greeted me with a lot of abuse: "Of all the fools I have on board," he shouted, "you are the biggest. Why in thunder did you not tell me that the fathers wanted to go to Spain? You said they were bound for Mexico. Are you such a blockhead as not to know the difference between Spain and Mexico? I have a good mind to have you flogged."

One of the priests interposed at this point. "Forbear, captain," he said, "by flogging the man nothing would be gained. We are sorry that through this misunderstanding we have put you and ourselves to some inconvenience. If you will kindly send us on shore again we, at least, shall forgive the man and hope you will do the same."

"I shall, since you wish it," growled the captain, "but as he must be punished, he will have to take you back again. Now, fathers, come down and have breakfast with me before you go." Turning to me he added: "And you get everything ready and lower the boats."

The captain and the priests disappeared below and I called up my same crews who had accompanied me ashore. They looked astonished when told to load the luggage and bundles back into the boats but no one said anything. As soon as it was all safely stowed I went down the ladder, followed by the priests, and we shoved off.

The priests did not care to return to the village, they said, and instead they directed us to land them in a small creek which they pointed out. Close to the beach was a small house and as soon as we had begun to unload the head priest went towards the house, bidding us to wait. As soon as we had finished unloading, however, we boarded our boats and pulled away, leaving the three priests and their luggage on the beach.

On the way back to the ship some of the men began to murmur and one of them, a Spaniard, said: "Carajo! Amigo, what is the meaning of this? Is the captain losing his senses? Sending the luggage of the priests back again when in three months we have not made a haul! Surely we are not sailing these seas for pleasure?"

"You heard the captain's order," I replied. "Why don't you ask him?"

"I will," retorted the man, "I and a few more will ask him the reason why, and that damned soon."

That closed the conversation but nothing was said when we came back aboard the brig, sails hoisted and we headed again up the coast. But a few days later mutiny broke out. I thought it would come to blows, but the captain had too many men on his side and the mutineers were afraid to rise. They did, however, obtain the captain's promise that he would heave to opposite Valparaiso and those who wished to go ashore for a little spree could have the use of a boat. He would wait for them three days outside the harbor, he said.

When we reached the latitude of Valparaiso, the brig was hove to, a boat was lowered and 17 of the mutineers sailed away. The captain promised he would wait three days for them, but they were no sooner out of sight when all the canvas was ordered set and we ran before the wind up the coast.

We did not sight any other sail until one morning about 16 days after the mutineers left us when the lookout reported a vessel ahead, two points on the starboard bow, close hauled and heading about west-south-west.

"Call all hands," shouted the captain. "Open the ports and clear for action. We are opposite the Guayaquil River, and this ship may be a Spanish galleon homeward bound, judging by the course she steers. Step lively, chicos, these tubs generally carry much treasure. Let us take her. We have been idle long enough."

We were running before the wind so the other vessel could not see our flag. "Hoist the flag in the foretop," shouted the captain, and up went our flag, while the other ship hoisted Spanish colors. At the same time her yards were squared and she came up before the wind about one mile ahead of us.

"Ho!" laughed our captain. "She's going to make a stand. That's the best she can do because she knows we could beat her in a race." The captain shouted orders to the starboard guns and the grappling irons and every man aboard was standing by ready at his post. We came abreast of the Spaniard in about an hour and poured a broadside into her, made fast with the irons and boarded her with the captain in the lead.

The fight lasted less than ten minutes. We greatly outnumbered the Spaniards and when their captain fell the rest soon surrendered. The name of that ship was the *Rosario*, 250 tons, bound for Cadiz with a crew of 50, of whom more than 20 were killed in the fighting and most of the rest were wounded. Our broadside of grape had done the trick. We transferred her bullion and valuables to the *Relampago*, along with ten pipes of wine and a few casks of beef. About a dozen of the prisoners took the oath and joined our crew, then the *Rosario* was scuttled and the dead and wounded went down with her.

That night our course was altered slightly to N.W. and the captain said we would make for Acapulco on the coast of Mexico.

This announcement was hailed with shouts of glee by all the men, for Acapulco in those days was a famous hangout for ships and men of all nations. But in the days that followed we began to have some second thoughts about sailing into Acapulco harbor with all the *Rosario's* booty aboard. As luck would have it, we happened on to a good solution to that problem a few days and several hundred miles from Acapulco.

9.

WE have spoken before of the uncertain maps of the Pacific. Many of these were still in existence and in use during the early days of the nineteenth century and it is easy to understand the surprise of the captain and the crew of the pirate ship *Relampago* when they stumbled onto a small island unnamed and unmarked on their charts. But the pirates turned the mapmakers' carelessness to good use, as we shall see, and thereby established another sequence of treasure legends about Cocos Island. Manoel Cabral's pirate grandfather herein recounts the action which inspired August Gissler to spend a lifetime in a fruitless search.

A few days after our capture of the *Rosario*, the lookout reported land ahead. I do not think the captain had any intention to stop there but as the land lay directly in our course we worked close in shore and discovered that we had come upon an island. From far off we could see a huge waterfall with high mountains on each side. We shortened sail and approached slowly, heaving the lead all the time. At last we dropped anchor in 14 fathoms, close to a small conical rock shaped something like a farmer's haystack. The island was covered with trees. Everything was green.

The captain called all hands on deck and began by saying that he was as much surprised as anybody to find an island here, as he did not expect to sight any until we had reached the coast of Mexico. Under the circumstances he thought we might pull in shore and replenish our water tanks, and at the same time sail a boat around the island to see whether there were human beings living on it.

That same afternoon the captain, myself and six men sailed away and rounded the island. We found a small bay at the N.E. end, but no signs of habitation anywhere. Returning on board, a council was held and it was agreed to bury on the island all the booty we had taken from the *Rosario*.

The next day three boats landed the treasure on shore near a coconut grove. The captain, myself and five men had come in one boat. After the treasure was unloaded and carried up on the beach, two boats returned to the ship to fetch the empty water barrels. There was a wide stream running into the sea close to us, but of the waterfall that we had sighted from the ship, we could not see anything now.

The captain and I, leaving five men with the booty, followed the stream. About half a mile inland we saw the water falling from a height of about 300 feet. The sides of the river were steep up and down, sloping a little toward the sea. The captain thought of burying the plunder somewhere near the waterfall, and I agreed with him, but while returning and following the stream on the other side we came to a small grove of coconut trees; here we eventually decided to conceal the treasure.

The captain remained in the grove, while I went to tell the five men to bring up the booty. We had taken some shovels with us in the first boat and with one of these I dug a hole in the ground. The soil consisted of a kind of gray sand, with very small stones in it. The treasure of the *Rosario* was wrapped in ship's canvas and piled into the hole, which is about 600 feet W. by S. from the mouth of the stream and about 20 feet back of the coconut grove. The captain took exact bearings, but he did not tell me what they were. I took my own bearings from the mouth of the stream in a line with the round rock.

All of us then returned to the brig and fetched the luggage of the priests. This was not so bulky as the other load but was more valuable I thought. The captain ordered us to carry the stuff to the coconut grove. There we gathered a lot of coconuts which the captain ordered carried to the boat.

Meanwhile, the captain told me to pick up a bundle as he did and follow him. A little farther inland we came to a small runlet which we traced a short distance until we reached a large tree.

"This is a good place," said the captain. "Put down your load and go back for another." When I returned to that spot the captain was not there but since I had more bundles to fetch I went back and forth several times. When at last I had all the bundles under the tree and the captain still had not returned, I shouted for him. He came shortly after and said: "Come along and bring the shovels."

We stepped across the runlet and not far away came to a small hill. "Here is a good land mark near this boulder. Now we will bury the treasure in front of the hill and drop the boulder on the top of it."

I dug a hole on the edge of the small hill, right in front of the boulder. When the pit was about four feet deep, the captain and I returned to the tree and fetched the bundles. We had to make several trips. As soon as we had everything placed in the hole, I shovelled in some dirt from underneath the boulder, which finally tumbled by its own weight directly on top of the grave.

While carrying up the treasure I had counted 85 steps from the tree to the hole. From the coconut grove to the tree I did not count the steps but calculated that it was about twice the distance, or at the most very little more.

The boat was waiting for us when we returned to the shore, but we lingered for nearly an hour. Not far from the stream lay a heavy rock. The captain, who had brought with him a hammer and cold chisel, went over to the rock and cut in the surface of the stone the letters D. P. I. 600 P.

By this time the tide had receded and we had hard work launching the boat, with heavy rollers rushing in all the time. There is very little sand beach at low water, practically nothing but boulders. At last all of us got into the boat and although we were very nearly swamped several times we managed to get aboard safely. As soon as the boat was hoisted we hove up anchor, sailed round the southern point of the island and struck for the western coast, heading for Acapulco.

About ten days later we had run down our latitude and stood toward the land under small sail. Close in shore we sighted a small sailing boat which we captured. There were two fishermen in her who informed the captain that two Spanish galleons were lying in the harbor ready to sail homeward. They were waiting now for a train of mules from the City of Mexico. Several pack trains had already arrived a few days before.

The captain decided to keep the two fishermen aboard and ordered them to change clothing with me and another man named Alonzo. We were to disguise ourselves and use their boat to sail into Acapulco and find out all we could about the two galleons.

The captain gave each of us ten gold ounces and advised us to try to mingle with the crew of the galleons and induce them to drink with us in order to obtain information.

Alonzo and I put off and sailed into the harbor. It was still daylight so we did not attempt to land, but lowered the sail and dropped the fishing lines overboard, pretending that we were fishing. In reality we were only looking around for a good landing place not too far from the town. We at last decided to run in close to a grass hut just on the outskirts of the town. Gradually pulling towards the hut, we landed shortly after dark.

We beached the boat and started for the town on foot. We traversed several streets without noticing any drinking place, but presently we heard music and through an open window noticed that dancing was going on inside. We thought this would be as good a place as any to get information about the Spanish ships.

We entered and stood just inside the doorway awhile, looking on. Two girls who had been sitting on a bench against one wall came up to us and asked us to come on in. When we asked for something to eat and drink they led us into another room furnished with several tables and benches. We ordered wine and edibles for the four of us. From time to time a couple from the dancing room, a sailor and a girl, would come in and order refreshments. The girls we had at our table invited other girls to drink with us, and in a short time we found ourselves with eight girls sitting at our table drinking wine.

We had to pay for the wine as soon as it was served and Alonzo took out a gold piece and paid for what he had ordered and gave the change to a girl.

It had been a long time since we had known the company of females so Alonzo and I sat there eating and drinking and talking to the girls for about two hours. But this monopoly of so many antagonized some of the sailors and finally a group of six or more came in and a fight started. Bottles and knives were freely used but we two were no match for the numbers that bore in on us despite some help from the girls. At last Alonzo and I both went down and lost consciousness.

When we came to our senses we were lying in a small room with our heads and other parts of our bodies wrapped in bandages. We were both so badly wounded we could not move without severe pain.

We lay there for several weeks while our wounds healed and the girls nursed us back to health, but it was a couple of months before we were able to walk on the street.

In the meantime the galleons had sailed and we heard that they had been captured by a foreign vessel. They had also captured a rich mule train in a raid ashore. Alonzo and I well knew the name of that pirate but prudence compelled our silence. However, we swore vengeance if we ever came face to face with our captain for thus deserting us, for we are sure he made no effort to find us.

After paying for our lodging and care we still had four ounces between us and with this capital we left Acapulco and journeyed to the interior in search of work. We found employment in the silver mines where we worked for two years. With a little money in hand we then made our way towards the Atlantic coast by way of the City of Mexico. We at last reached Vera Cruz where we hoped to learn something about the whereabouts of the *Renard*. While waiting, Alonzo caught the fever and despite anything I could do for him he died.

I was very anxious to get back to sea but after several weeks I still had heard nothing of the *Renard*. I did, however, hear that the *Relampago* was back in the Caribbean, and then word came that she had been captured by an English frigate and 81 of the crew hanged in Jamaica. Perhaps this was the fate of the *Renard*, for I never heard anything more of her.

I eventually worked my way to Cadiz on a Spanish vessel, and from there went to Lisbon. While crossing on the Spanish vessel, I came to realize that I could no more do the work of a sailor but I still could ship as a cook and from Lisbon I sailed in that capacity on an American ship. From there I transferred to an American whaler which I hoped would return me to Pacific waters.

While Alonzo and I were recuperating in Acapulco I learned that the island where we had buried the treasure was known along this coast as La Palma. It was my object now to return to the island and try to recover some of the treasure, but though the American whaler did operate for a while in the Pacific we never did call at La Palma, though it was the habit of most whalers to call there for water.

I remained three years aboard the whaler and left her in Fayal, where I was paid off.

After I left the whaler I did not try again to get to the island. I was married soon after I left the sea. My wife's father died leaving her this place in San Miguel. We moved over here. A little later a boy was born who did not live long. When my daughter got married I thought her husband ought to seek the treasure, but he proved to be useless for the purpose. Now my only hope is that little Manoel will do it when he grows up.

Thus ended the strange tale of the old pirate, grandfather of Manoel Cabral. When Gissler had finished reading and transcribing it, Manoel asked him what he thought of the story. The German exhibited some skepticism and said there were several things in it which he could not understand.

"These papers are nicely written," he said, "and I can see, judging by the Portuguese we have on board here, that very few of them can read and write. How then could your grandfather have written these pages?"

"My grandfather," answered Cabral, "was not a common man like these emigrants. He was well educated and I know this to be his handwriting from some letters he wrote to me while I was in San Miguel."

"On the other hand," Gissler argued, "I cannot understand

why he did not persuade your father to go after the treasure."

"My mother," said Manoel, "told me that shortly after their marriage grandfather told both her and my father this story in the hope of inducing my father to ship on board a whaler and make his way to the island, find the church treasure and break out the jewels, as they were the most valuable. This portion of the treasure he could easily conceal on his person and nobody need have been any the wiser. But my father refused to have anything to do with stolen church property and mother always thought that it was through him that people came to know that my grandfather had been a pirate.

"From this time on grandfather took little notice of my father and after I was born grandfather told my mother he would look after me and bring me up to be a different man from her husband. As long as I can recollect, grandfather's will was the law in our house and when he died it was mother who ruled."

The young Portuguese earnestly believed his grandfather's story, but the stolid German was slow to accept it. He put his copy away, however, and jotted down in his diary all the other details about the island of La Palma.

A week or ten days later the emigrant ship *Highflyer* anchored in the harbor of Honolulu. Gissler recorded in his diary that it was on a Saturday morning, 169 days after they left London. According to the diary:

Doctors came on board, the crew was mustered aft and those who had no distinct marks of vaccination were vaccinated again. On the following Monday all the passengers were taken in tugboats to the quarantine station on the other side of the bay.

After the passengers and their luggage had been landed, the barque was made fast alongside a wharf and the discharge of the cargo began. The next day the passenger cook, the steward and several sailors, myself included, were paid off at the consul's office and that same day having found rooms on shore we all left the ship.

Gissler's account of his first few weeks in Hawaii gives us a vivid description of the islands at this period, his adventures in Honolulu during a smallpox epidemic, and his wide-ranging search through the islands for work. Being a little more frugal than most, he chose to do most of his traveling by foot, his bedroll on his back, or by working his way in one of the small native schooners that plied the islands. His description of these travels reveals a man of keen perception, unusual physical stamina, and a real zest for life.

Eventually he found employment on the plantations around Pahala where he worked for a couple of years. In his account he says:

While in Pahala I had bought a saddle horse, and often in the evening I would ride into Waiohinu to purchase what I needed at one of the various stores. Thus I became well acquainted with a storekeeper by the name of Charley Meincke. We used to shake dice over the counter for a bottle of beer and I seldom went there without encountering an old man who went by the name of Mac. Mac would often shake the dice with us but he never talked much.

Seeing old Mac around the place so often, I finally ventured to inquire of Charley what the old man did for a living. Charley said he owned a patch of land on which he grew vegetables and raised hogs, and sometimes he did a little work as a carpenter.

Later Gissler met a young farmer named Bartels. He was married to a half-caste girl who was the daughter of old Mac. Bartels and Gissler became very good friends and one day Bartels, with his wife's help, told Gissler in confidence something of the interesting background of old Mac, her father. It turned out to be another link in the chain of evidence that was to bind Gissler to the life of a treasure hunter.

10.

ONE Sunday afternoon Bartels and his wife came to visit Gissler at the latter's house. It was in the course of their conversation on this occasion that Gissler learned for the first time that Bartels' wife was the daughter of old Mac. Bartels also disclosed that he had sold his ranch for a good price and when Gissler asked him what he intended to do now, Bartels said he had come to see him for that very reason.

With a glance at his wife, Bartels said: "Maybe I'd better tell you first what I know; afterwards my wife can relate what she recollects and fill in the points I overlook."

August Gissler was always a good listener, and he seemed to have a knack of winning the confidence of those he met, as witness the circumstances under which he acquired the autobiography of the old Portuguese pirate. The story which Bartels and his wife told was somewhat diffuse but, briefly, it was this:

In 1851 Mac, his Hawaiian wife and their two small children, a boy and a girl, started from Hawaii on a trip to an island off the west coast of Central America. Mac had long been in possession of certain maps and information relative to a treasure buried on this island and he had no doubt at all that once he got there he would know how and where to recover the treasure.

This family expedition, however, failed to reach the island. They got only as far as La Paz, Baja California, when their funds gave out. Here Mac found work as a carpenter. The intention was to remain in La Paz only long enough to raise the money to continue the trip, but they never went any farther. Mac was injured in a fall and since his wife still owned some land in Hawaii, they decided to return there and wait for another chance.

Mrs. Bartels remembered that they had been for several years in La Paz, and that they returned home by way of San Francisco.

A few years later Mac had a chance to go to the island with an expedition set up for the purpose of hunting for the treasure. But before the old salt went aboard ship he asked the captain what would happen in case the treasure could not be found.

"If we don't find the treasure, we throw you overboard," said the captain, half in jest.

But Mac was no fool. "You'll throw me overboard if we don't find it," he said, "and you will not hesitate to throw me overboard if we find the stuff, so I think I'll not go." It was the last time Mac had tried to recover the treasure.

"He is afraid for his life," said Bartels, "but he has a chart and detailed plans that show where the treasure is buried. And for some reason he knows them to be true, so he grows more anxious every year to go to that island."

Bartels then explained that he himself was convinced the old man knew something he was not telling, but above all he believed too that the chart was authentic. He and his wife thought they could persuade old Mac to lend them the chart and he invited Gissler to "come along with me to the island and we will have a shot at discovering the treasure."

Gissler by now was remembering Manoel Cabral and his strange documents and wondering if there could be any relationship between the island of La Palma and old Mac's "island off the west coast of Central America."

Bartels and his wife returned a couple of weeks later and it was evident at once that they were in very good spirits. They not only had old Mac's papers, but a more detailed story of the treasure. Mac had told them that a captain he knew by the name of Benito had taken a Spanish galleon off Acapulco, Mexico, and had sailed to Cocos Island and buried the treasure there. But before he could remove it again the captain and his pirate crew were caught by a British man-of-war and all hands with the exception of two men called Chapelle and Thompson were hanged.

How old Mac came into possession of the chart he had not explained, but he had assured Bartels that he had proof the treasure was there, and that part of it was buried only five feet underground.

Bartels then showed Gissler the papers. They were obviously very old and written in Spanish, but the drawing was plain. It showed an island with two bays at the N.E. and N.W. ends with several mountains in the center. The island's position was given as latitude 5' 27° N. and longitude 87° W. Compass bearings from two points were given, and where these two lines crossed, the treasure's hiding place was marked. Near this spot there were written the words *tierra alta* which means *high land* in Spanish, but Mac had said that the treasure was lying right under a high bluff.

"Well, what do you think of it?" asked Bartels.

"I wish I had an atlas," said Gissler.

"Wouldn't help you much," said Bartels. "I looked over several but I never did find the island."

"Then the only way to find it," said Gissler, "is by looking up a navigation chart." But by now Gissler was convinced that Mac's Cocos Island and the island of La Palma, spoken of by the Portuguese Manoel Cabral, were one and the same.

"That day," records Gissler, "I decided to accompany Bartels, informing him that I would meet him in about two weeks in Honolulu where we would proceed first to look for a small schooner for our needs."

Bartels and Gissler met in Honolulu as arranged, but no schooner was available for such a long trip. While they were combing the waterfront they received a last note of instructions from old Mac. In it he advised them not to take too many hands to the island. The best way, he said, was to go to San Francisco, thence down the coast to Costa Rica, where they might procure a small craft that would take them to the island. Once there they would be able to dig up the treasure and carry enough of it away to charter a steamer to take away the balance. And, he added: "Don't let a living soul know what you are after or you will have trouble. People might follow you and watch you, and you might not only lose the treasure but also your life."

Bartels and Gissler agreed to follow the old man's advice and so took with them only Bartels' eleven year old boy. They booked passage to San Francisco on the *Mary Winkelman* and left Honolulu on May 18, 1888. They arrived in San Francisco on June 3 where they purchased "an outfit" (probably mining equipment) and a few days later sailed on the steamer *San Blas* for Puntarenas, Costa Rica, which they reached "one Sunday morning about 22 days out from San Francisco. As soon as the steamer came to anchor in the harbor of Puntarenas, we noticed a small craft flying the Nicaraguan flag lying close by."

102

August Gissler had his eye on that small craft as a possible means of getting over to Cocos Island. Here is the story of his adventure for the next few months as he gave it to us:

Not far from the wharf was the Hotel McAdams, where we took lodgings. After breakfast there, Bartels and his boy went to their room and I, remaining on the veranda, was enjoying a smoke when three white men came up to me and asked whether I spoke English. I answered in the affirmative and they inquired what chance they had of obtaining work in town. I explained that as I had only landed there that very morning I could not give them much information. I had heard about several gold mines in Costa Rica where a number of Americans and Englishmen were employed and, judging from these men's appearance that they were miners, I asked them whether they had been working in the mines. One of the men answered:

"We are not miners. We belong to the schooner that is anchored in the harbor."

"Why do you fly the Nicaraguan flag?" I asked. "Have you been smuggling?"

"No, we have been hunting a pirate's treasure," he replied.

"Hunting a pirate's treasure? Where?" I asked, at once becoming tremendously interested in this colloquy.

I almost expected it, but when the man said Cocos Island I nearly jumped from my chair. Here we were, Bartels, his son and I, fondly imagining that no one knew anything about this treasure, and the very first men I spoke to had been on the island hunting for it. I was astonished and perplexed, assailed by doubts for which I could not account.

Later I learned that the men were from Ottawa, Canada, and that a certain Captain Carr had told them he had authentic information of treasure buried on Cocos Island. They had fitted out in San Francisco. But Carr was unable to show them where the treasure was and they had given up the search and sailed for Panama. Here Carr had left them and they had come up the coast to see whether they could sell the schooner.

As soon as the three men left, I want to Bartels' room and told him what I had learned. He, of course, was as astonished as I had been. But we made up our minds to visit tho schooner tho next morning and see if we could hire the vessel or, if the owners did not ask too much, to buy it outright.

When we came down to the wharf the next morning we found the schooner lying on shore, a total wreck. The anchor chain had parted early in the night and she had drifted on the beach. The tide was ebbing and a couple of hours later the little vessel lay high and dry.

We were still interested, however, and concluded to go aboard, but we soon saw that the schooner was old and in a very bad state. She lay on her port bilge, the starboard side high up. Between her timbers she leaked like a sieve. Not being copper sheathed, and having been eight months in the tropics, worms had eaten through the planks. We found out later that she had lain six months at anchor in Panama while two of the men had gone to work on the canal [under the French concession].

It was not worth trying to tow her off, so the owners sold her as a wreck and a few days later they left for the interior of Costa Rica, hoping to find work enough to earn their passage home.

During the few days that they remained in Puntarenas we saw a good deal of them. Thus we learned that Carr pretended to have obtained the information about the treasure from a man by the name of Keating who had been on Cocos in 1844, had found the treasure, and taken away only as much of it as he could safely conceal on his person. On this trip a certain Captain Boag had been with Keating but he was never seen any more.

Keating had said, upon his return to St. John's, Newfoundland, that Captain Boag had fallen overboard and been drowned. The authorities prosecuted Keating in an attempt to prove foul play, but in the absence of evidence they were forced to let him go free.

After the Canadians left town we hunted around Puntarenas for a craft. At last the manager of a pearl fishing company promised us that in about three weeks one of his schooners would come back from up the coast and he would send her to Cocos Island to hunt for pearls and we could have transportation on her.

During our wait, we journeyed up to the capital, San José, on a little sightseeing excursion. We were back in Puntarenas in two weeks but though we went to the office of the pearl company every day, we could never ascertain when the schooner would arrive.

In the meantime Bartels' boy came down with the fever. His father became alarmed and wanted to return to Honolulu. He said we could start anew from there in our own schooner. But I declared positively that I would not return to Honolulu until after I had been on the island, and that if he wished to go back he must leave me the chart. I would try on my own hook, and if I succeeded in finding the treasure, he and old Mac should get their share. Bartels agreed, gave me all old Mac's papers, and left a few days later by the steamer for San Francisco. I never saw him or heard from him again.

For another two weeks I waited around for the pearl schooner without results. Eventually a Swedish barque with a cargo of cedar wood from the West Coast came into port. I soon found out that she was shorthanded, but no sailors were to be had in Puntarenas. I made the acquaintance of the captain and learned that he was bound for Fleetwood for further orders, but as he had a brother in Chile and also needed a new set of sails, he would run into Valparaiso on his way down.

I saw a possibility here and so I proposed to the captain that I would go to Valparaiso with him, provided he would land and stay at least a week on Cocos Island. The captain agreed, and I helped him pick up two green hands to make up for the shortage in his crew. Even then, however, we were far from being fully manned. We could not even heave up anchor when leaving port, and had to send for help to a German barque that had arrived the day before.

We were only 350 miles from the island and thought we could easily make it in a week's sailing, but very light winds prevailed, and 14 days elapsed before we sighted Cocos. At that point we were becalmed again and that night we lost sight of the island completely. For another week then we drifted around without having a glimpse of it and finally we gave up and headed for Valparaiso, where we arrived 73 days out from Puntarenas.

Thus August Gissler laconically describes his first attempt to reach Cocos Island. There is little hint of his great disappointment in coming so close and yet not even setting foot on the island, but we can assume that by this time he was thoroughly convinced that treasure was buried on Cocos and for the rest of his life he would stubbornly persist in the search. Here, too, we find his encounter with still another treasure map and the Keating sequence. He admitted to astonishment and perplexity, ". . . assailed by doubts for which I could not account." But he was to meet many more such currents and crosscurrents in his search for Cocos treasure, though none ever threw him far off his determined track.

11.

ONE could hardly call August Gissler's first inoculation of the treasure bug anything but coincidence, but when circumstances brought him in contact with a second Cocos Island treasure story he was ready to undertake the quest. And, typically, he set about preparing himself for the role of treasure hunter with more intelligence than most. Among the first things he purchased in San Francisco en route to the island were a sextant and navigational instruments. He had already among his possessions a navigation book which he had purchased years before in London. Thus he knew the theory of navigation but he lacked practice under actual working conditions. All this he learned, however, on the long run from Puntarenas, Costa Rica, to Valparaiso, Chile, aboard the Swedish barque. And his inventiveness and natural resourcefulness were thenceforth to stand him in good stead, for everything he did from now on was to one purpose and one purpose only—to find the treasure, or one of the treasures, buried on Cocos Island.

He continued, too, to check his original charts and treasure data against every new scrap of information. In Valparaiso the captain of the barque, true to his promise, immediately introduced him to his brother who was in the shipping business through whom Gissler hoped to acquire a boat for a return to Cocos. As the German tells it:

"That morning the captain and his brother invited me to go ashore with them and in the afternoon we called on Captain Howland, the superintendent of the Valparaiso Whaling Company. He was a New Bedford man and he told us that he had been several times on Cocos Island. Once, in 1875, he had fallen in with an American expedition looking for the treasure. He showed us on a chart where they had been digging close to the beach. This interested me, as the plans in my possession pointed to the cache being a good way inland."

Through these contacts Gissler was able after several months (during which he found employment in Valparaiso) to form a syndicate of 14, consisting of himself and local merchants and dockside workers willing to take a shot at locating the buried treasure on Cocos. A small barque, the *Wilhelmina*, of 350 tons was chartered and from Gissler's account it would appear that every member of the syndicate was on the expedition. It arrived in Cocos waters near the end of February, 1889.

"We had a good run of 18 days and sighted the island one afternoon, but when about four miles from the harbor the wind died down and we began to drift away. We launched the large boat and tried to tow the barque in, but although we were six good men at the oars and pulled for more than an hour, we did not succeed in making any headway. We simply drifted farther away."

They gave up the struggle after awhile and that night lost sight of the island. They continued to beat around but it was another week before they saw it again. Then ". . . the breeze was light and blowing dead ahead. Our water supply was getting low and that little we had was contained in old wine barrels and had turned almost black. On the following Sunday, four weeks after leaving Valparaiso, the day being nice and calm, we held a consultation and concluded that if we could reach the island in a small boat, one man and I would remain on shore, while the mate and three other men should return with water for the barque."

The boat was provisioned and loaded and they cast away about 10 A.M. The boat was equipped with a small mast and a sail, but the day was a dead calm so they rowed. There were six men aboard.

"The day was warm and sultry. Rowing for a whole day in the damp, suffocating atmosphere, under a burning sun, was a severe trial, and all of us were very glad when the sun went down. Immediately before sunset, however, we took bearings by compass to verify the course we had to steer."

During the night a sudden squall struck them and nearly capsized the little craft, but daylight found them near Chatham Bay. It was noon and several adventures later, however, before August Gissler set foot on Cocos Island for the first time.

They filled the water casks and Gissler took a preliminary stroll around the beach. Later that afternoon, after returning to the barque, ". . . I spread out my chart on the cabin table and we made comparisons with the surrounding land.

"The barque rode at anchor about the middle of the bay. To the eastward stood a high mountain; to the westward another mountain with two distinct peaks dominated the surrounding scenery. The two were marked on my chart, one on each side of the anchorage. From these mountains two lines were drawn which joined a good way inland, and a large square had been drawn round the point where the lines intersected. The writing on the plan was in Spanish but Matton, the mate, who knew Spanish well, translated it for us as follows:

"'This island lies in latitude N. 5 deg. 27 min. longitude W. 87 deg. It is a healthy place. In the year 1821 we buried here a treasure of immense value. After we had buried the treasure we planted a coconut tree on top and took bearings by compass which showed locations to be N.E. by E. 1/2 E. to the east mountain and N. 10 deg. east to the West Mountain.'"

A base camp was set up and the expedition remained at the island for several weeks, suffering a daily series of extraordinary adventures and hardships; but in spite of extensive and difficult surveys which they made through the tangled jungle, and numerous excavations under likely rocks and less likely palm trees, they failed to find any treasure.

By the end of a month that had been a constant battle against tropical downpours, heat and hard work, most of the treasure hunters were ready to give up. Gissler, however, refused to leave and three others, Anderson, a marine engineer, Mike, a deep sea sailor, and Holm, a former Swedish army officer, elected to stay with him. The dwindling supplies of the *Wilhelmina* were divided equally into 14 parts and the four for Gissler and his companions were transferred to the base camp on shore. The little ship with her disillusioned treasure hunters returned to Valparaiso, with the promise to return to Cocos within three months with more supplies.

Meanwhile, the four who remained on Cocos continued their search, digging under every palm tree within a wide radius of the spot marked on the chart. "Although we were wet day and night, everybody kept in good health; but of course we all realized that if the rain did not cease we should have to build a better camp."

And one day ". . . instead of going to the diggings, we went on a hunt around the place where I had seen some sheet iron lying on the day we landed. We found the spot easily, and a little farther away part of a house was still standing, entirely covered by creepers. In clearing the creepers we uncovered a door and went inside the house. At a glance we perceived that it could be made habitable with very little repairing.

"On the door we found this notice plainly written in English and Spanish: 'On the 31st day of January, 1884, Captain Schwers of the steamer *Neko* found this island uninhabited and took possession of it in the name of the German Emperor.'"

The treasure hunters cut away the jungle and repaired the shack and forthwith moved in. But it was some time before they saw another ship.

The *Wilhelmina* failed to return to Cocos Island as agreed and for many long months the four treasure hunters remained alone on the island. Eventually, they began to fear that their companions had forgotten them, and with supplies running out, they started to build a boat with the few simple tools they had at hand, with the idea of sailing it to the mainland.

Then, in September, just as their little boat was almost ready for launching, some of the original members of the *Wilhelmina* expedition returned to the island in the barque *Clorinda*, which they had chartered and stocked with relief provisions.

Rough weather, however, prevented the ship from getting close inshore for 22 days. To help the marooned men—who, it was feared, might well be starving by now—the captain ventured one day to send two men ashore in a skiff with food, but they never reached the island and it was presumed that they were wrecked and devoured by the sharks. (The fate of

111

these two men was not explained to Gissler until nearly a year later when he learned that they had been blown away from the island and landed eventually, after many hardships, on the coast of Panama. From there they made their way back to Chile.)

Eventually, a landing was made, and after a few weeks of further fruitless digging, Gissler and the others left the island at the end of December, 1889, and returned to Chile.

For several months after Gissler returned to Valparaiso he was engaged in "various trading ventures" in that city. From these he seems to have profited and he also managed to retain the confidence of his stockholders, for by October, 1890, he was back on Cocos with another expedition, better equipped and more generously supplied than the previous one.

This expedition spent several months on the island "digging and boring . . . until . . . we were forced to admit that we had no sure signs that we should strike anything in the near future. We therefore hove up anchor and sailed for Puntarenas which we reached after a week's voyage."

Gissler by now was of the opinion that the treasure on Cocos was not to be found by a quick perusal of some old chart and a few moments of easy digging in the island soil. The way to find this treasure, he reasoned, was to begin with the known clues, then explore in an ever-widening perimeter around that point until, if need be, he would have covered the whole island. But such a long-drawn-out procedure was not possible with the kind of expeditions he had organized. Even though he had been able to remain on the island for several months and he and his companions had explored a great many possibilities, this hit-or-miss approach to the problem was not to his liking. Gissler reasoned that some system and organization should determine his digging and to do this he would have to spend more time on the island.

Indeed, if possible, he should take up residence on the island and prepare to spend the rest of his life, if necessary, in the search for the treasure.

Thus it was that Gissler hit upon the idea of forming an agricultural colony on the island. Nearly anything could be raised in the climate and rich soil of the island valleys and there was an abundance of wild pigs, deer and goats. With only a minimum of help, a colony could gain a foothold on the island and in a short while be completely self-supporting. And in between times the whole colony could dig for treasure, according to a plan which he would set up.

Fired by this idea, Gissler left the Chilean ship when it put in at Puntarenas and proceeded to San José, the capital, where he made application for a concession to establish a colony on Cocos Island. But these things take time and while he waited he found work in one of the mines in the interior of Costa Rica. Finally, in July, 1891, President Rodriguez granted him certain rights to develop the island agriculturally. "I obtained the concession under the condition that 50 German families should be brought to settle on the island."

Also ". . . A government official gave me a copy of a chart showing where the treasure was buried. Taking the precaution to compare the original with my copy, I found them alike. This chart pointed to a spot not far from shore and was somewhat similar to the plan I already had, except that mine showed the treasure lying farther inland." This was the Jimenez copy mentioned before and was, obviously, the same as the Forbes chart as we shall see.

With the colonization concession in his pocket, Gissler went to Germany "in an endeavor to interest capital in the Cocos Island scheme, but in this I was not successful, the reason being that the concession was too much in favor of the Costa Rican government. At last, after a stay of four

113

months in Europe, I sailed for New York and proceeded from there to San Francisco by way of Panama."

One day, while he was still in San Francisco, he read in a newspaper that a man in Stockton had invented a divining rod by means of which he could locate lines, wells, buried treasures, etc. It was even said that he had already succeeded in locating several valuable gold veins in the Sierras.

"I thereupon decided to go to Stockton and inquire about the invention. Taking the river boat, I proceeded to Stockton and hunted up the man at the address given in the paper." After a long conference ". . . I spoke to him about the Cocos Island treasure. He said that he had intended going to the island to see what he could accomplish with his novel device."

The following morning the man took Gissler around to visit several well-known local citizens, all of whom vouched for him and his ability with the divining rod. But Gissler was hard to convince. He wanted to see the instrument in action, so "we buried $300 in gold in a vacant lot and he located it without much difficulty." This convinced Gissler, and they immediately set about forming a company and raising capital for an expedition to Cocos.

Gissler saw a little 32-foot sloop named the *Hayseed* lying on the muddy river shore. "She looked rather small for a voyage of 4,000 miles but on the whole she seemed to be a good sea boat."

On the voyage up to San Francisco from Panama he had made the acquaintance of a former mate in the employ of the Pacific Steam Navigation Company, a man by the name of Hamlyn, who had been a fisherman in his younger days and had sailed many a mile in small crafts in the North Sea.

"I wrote to Hamlyn, who was in San Francisco, to come to Stockton and have a look at the sloop. When Hamlyn saw her he at once said that she was fit to go anywhere and he would not hesitate to go in her to Cocos Island with me. His decision settled all doubts, so we bought the boat. We put her on the ways, did all the necessary repairs, and the shareholders were very glad indeed when at last we were ready to sail. A blacksmith by the name of Joe Reine, one of the shareholders, came along with us, but the inventer of the divining rod backed out at the last minute, giving as his excuse that the boat was too small."

The *Hayseed* was too small to hold all the provisions and equipment which they purchased so most of it was sent to Puntarenas by steamer and the little sloop put out to sea.

After a succession of squalls, calm and rain, and a near disaster in a gale off Acapulco, they finally dropped anchor in Puntarenas 57 days after leaving San Francisco. It was another few weeks, however, before they landed on Cocos, what with a series of mishaps, contrary winds, a broken rudder and torn sails. Even then, they were able to make it only by passing the island and coming up to it from the opposite side.

Without wasting time in clearing away the debris and tropical growth that had taken over the camp in his absence, Gissler and his companions got immediately to the business at hand:

"The same afternoon we took out the ship's boat and rowed on shore to locate the spot where the lines on my new plan would cross. We soon saw that the line N. 20 deg. W. was taken from the inner point of Nuez Island, while the other line north 63 deg. E. was taken from Conic Island. As we could see, the plan was not quite correct because the lines crossed on the gravel beach about 20 feet seaward from high water, whereas by taking the inside point of the Nuez Island we should come to about 50 feet inland from high water.

"This last place we thought more likely to be the right spot, and we began working at it the next day. We dug down about five feet through the gravel, but the water rushed in so quickly that we had to keep on bailing all the time. We dammed the stream above to deflect its course, but after working a week we had not been able to stop the inrush of water to the hole. We could not use augurs on account of the coarseness of the gravel, intermixed as it was with small stones, and finding it too hard to dig any lower at this place we tried the other spot, starting work at low water. Although we covered the hole with sheet iron, the incoming tide quickly filled it up with sand again.

"Undismayed at the prospect of having to do our work over again every day, we kept at it until we reached a depth of eight feet, where we came on standing water and could not dig any deeper. We worked all around this place as deeply as we could, but although we covered an area of about 400 square feet still nothing was found. Like the plan I had originally brought with me from Honolulu, the plan from Costa Rica proved useless. At any rate no treasure was buried at the point where the lines crossed. After digging for a month we gave it up in disgust, took on water and firewood, and set sail for Puntarenas where we arrived five days later."

Before leaving the island they went into Wafer Bay and discovered on the door of the house which Gissler had built on a former expedition a notice that the steamer *Eliza Edwards* had come there with a party that dug 20 days for the treasure. "We looked for their diggings and found that they had run a tunnel for about 50 feet through a small hill on the N.E. corner of Wafer Bay. And the notice written on the door also reported an expedition which had come in the schooner *Lucia* from Panama. We found their diggings a short distance inland up the stream."

At Puntarenas Gissler came across a clipping from the *New York Herald* which stated that a certain Mr. Young of East Boston, who had information from his father-in-law,

John Keating, had gone to Cocos Island on an expedition organized in Panama. In the article Young complained that he had been ill treated by the crew because he would not tell the exact spot of the treasure according to Keating's information. Gissler wrote:

"I had previously heard that Keating had taken away some valuables from the island in 1844, and the reading of this article decided me to go to Boston and see what I could learn from Young. I thereupon left Puntarenas for Colón, where I took passage for New York, proceeding thence to Boston."

12.

It is our considered opinion that there are three stages through which a man must progress before he becomes the ultimate, the dyed-in-the-gold treasure hunter. The first, naturally, is the educational or indoctrination period. This involves a softening up process wherein all his faculties are remolded to fit the new character. It is the result of a diet of treasure stories.

If he can get hold of some secret information then, or a hitherto unknown angle on some particular treasure story, he is hooked, and impatient for the second stage. This is a period when he will spend money, time and energy "proving" his clues in search of the treasure. If the search is successful, then his expenditures are justified; but if all his efforts are in vain and the treasure continues to elude him, then his search becomes more frantic with each failure. This, the frantic period, is the third stage.

August Gissler's long trip to Boston on the slim tip given in the newspaper article may seem a little farfetched and out of character for the German "Hermit of Cocos Island," but the fact is that Gissler was by now in the third stage and becoming a little frantic. He would follow up any lead no matter how faint, because all his failures had only convinced him that the treasure was still there.

Gissler found his man, Young, in Boston without much difficulty, but getting the treasure information out of him was something else again. In Gissler's account of this trip a lot of cloak-and-dagger shenanigans are played by several interested characters, but after weeks of negotiation, Gissler and two New York promoters put together an organization and Young put up the Cocos data as his collateral. Gissler says that between them they gave Young $700, but it is our belief that if Gissler put up anything it was his promise to pay a percentage of any treasure found by Young's instructions. Certainly, after a glance at Young's papers he knew every rock and tree mentioned on them and he so informed his partners. He also told them he had already explored the spot marked on Young's chart and he believed the clues were all wrong.

Nevertheless, an expedition of ten men was organized and it sailed from New York in the steamer *City of Para* for Colón. Young was too ill or too senile to go so he sent a friend along to watch out for his share of the booty—if any. From Colón the party crossed the Isthmus of Panama and boarded the Pacific Mail Steamer *Acapulco*. Captain Clark of the latter ship gave them a whaleboat and left them and their supplies off at Cocos Island. He promised to arrange for another ship to pick them up in two weeks, but long before that short time expired, Gissler had proved to the other expedition members that Young's information was erroneous. It was a discouraged and disillusioned bunch of treasure hunters that stood on the beach of Wafer Bay when the Pacific Mail's *San Blas* stopped by to take them off.

Gissler returned to New York with the others and went on to Boston to confront Young with the failure of his instructions. We do not know why he would go to such expense unless he had some hope of getting more explicit or more accurate information from the ailing Young, or the hope that he could interest capital in another Cocos venture. In any case, we find Gissler back in Costa Rica after a few weeks, the object of this trip being "to obtain another concession from the government. I explained to the president (Rafael Yglesias) that it was impossible to raise any capital on the concession I had received in 1891, and he requested me to put down what I now desired, and he would see what he could do.

"My demands were for a gift of one-half of the island for myself, the other half to be laid out in sections for the settlers I proposed to bring. It took some time to win my point, but eventually the terms were granted."

Gissler now made another trip to Europe where he was able to raise some capital and colonists among his relatives and friends. He also got married, and "my wife went with me to the island where the Pacific Mail Steamer *Costa Rica* landed us on the 13th of December, 1894. We were in all six families. From New York we brought lumber and building materials, provisions and seeds. In Panama we secured tropical plants, chickens, ducks and turkeys. The first thing we did was to build more houses and clear the land to plant cane, bananas, vegetables and coffee." The limes which recent visitors have reported using in their cocktails were from trees planted by Gissler's colonists.

In February, 1895, the Costa Rican government's steam launch, *Turrialba,* under the command of Captain R. McCartney Passmore, visited the island for the first time. Captain Passmore, aided by Gissler, took a series of soundings and obtained other hydrographic data from which he subsequently made a chart of the island to supplement the earlier British Admiralty charts which, up to that time, were the only ones available.

Gissler sent off a letter by the *Turrialba* telling his friends not to send any more families until he had more housing accommodations ready for them; nevertheless, in May, four more families and three single men arrived. They brought with them not the provisions which Gissler asked for but more building material, lumber and tools, none of which was really needed. "As no more ships came in, it was not long before we ran short of provisions. One of the settlers fell ill, his limbs became swollen, and soon afterwards he died of dropsy."

At last Gissler realized it would be necessary to go to the mainland for help and so once again he set about building a boat. "To save time, we made her flat-bottomed. She was 26 feet long, eight feet beam, and for sails I used my wife's bed sheets."

He took four men in the boat with him, not one of whom even understood the use of a compass, but with the German's good knowledge of navigation they made Puntarenas in four and a half days.

Gissler took this opportunity to make a more favorable contract with the Costa Rican government, under which it was stipulated that the government launch *Turrialba* would make a regular monthly visit to Cocos Island with provisions and mail. When Gissler was ready to return, three of the men who had accompanied him to Puntarenas refused to return to the island. "All I could get out of them was that they did not intend to go back to Cocos, and that their wives could come to Puntarenas on the government steamer if they wanted to. There was no use in trying to reason with these men and telling them what a cowardly thing it was to leave their wives. . . ."

It was several weeks, however, before Gissler himself got back to the island and when he did arrive he found the rest of the colony in rebellion. "All were complaining and had made up their minds not to remain there any longer. To bring the settlers over had cost a lot of money but I thought it would be cheaper in the long run to get rid of them."

Gissler shipped the three deserted wives to Puntarenas when the *Turrialba* made its first call at the island. Thereafter, the government launch made its monthly trips fairly regularly for a few months but, after a while, it failed to return to the island. In 1897 provisions had got so low that Gissler patched up an old open boat and set off for Puntarenas with two men. They made it to Puntarenas this time in 52 hours, something of a record for small sailboats.

While Gissler was in Puntarenas on this trip, a British man-of-war, *H.M.S. Imperieuse*, Admiral Palliser in command, landed at Cocos. The admiral sent several platoons of bluejackets ashore with shovels and picks and large quantities of dynamite. Without permission or government authorization, and despite the remonstrances of Mrs. Gissler, they dug and blasted huge holes all over the place for several days. When Mrs. Gissler protested she was curtly told to mind her own business. When Gissler recorded this sorry incident, he added: "For the sake of the British Navy, I hate to believe that Palliser acted under instructions from his government, but if greed of money can lead a British admiral so far to forget himself as to violate private rights, what can be expected from the rough sailors who carried out his orders?" In fairness to the admiral's superiors, and British diplomacy, let us say here that the admiral was severely reprimanded for his unwarranted intrusion on Cocos Island.*

It was in 1897 also that John Keating's widow, now Mrs. Brennan, arrived at Cocos Island on the schooner *Aurora*

* See Appendix V.

and tried to locate the treasure on information she said Keating had given her. Nothing was found, but several years later Gissler happened upon the spot described by Keating, to wit, a large boulder inscribed with a "K" and an arrow pointing towards a hollow tree. He found no other indications of the treasure, however, and finally gave it up as another mystery of the island. Curiously, this boulder, with the mysterious markings, was unearthed by the Forbes-Lewis treasure hunting expedition 43 years later, in March, 1940.

On November 11, 1897, by a formal presidential decree, August Gissler was appointed Governor of Cocos Island. He had become a naturalized citizen of Costa Rica a short while before and this honor was the climax of his Cocos Island experience. He was the first and only governor ever appointed to the island.

But Gissler's colony was disintegrating. By 1898 only three families of his original settlers remained on the island, the others having left as opportunity offered. And sometime during this year these last three families left, disgusted with the rugged island life.

For 22 months, then, Gissler and his wife and one Costa Rican peon remained alone on the island without any communication whatsoever with the mainland. Again provisions ran low and again Gissler built a small boat in which the three survivors eventually reached Puntarenas. Gissler left his wife there and proceeded on to the United States in an attempt to interest new capital in his Cocos project. He returned a year later in December, 1902. A Norwegian vessel carried him and his wife back to Cocos and from then until February, 1905, they were alone on the island.

In that month the yacht, *Rose Marine*, owned by an Englishman named Gray, arrived at Cocos to search for the treasure. Gray immediately entered into partnership with Gissler, but after some weeks of unsuccessful digging the

Rose Marine returned to Panama and Gray went on to Europe to obtain more capital and more people to assist him in continuing the search for the treasure. He returned several months later and worked with his men for a long time without finding any trace of the treasure.

In the Costa Rican National Museum in San José there hangs a half-section of the trunk of a large coconut tree. The chunk of wood is about two feet long and nine or ten inches wide. From its weather-beaten appearance the wood is obviously of great antiquity and the tree from which it was cut must have been a very old one. Deeply carved in the wood, in legible English and in letters two inches tall, are the words: THE BIRD IS GONE.

The tree bearing this strange inscription was found near Chatham Bay by August Gissler. He cut out the section and for a long time it adorned a wall of his house on Cocos Island. When he eventually left the island for good, the piece of wood passed into the possession of the National Museum. How old the chunk is no one can say, but it is obviously very, very old.

What does it mean? What message does this short inscription convey? And to whom?

The opinion among most Costa Rican treasure *aficionados* is that one of the men who buried the treasure, or one of the treasures, on the island returned many years later to unearth it only to find that somebody, perhaps one of his former shipmates, had got there before him. Whatever the reason, whoever carved that line had a fine sense of irony, as more than one treasure hunter in recent years will agree.

Altogether August Gissler spent 17 years searching for the Cocos Island treasure—need we add, without success. His efforts cost him at least $50,000. On several of his periodical visits to Puntarenas he disposed of odd ancient Spanish gold coins in order to obtain funds with which to buy the provisions he needed. When questioned about the origin of these gold coins, Gissler always explained that he had simply picked them up by sheer accident on the island beaches. The inference, of course, was that the coins were the flotsam from a larger hoard buried somewhere on the island or washed up from the sea. In a letter which he wrote to a correspondent in 1927, Gissler stated that he had found a total of 33 gold pieces minted between 1773 and 1799, and a gold gauntlet during his sojourn on Cocos Island.

But perhaps the most extraordinary story of August Gissler's hermitlike life on lonely Cocos Island occurred near the end of his residence there. Once again he was faced with the old shortage problem. Even his ammunition had run out or been spoiled by the incessant rains so that he could not hunt wild pigs, always an important food source for the island adventurers. No ship had called at the island for almost a year. Thus, once again he patched up his little sailboat and set out for Puntarenas to buy supplies. He left his wife behind on the island, telling her that he would be back in a matter of four or six weeks at the most.

But six long months passed before Gissler got back to the island. Shortly after leaving Cocos he ran into a storm and the little craft was swept far off her course. When Gissler finally did make his landfall in the leaky and all but useless boat, it was not at Puntarenas but in distant Panama.

Broke and unwilling to spend the few dollars he had set aside for provisions, it was several months before he was able to work his way up the coast to Puntarenas. Even then a lot more time slipped by before he was able to get his supplies and find a boat that would take him back to Cocos.

Six months later, when he eventually got back to the island, he found his wife not only alive but well and apparently none the worse for her long vigil—and this despite the fact that on the day after Gissler left the island she had fallen and broken an arm! She had managed to set the arm herself and it had healed nicely, and she had set traps and snares for wild game with sufficient success to provide something more than a starvation diet.

Perhaps that experience was the factor that decided Gissler to abandon the island which had been his home for so many long years, for shortly afterwards he and his wife left Cocos and neither of them ever returned. They went to New York where Gissler spent his last days, supported by relatives. When at last he died in the big city on August 8, 1935, at the age of 78, it was towards Cocos Island that his last thoughts turned.

August Gissler's will was filed for probate in the Surrogate's Court of New York on November 12, 1935. In his will he bequeathed half of Cocos Island to various relatives and friends. He estimated the value of his legacy at not less than $200,000 but for probate purposes he had suggested that his estate be valued at a paltry $500.

One can understand the elation of Gissler's beneficiaries when they learned that they had fallen heirs to a treasure island in the Pacific Ocean, but they were soon to suffer disappointment. When some of them wrote to the Costa Rican government to ask about the value of their inheritance and to inquire when they could take possession, they were politely informed that inasmuch as Gissler had never owned Cocos Island, but had merely been the incumbent as nominal governor of the island, the "inheritance" was worth precisely nothing.

Among August Gissler's papers we find these lines, perhaps the last he ever wrote: "The treasure is on the island, but it will take money and a good deal of effort to unearth it. . . . I have gone through many hardships and dangers and perhaps shall have to do so again, but this will not keep me away. . . ."

THE LOST TREASURE OF

13.

THE only period in contemporary history entitled to the nostalgic panegyric, "The good old days," was the decade that immediately preceded the Great Depression. It began with the ending of the first World War; it sprouted new wings in industry, art, science and the social graces; it developed these to a perfection which the world labeled American Standard of Living; it ended with Black Thursday and the stock market crash of 1929. Any oldster who remembers earlier times must compare his Stanley steamers and outdoor privies unfavorably with this colorful decade, while most of those who knew it and the bitter years that followed have no argument either. It was a period of extreme fads and revolutionary fancies, profusion and Prohibition, Florida booms and F. Scott Fitzgerald, the Charleston and Al Capone, swivel-hipped Red Grange and long-clouting Babe Ruth, Dempsey and Firpo, Gertrude Ederle and Slim Lindbergh. It was a time like nothing that had gone before, or anything that has followed.

The American born during this period has lived his entire

life in a succession of crises. His childhood was spent amid the financial problems that beset his family for ten long years during the world's worst economic depression. Grammar school and high school were clouded with the burden of insufficiencies, and before he could experience any measure of normal adult attainments, he was saddled with the responsibilities of World War II. He has never had the opportunity of experiencing the feeling that the world is peaceful and essentially benign. He remembers not a single year that could compare with any one of the 1920's. It was a period and a time when a man of prominence could relax with his dreams and state without embarrassment that "without the least intention of blushing, I regard treasure-seeking as a praiseworthy and legitimate pursuit!"

We find that line among a considerable pile of correspondence and published material we have collected on Sir Malcolm Campbell (for one of us was a fan of the speed king before we ever heard of Cocos), and it is not a line lifted out of context contrary to the real character of the man. It was a concept he maintained throughout his own praiseworthy life and he found it easy to justify:

"In these days," he wrote, during the height of his racing career, "when life tends to become at once more complex and more prosaic, it is pleasing to find something which still retains mystery, which still defies analysis, which is still capable of lending a touch of romance to things, of kindling sudden enthusiasms. Treasure-seeking does all this. It appeals to the perpetual boy in every man."

Sir Malcolm (at that time he was Captain Campbell) made a trip to Cocos Island during February and March, 1926. In July of the previous year he had become the first man to drive an automobile faster than 150 miles per hour. He continued to break his own records until ten years later when he pushed his Bluebird Special over the 300 mile mark.

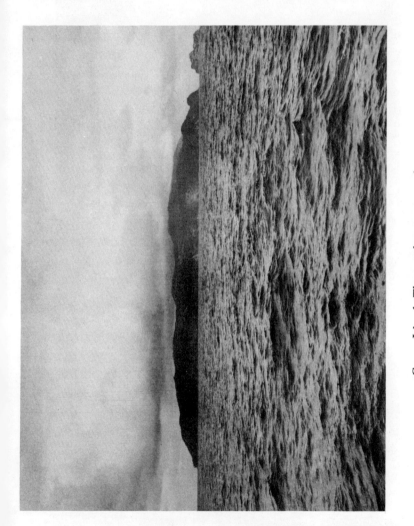

Cocos Island. The northeast approach.

Wafer Bay.

Chatham Bay.

The sign supposedly made by John Keating in 1846 to indicate the position of the treasure. *Photo: Bert Roe*

"The Bird is Gone" — the sign cut from an old palm on Cocos Island by August Gissler. It is now in the museum in San José.

August Gissler as he looked when he was Governor of Cocos Island.

The *Veracity* at Puntarenas.

Members of the *Veracity* expedition.

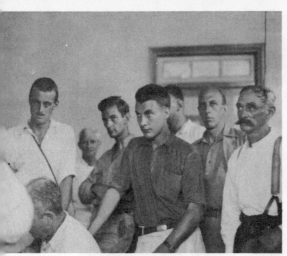

aptured British treasure hunters of the *Queen*
Scots expedition in court at Puntarenas.

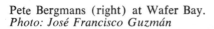

Pete Bergmans (right) at Wafer Bay.
Photo: José Francisco Guzmán

President Roosevelt on Cocos Island.

A carved boulder on Cocos Island bearing dates of visits to the
island over a hundred years ago. The tent at the right gives the
scale. *Photo: Bert Roe*

James Forbes of Riverside, California, the promoter of several
treasure-hunting expeditions to Cocos Island.

The *Spindrift* in the harbor at Puntarenas.

The yacht *Stranger*.

An old wreck on the beach at Cocos Island.

It was in the midst of such concentration and physical stress that he wrote the following letter on April 29, 1930:

I visited Cocos Island in 1926 with a small party of friends who were not really enthusiastic over this treasure hunt, they all being too sceptical and believed that the whole thing was a fairy story.

I already had in my possession the clue to the *Mary Dear* treasure, which I had received from the most reliable sources possible, this clue having been held for many years by the late Admiral Curzon Howe, who received it first hand from a seaman whose life he had previously saved. The veracity of all this can be definitely vouched for.

My friends expected that they would come across the treasure five minutes after landing, and because we were not immediately successful they lost heart. I lived on the island with two seamen in a tent for a matter of seventeen days, and we had to leave hurriedly since the yacht on which we had made our voyage was due back in England in April, as it had been sold and a definite delivery date named. In addition, both my seamen companions were losing heart owing to the privations which we endured, and one of them fell down the hillside and nearly broke his back, and, therefore, we had to leave in great haste with the sick member of the crew.

I was actually there during the months of February and March, 1925, and we only had rain for about a quarter of an hour one night, the weather being exceptionally hot but fine.

I should be extremely indebted to you if, when next you write, you would let me know definitely what are the best months of the year for spending on Cocos. From previous experience I rather gathered they must be January, February, March—April to August being the wet season and much rain is experienced also during September to December. I should be very greatly obliged if you could enlighten me further in this respect, as although I have endeavored to get definite news from reliable quarters concerning the general weather conditions, all the information I have so far obtained has been rather vague.

I found certain markings on stones when on Cocos, but was absolutely unable to fathom the sense of these, but since Gissler had apparently made his own markings, having removed the genuine ones, this would account for the mysterious letters and words which I came across, and which I could not make head nor tail of.

As far as I know the treasure is buried quite close to the coast, if the clue which I still have can be relied upon. There has been a landslide over this particular spot, although there is not a terrific lot of material to clear away in this area, if the treasure still lies beneath.

I have heard rumors, however, that the treasure was removed thirty years ago from its original hiding place and secreted elsewhere. This may or may not be true.

I had a most interesting letter from another correspondent abroad, who states that he himself has been to Cocos, unearthed half the treasure and upon returning for the remainder some years later was nearly engulfed himself in a landslide, and was unable to enter the cave in consequence. I am following up this information also, as I agree in sifting out every scrap of news, as one never knows what this may lead to.

I met Captain Polkinghorne several years ago, before undertaking our first trip, but we were unable to take him with us and I have not seen him since.*

Re Ants: We certainly had our full taste of these pests, as we actually could not keep these out of our tent and they swarmed over us all night. In any case, none of us could sleep properly owing to the terrific heat which prevailed at the time.

No one realizes more than myself the extreme hardships which have to be undergone in an expedition of this description, and I fully agree with you that success can only be achieved by patient and systematic work, which is backed up by a tremendous amount of determination, and no expedition can hope to be successful unless all members of the party have a single minded purpose and are really determined to win through.

The reason why the *Mary Dear* treasure was not discovered almost immediately after it had been secreted, was due, in my opinion, to the fact that it was hidden in a cave, no digging operation having been necessary. I think this must definitely

* Authors' note: We meet him later.

prove that this was so. There are two other treasures to be found in addition to this one. . . .

Sir Malcolm, in his day, was not only the world's fastest man on land (airplanes weren't much faster in those days), but he was undoubtedly the foremost thinker where Cocos Island treasure was concerned. It would be interesting to know, therefore, by what incentives and what reasoning he concluded to organize an expedition to Cocos to hunt for the treasure. He once confessed that his interest in buried treasure began "when I was a very small boy. I loved pirates and their treasures then and I love them even more now. Those dirty, illiterate, bloodstained old brigands of the sea who looted and plundered, swaggered, drank, fought and died, who stormed towns and sank Kings' ships, raised their own armies and captained their own navies, put into practice an impulse which is submerged in almost every man although it may seldom come to the surface."

It was a false picture in many ways, he admitted, for more often the pirate was a brute pure and simple. There were exceptions, of course, but one cannot play at piracy today, nor would he if he could. Nevertheless, there is a remnant of the urge in every man today, for, as Campbell said, "what able-bodied man is there with time, money, and imagination, who would not trim his sails and set his course for salty horizons tomorrow, if he had a clue in his pocket, a treasure to find!"

But with all his background of romantic thinking, Sir Malcolm had a practical, adult head on his shoulders and no Cocos Island clue would send him half way around the world unless it had some foundation in fact.

Like us, he believed there were three separate treasure troves on the island. Somewhere on Cocos, he said, "lie three treasures of gold and silver, jewels and plate, images and weapons, which I honestly believe are the richest and most authentic pirates' treasures in the world." Estimating their value in 1930 he said, "I think that twelve million pounds is a conservative estimate."

He listed the three main treasures as we have: "The first is that of Captain Edward Davis, a partner with Dampier in his privateering adventures, when he blockaded the Bay of Panama and sacked the City of León in Nicaragua in 1685. The second is that of Benito Bonito, 'Bonito of the Bloody Sword,' a pirate of the early eighteen hundreds, and the third is the famous treasure of the City of Lima, which was buried on Cocos in about 1821, by a Captain Thompson, a Scotch merchant skipper, who turned pirate. . . ."

Further, when he had gone over some of the same research ground we have covered, he said of the treasure, "the historical evidence of its reality was beyond question."

It was one thing, he said, "to fix on a treasure and quite another to discover ways and means of getting it. Cocos Island offered hidden millions, but so far I had no clues. These, however, eventually turned up in the most extraordinary manner."

Campbell's background reading was largely influenced by Ralph D. Paine's original account of the Thompson-Keating sequence. Paine (whose son, Ralph Delahaye Paine, Jr., was editor of *Fortune* Magazine from 1941 to 1953 and its publisher since), an authority on American naval history, held with the theory that Thompson was the captain of the *Mary Dear* and that the Lima treasure was buried in a cave.

After Keating met Thompson aboard ship en route to Newfoundland (it was assumed that Thompson had been hiding out in England for the past twenty years), and took him into his house in St. John's, and Thompson confided to Keating his part in the hiding of the Lima treasure on Cocos Island, the rest of the story was interpreted by Campbell as follows:

Keating had little difficulty in persuading one of the rich merchants of St. John's to fit out a vessel. He stipulated that the expedition should sail under the command of a Captain Boag, a trusted friend and reliable mariner. In the midst of the fitting-out Thompson died. He did not forget to leave his chart and clues to Keating and, armed with these, the expedition sailed.

Cocos was reached after a terribly rough voyage, which set up much discontent among the crew, who were in a state bordering on mutiny.

Keating and Boag were both rowed ashore and landed on the beach of Chatham Bay, where the little stream runs over the shingle into the sea. They followed the course of this stream as directed by their chart, reached the great rock, found the secret door, opened it and discovered the dazzling treasure of Lima. It is easy to picture the excitement which seized them. Few men could be expected to keep their heads under such circumstances. Here was enough treasure to make them two of the richest men in the world. . . .

The two promptly stuffed their pockets with as much gold as they could carry and returned to the ship. Their plan was to tell the crew that they had discovered nothing, and to go ashore each day and remove as much treasure as possible, without exciting suspicion. It was a stupid plan, which obviously would never have succeeded. In any case, they had no chance to attempt it, for when they reached the ship their excited manner betrayed them. The men, who were in a very ugly temper, insisted on going ashore at once to look for the treasure and divide it among themselves. They tumbled overboard into the boats, rowed ashore and spent the whole afternoon searching the undergrowth for the cave. Naturally, they found nothing. Nightfall came and they returned to the ship in a worse temper than ever.

The mate got hold of Boag and Keating and told them that unless they led the crew to the treasure next morning both their throats would be cut. Keating saw that the crew would most certainly act on their word, so he promised to show them the cave in the morning.

In the middle of the night Keating and Boag slipped out of their cabins, swarmed down a rope into a small dinghy which was trailing astern and rowed ashore. They landed under the stars in the warm velvety darkness of the Pacific night and scrambled through the dense undergrowth inland. They hid themselves somewhere high up among the gullies of the hillside and awaited the morning.

Dawn came, the first blue smoke of the cook's galley rose up from the ship, voices and the rattle of ropes came across the still waters from the decks and then suddenly there burst out a storm of shouts and cries. The mate had gone to the cabins and found that both the birds had flown.

Bedlam broke loose, whistles sounded, commands were shouted, barefooted sailors tumbled up on deck and lowered away the boats, while others, tousle-headed, bleary and unwashed, stuck their heads out of the ports, still rubbing the sleep out of their grimy eyes. The first boat to touch the water was filled with men and shot for the shore. Another followed and another, and within half an hour of the alarm being given, practically the whole ship's crew was searching the island with axes and muskets, looking for their captain and supercargo. Shouts and cries rang through the palm groves, mingled with blasphemous announcements of what they would do to the two men if they did not surrender immediately.

Keating and Boag both lay low, and after a day or two of toiling and sweating through the almost impenetrable jungles the crew gave up the job and sailed away leaving the two men marooned. Not long after the vessel was wrecked, owing to bad navigation, and I believe I am right in saying that the entire crew was drowned.

Months later, as Campbell believed the story to be, a whaler put into the island for fresh water and discovered Keating, alone and half-starved. Boag had disappeared. Keating said that Boag had been drowned on the night they fled from the ship. Boag had stepped overboard into deep water, with his pockets so full of gold he sank like a stone.

"I do not believe this story for a minute," wrote Sir Malcolm. "I am certain that Keating murdered Boag by shutting him up in the treasure cave and leaving him there to starve. What is more natural than that, when the two men had seen their ship and crew depart, they should go at once to the cave to gloat over the treasure and make plans for its removal when rescue should come? What, also, is more natural than that a man like Keating, who, by all accounts, was a villain, should suddenly stun Boag as he was bending down over the treasure and shut the rock door on him, leaving him to die in the darkness? It was a quick and easy way of making sure that there would be no one else to share the final booty.

"I am convinced of the truth of this theory by the fact that when in later years Keating had escaped and was asked to lead another expedition to the island he agreed to do so on the one condition that he should not be asked to enter the cave. He was so point blank in his refusal to do so and showed such nervous dread of it that, to my mind, there is no doubt whatever that he feared the ghost of Boag."

Sir Malcolm Campbell was convinced that one day when the cave was found and the rock door was opened the discoverer would see beside the heaps of gold and jewels, the boxes of silver, and the bars of gold, the skeleton of Captain Boag, doubled up as he died in the last agonies of starvation, in that black abyss of nightmare horror. But if that be so, then his is only one of the many ghosts which haunt that mysterious island as we know.

Keating suffered great hardships after his escape from the island and in the years before he died, for he never gave up trying to recover the treasure. Campbell reported that "He was wrecked in 1867, and a year later he met a master mariner named Nicholas Fitzgerald, who found him, an old man living in a broken-down hut, penniless and half starved. Fitzgerald took him home and tried to nurse him back to health. It was no use, Keating died; but on his deathbed he told Fitzgerald the full story of the Cocos Island treasure and gave him a map and clues which he had received from Captain Thompson.

"A few months later, Fitzgerald, who was employed in the Newfoundland Cod Fisheries, was wrecked. He was only saved from drowning by the prompt action of Commodore the Honorable Curzon Howe, who happened to be in command of vessels in the locality. This happened in about 1870, two years after Keating's death.

"Fitzgerald never forgot Commodore Curzon Howe's kindness, and when, in 1894, he was lying ill, near the point of death, he wrote to the commodore, giving him all the information that he had received from Keating twenty-six years previously."

Through all those years, Fitzgerald had clung to the hope that he would one day raise enough money to fit out an expedition but, tragically, he was never able to bring it off, though he was instrumental in promoting others.*

Fitzgerald's letter greatly impressed Curzon Howe and he determined to visit the island if ever he got the chance. He placed the map and letter in a safe deposit box at his bank and there they remained until he died.

His son had some hope that he might one day go to Cocos and look for the treasure, and while he was in the navy he once came close, but he, too, was unable to visit the island. However, when he heard that Campbell was outfitting an expedition, he turned over to the famous sportsman all his father's papers. These, and especially the letter from Nicholas Fitzgerald, inspired Captain Campbell to undertake his first visit to Cocos Island. This was the letter which Nicholas Fitzgerald wrote to Commodore Curzon Howe on September 10th, 1894:

* See page 44 and Appendix V.

136

To the Honble.
Commodore Curzon-Howe

Dear Sir,

I presume to address you on what may appear to be a very strange and romantic subject; what induces me to do so is from what I have heard of your gentlemanly and honorable disposition, hoping that you will not treat the matter light, but give it your consideration.

It has been on my mind for many years, and now I have come to the conclusion of confiding to your Honor the information that I received as a secret from one who was under a great obligation to me, and that one was an actual factor in what I am about to disclose to you, allowing that you entertain it.

I believe there is a treasure lying concealed in the Cocos Island, Pacific Ocean; believe that I am the only person who knows the secret where it lies.

Now, as you are occasionally on duty in the Pacific and as a warship is the most suitable means of carrying out such a project, I thought that it would be to my advantage to write to you and explain the facts of the matter to you.

How I came to the knowledge of this: In the year 1868 fortune had thrown me as a shipwrecked sailor from a sailing vessel on the shores of Codroy Village on the west side of Newfoundland, and there I met the owner of another schooner that had been lost in the ice at the same time that we were. This man's name was Keating, a native of this country, and generally known at least by the old inhabitants of St. John's as the man who was on two occasions fitted out with vessel and crew to bring the treasure that still remains hidden in a very secure way at Cocos Island. When I met Keating in 1868 he was in great distress on account of the loss of his vessel and want of provisions for himself and crew; and he was also sick and living for the time in an old deserted house, sleeping in a vessel's sail lying on the floor, banked with ice and snow.

In these difficulties I had the power to assist him, which I did; bringing him to my lodgings and my own bed, caring for him in his sickness. In return for acts of help on my part he en-

137

trusted to me the secret of where the treasure lies hidden at Cocos Island. We drew up an agreement, one of the conditions being that I should go with him for the treasure; another condition was that I should enter the cave alone, as he had pledged himself never again to enter it. I attribute that to fear of something. However, the agreement was not carried out because I, having a family to see to and believing that Captain Boag, the only man who had the secret from Keating at the time, had mysteriously disappeared in his company while at the Cocos Island, I thought I would be running grave risk of my life to go single-handed with him. This disappearance of Boag was unsatisfactorily explained to me by him.

Therefore I believe that I alone possess the secret of where the treasure lies hidden at Cocos Island. I am the only person who can find it or show how it may be found. I am anxious therefore that you, Sir, should give this matter your most careful consideration, and if you arrive at the same opinion as I have concerning the matter you will be more convinced when you have the secret disclosed to you.

The conditions that I will disclose the secret are these: That you will send me an agreement signed by you, Sir, that if you or any person acting for you or any way on account of this information get the treasure you will hand over to me one-twentieth part of the gross value of what is in the cave. The treasure comprises gold coin, silver coin, gold images of the Madonna, life-size church images.

If you desire any further information on this matter I shall be only too happy to supply it you, or any question you may be pleased to put.

I would wish to refer you concerning Keating's expedition to Messrs. Bowring Bros. or Messrs. Job; one of these houses should have some knowledge of the fitting out of the vessels. I think it was in 1843 or perhaps a year or two later. I do know that there is now living in St. John's a man who was an officer on the vessel that went with Keating, who was on his second expedition, and that man's name is Captain Richard Kearney, his address is George Street, St. John's.

I believe Kearney left the vessel before she got round the Horn on account of mutiny. Keating told me that mutiny took place on board of each vessel that he went in, and that was the cause of his not putting the gold aboard of them. He left the vessels each time at the Cocos Island, there was no inhabitants on the island then, he lived fourteen days on ground roots and got taken off by whalers putting in for water, bringing with him what gold he could conceal on his person. Keating's map was held by his wife in Sydney, Cape Breton. It is no use without the secret.

Yours Faithfully,
Nich. Fitzgerald.

A copy of this letter came into our hands via Sir Malcolm and became one of the first pieces of Cocos lore in our collection. It spurred the interest of Commodore (later Admiral) Curzon Howe who signed the agreement Fitzgerald requested. The latter, in turn, gave Curzon Howe the vital clue. These were the documents that caused the King of Speed to "waste at least a year of his life in going off to hunt for a hidden treasure," as he once put it, but "I warrant that under such circumstances the ordinary man would behave just as foolishly as I behaved, as I intend to do again."

We like that. It restores our faith in human nature, to say nothing of the pedestal it makes for a boyhood idol.

14.

Finding a treasure on Cocos Island, we think, is a job for someone with a combination of talents. He should have the deductive powers of a super Sherlock Holmes, with the basic practical knowledge of a geologist, a psychologist and a civil engineer. A few of the lesser sciences—i.e., woodcraft, seamanship, lifesaving—would be helpful, but in the main, the ideal treasure hunter should have a finely devoloped sense of deduction. Such a man could take all the maps, charts, clues and legends, shuffle the deck and deal out a handful of directions that would lead him straight to the most fabulous hoard in the world.

We have arrived at this conclusion from watching innumerable others demonstrate how not to find the treasure on Cocos Island. Sir Malcolm Campbell's expedition to Cocos in February and March, 1926, was a good case in point.

To begin with, he surrounded himself with top-notch sportsmen like himself. As he said: "It is absolutely essential on such an expedition to get the right type of man. First, he must be a good fellow and a good sportsman, willing to go anywhere and do anything. Secondly, he must have sufficient means to be able to foot his share of the bill. Thirdly, he must be able to spare the time."

K. Lee Guinness, whose large yacht, the *Adventuress*, they used for the trip, was typical of Campbell's companions on this expedition. Guinness was himself a racing driver of note, independently wealthy and certainly able to spare the time. But if there was one among them who could have qualified as a first-rate detective, no one ever knew it. Thus the expedition was doomed from the beginning for it foundered on the correct interpretation of the Keating-Fitzgerald clue and other data which Sir Malcolm had in his possession.

"The clue," the full details of which, for obvious reasons, Sir Malcolm would not release, "stated that one had to reach the high-water mark of a creek or stream, strike off so many paces in a certain direction, turn looking due north, and then come face to face with a great square rock in whose side was a hole large enough to take the end of an iron bar."

If a crowbar were inserted in this hole, according to the clue, and used as a lever, the side of the rock would swing open and disclose the entrance to the cave. There, in heaps and boxes and decaying leathern bags lie the plate, the bars and ingots and precious jewels, guarded by the life-sized Virgin and probably the mouldy skeleton of Boag.

Before they went ashore they examined the coast carefully through glasses and spotted what they thought was the entrance to a creek. On landing they made for this point and though it was low water, the high-water mark was easily found. With compass in hand, Sir Malcolm quickly stepped off the number of paces, though it must have been quite difficult what with the enormous boulders strewn over the beach and the dense undergrowth which comes right to the waterline around the bay.

When he had stepped out the distance he' stopped and turned north, but the only bare rock he could see was a huge boulder which stood in the water some distance from shore. Even at low-tide it was almost covered by the breaking surf.

The steps were retraced, from another high-water mark, but this time everyone got hopelessly entangled with the bushes and vines of the undergrowth. At the end no bare rocks of any description were visible.

There followed a consultation and the party split up, one lot worked north-east along the beach and Sir Malcolm turned to a closer examination of the boulder in the surf. This latter was risky, what with the giant sharks that threatened to snatch a leg at any moment, and in the end it proved fruitless anyway. There was nothing on the rock that remotely fitted the clue.

When they gathered again on the beach to compare notes and report no encouragement, most of the searchers came to the conclusion that either the clue was a fake or else it referred to Wafer Bay and not Chatham Bay where they were.

"I pointed out," reported Campbell, "that Wafer Bay could not possibly fit the chart, but the rest of them seemed to think that when the treasure was buried the compass used was not reliable—which was often the case with compasses in those days—and that therefore Wafer Bay could just as easily be meant as Chatham Bay."

But after a long hard day of search in Chatham Bay without uncovering a single likely spot, Sir Malcolm gave in and the scene of operations was transferred next day to Wafer Bay.

Chatham Bay and Wafer Bay are divided by a point of land and a steep conical hill with a flat top. From a distance it appears like a grassy knoll, with here and there a single large tree to add shade and picturesqueness. Campbell had spotted this hill and what appeared to be a zigzag trail winding up its side. He had also read the few rare accounts which told of a pirate's lookout having once been established on this hill and he determined to investigate it.

After a day of fruitless search in Wafer Bay, the expedition returned to the Chatham anchorage. Sir Malcolm took with him two hearty seamen and established camp ashore, and there then followed two weeks of the most gruelling labor either of them ever knew.

After several of "the hottest days of hard work I have ever tackled," when "The heat was terrific and the bugs bit all the time," all they had to show for their efforts were a few short trails cut through the brush and half a dozen "dry" holes in the rocky ground. "Our faces and necks were livid with bites and scratches and the perspiration poured off us, until our khaki drill shorts and shirts clung limply to our bodies, as wet as though we had just come soaked out of the stream."

Eventually, "We found one big rock, completely covered by moss and ferns, partly enveloped in the roots of trees and half-buried under earth from the hillside above, which lay exactly on the correct bearing according to the compass. We spent hours clearing the earth away from the sides, working like niggers, as we were convinced that here was the right spot at last. Imagine our excitement when we found a crack round three sides of the rock which looked as if it marked the door to a concealed cave underneath! Unfortunately, there was no fourth crack, which ruled out the chance of the rock opening.

"Nevertheless we drilled holes all round it, plugged them with dynamite and blew great chunks out until we had completely blasted the top away. There were no traces of a cave, and the rock . . . seemed to be solid right through. We blasted several other large boulders in the immediate neighborhood and finally came to the conclusion that it was a waste of time and dynamite to hunt round any further in that locality.

"None the less, I am still of the opinion that the treasure of Lima is buried beneath that spot. Had I had another two months to spare and a gang of men at my disposal I would have cleared the whole of that area and grubbed it all up, even though it would have entailed an enormous amount of labor."

Later they turned their attention to the zigzag trail Campbell thought he saw leading up the side of the knoll that divides the bays. But the knoll turned out to be a succession of steep rocky inclines, covered in the densest possible thicket, and the grass on the shady top was the tough Cocos grass that grows higher than a man's head and is almost impossible to get through even with the sharpest machete.

After several days of struggle, however, during which everyone received some kind of injury, they gained the top and here Sir Malcolm made discoveries which were the only contributions of value from this expedition. They uncovered the stone foundations of a house and what might have been a cannon emplacement on a shelf below it. They uncovered, also, several yards of sheet iron buried at a uniform depth, with nothing below it or above it but dirt. Here in this vicinity they found an ancient ring bolt that may have been the handle on a treasure chest, and an old shovel, its handle disintegrating into dust when they picked it up. This was all.

When one of the seamen fell down a jungle-covered cliff and injured his back and their allotted time was up, they pulled up their anchors and reluctantly headed for home. Sir Malcolm Campbell's last words in the matter contain some good advice:

"To do the job properly one needs to go out to Cocos with a well-equipped, thoroughly seaworthy boat, accompanied by a few friends who are determined to put their backs into it, and aided either by a strong, able-bodied crew or a gang of native workmen who can stand the heat. With those human factors and with good tools and blasting apparatus, plus a really efficient electrical divining apparatus, I am convinced that the treasure could be found. For that matter, I am still certain that it lies somewhere near the spot where we found the jumble of rocks and blasted the top of the great rock that had three cracks in it.

"One of these days I shall return to Cocos, and when I do I shall not give up the search until I have either found the treasure or convinced myself that it is humanly impossible to discover it."

15.

ONE thing leads to another in this treasure hunting business. So far as we have been able to understand it, every Cocos Island treasure chart (original or purported copy—of which there have been dozens) started its own chain of events which continue right up to the present and, no doubt, will father countless others tomorrow. For instance, we have sketched the sequence that put a treasure map in the hands of Sir Malcolm Campbell and prompted his interest. But his failure to find the treasure did not end that chain. No, indeed. As in the case of all the others, the failure of this one simply inspired his successors and the chain wasn't broken but strengthened. Thus, as Shakespeare might have said, doth fiction become fact and the hopes of men are based on questionable origins.

And there were many men with nothing but hope in the early 1930's. There were breadlines in every city and people who learned for the first time that "dole" meant something besides pineapple. So a lot of wishful thinking was inspired by old treasure maps, of which there seemed to be a plethora in 1932, '33 and '34. At least, these were boom years for Cocos Island treasure hunting. During 1932 alone three or four expeditions were at Cocos or on their way there simultaneously. In legal occupation of the island was the expedition organized by the Clayton Metalphone Company, an outfit whose headquarters were in Vancouver, British Columbia.

This company had its origin in the expedition headed by Sir Malcolm Campbell, for the records show that he was connected with it in its early days but, for some reason or other, took no active part in the actual treasure hunt. Colonel J. E. Leckie, C.M.G., C.B.E., D.S.O., F.R.G.S., an old friend and associate of Sir Malcolm, was one of the directors of the company.

The Metalphone Company had, late in 1931 and through the agency of Mr. Frank Nutter Cox, the British Consul at San José, obtained an exclusive concession from the Costa Rican government whereby they were to have a free hand to look for treasure on Cocos Island for a period of twelve months, renewable for further like periods, on the understanding that the government was to receive one-third of any treasure found on the island.

The British Consul and his partner, Mr. Alex Murray, Sr., the vice-consul, were awarded, as compensation for their services in obtaining the concession, a ten per cent holding in the treasure hunting company. This fact was later to become one of vital importance.

This expedition of the Clayton Metalphone Company (which we shall henceforth refer to as the Canadian company), when it commenced operations early in 1932, was probably one of the best equipped and organized of the many which have gone to Cocos Island. They proposed to search for the treasure with the aid of a sort of ancestor of the Geiger Counter. It was an electrical, hoop-like device

147

called the "Metalphone." It was invented by Clayton, a member of the enterprise, and it was supposed to react in the vicinity of buried metals when carried over any such spot.

The invention got a lot of publicity in the papers, at least in San José, and it was said to have been used with considerable success in locating hidden metals elsewhere. But we are inclined to think that whatever the merits the contraption might have had, the Canadian company soon found that its use was extremely limited on Cocos Island, owing to the precipitous and jungle-covered nature of the terrain, which made it difficult if not impossible for a man to move about while carrying the cumbersome Metalphone.

However, the "field" personnel of the company put in a lot of hard work. They were assisted by the dozen or so Costa Rican policemen who had been sent over to keep an eye on the treasure hunters and see that they did not get away with any treasure surreptitiously. Their supply ship was the *Silver Wave*, a small auxiliary schooner which made frequent trips between Cocos Island and Puntarenas carrying provisions.

Our interest in Cocos Island and its treasure-trove does not date from this year (1932), but our scrapbooks show that the news which the expeditions made this year was among the first stories on Cocos we filed to our papers and press associations in the United States and England.

While the Canadian company was hard at work on Cocos, three other expeditions arrived—all at about the same time. The exact order in which they came is neither remembered nor of importance, but there is one we must mention. It was brought by the *Vigilant*, a converted Brixham trawler, which had left England in March, 1932, with eight enthusiastic Englishmen in search not only of treasure, but also adventure. It was under the command of Stratford Dowker Aird Jolly, an elderly gentleman adventurer who had already taken part in several treasure hunting expeditions in various parts of the world.

The names of the other members of the *Vigilant's* crew were Sheffield, Plumpton, Tracey, Cooper, Milburn, Howe and Finnis. The last named, Lieutenant Commander Frederick C. Finnis, was a retired officer of the Royal Navy.

The *Vigilant's* voyage was dogged by bad luck from the day she left England. The various members of the expedition had each subscribed a fair amount of money for the privilege of participation in what was to be their own private treasure hunt on Cocos Island, but by the time the *Vigilant* reached Trinidad, about the middle of 1932, the common funds had almost run out. This state of affairs naturally caused considerable dissension among the members and the expedition would probably have collapsed then and there had it not been for the generosity of Sheffield, who was the only rich man in the party.

Sheffield provided out of his own pocket sufficient cash to enable the *Vigilant* to proceed in easy stages to the Panama Canal and thence to Cocos Island. But there, to their surprise, the adventurers found the Canadian company in legal occupation.

We stress this point of legal occupation now because the Canadians had a valid exclusive concession to search for treasure, and any expedition which went to the island without first obtaining the permission of the Costa Rican government was *ipso facto* guilty of quite a number of serious offences, not the least of which were illegal entry into Costa Rican territory and noncompliance with the customs and consular laws which require all ships going to Cocos to call first at Puntarenas to obtain proper customs clearance. If this latter requirement is not complied with, the visitor to Cocos is automatically guilty of smuggling should he land anything on the island. By the 1930's the world was becom-

149

ing aware of Costa Rica's claim to sovereignty over the island, though ignorance would continue to cause certain adventurous foreigners a little embarrassment, as we shall recount.

And we shall take no little credit for the part we played in fixing this sovereignty once and for all in the international consciousness. Thus the *Vigilant's* arrival at the island provided one of our first moves in this direction as it was one of our first news stories on Cocos.

The *Vigilant* arrived at Cocos near the end of August 1932, and the adventurers on board, discovering that another expedition was already at work there, did no more than hang around the island for a while, helping the Canadians more or less for the fun of it. Eventually, funds being completely exhausted, the *Vigilant* returned to Panama, via Puntarenas, at the end of 1932. In Panama, the crew split up, most of them making their way back to England as best they could. Percy Howe remained in Costa Rica in the hope of picking up a job of some kind, while Sheffield, a man of private means, after a brief stay in San José, went on his leisurely way to Tahiti.

The *Vigilant* was seized and embargoed by the Canal Zone authorities for nonpayment of harbor and canal dues and she lay at anchor in Gatun Lake for many a long month until some enterprising Panamanian bought the vessel and converted her into a banana boat to carry fruit down the coast.

Another craft to arrive in the vicinity of Cocos Island, although she did not actually stop at the island while the Canadians were there, was the ketch *Southern Pearl*, manned like the *Vigilant* by a handful of adventurous Britons who had come all the way across the Atlantic in search of treasure and excitement.

And, like the *Vigilant*, the story of the *Southern Pearl* was one of lack of funds to carry on. The little auxiliary ketch, which had passed through the Panama Canal just prior to the *Vigilant,* first cruised among the Galapagos Islands and then proceeded to Puntarenas where she hung around for several months. During this time the crew met and got friendly with the Canadian treasure hunters whenever they came into port from Cocos.

Eventually, the majority of the disheartened co-owners of the *Southern Pearl* returned to England and left the boat at Puntarenas in the hands of two of their party, Palmer and Edwards, who had determined to stick to their ship to the very end. They took aboard as co-owner Howe of the recently departed *Vigilant* and for a long time the three of them lived on the boat while it lay idly at anchor in the backwater at Puntarenas.

But income was lacking and there came a day when Palmer, who held the biggest share in the boat, was compelled to sell her to a *tico* (a Costa Rican) who converted the vessel into a freight boat for trading along the coast.

Howe went alligator hunting for a time in the rivers and swamps which line the Gulf of Nicoya and later on he worked at a gold mine in the interior, to the owner of which he lent a hundred pounds or so, which he had received from his family in England. However, failing to receive his promised wages, or to recover his loan, Howe took his satisfaction out of the owner of the mine, a German, by beating him up publicly one night in a Puntarenas saloon.

Shortly afterwards Howe left Costa Rica and returned to England. Palmer fared a little better. He became a partner in a small Costa Rican coffee *finca* and married a Costa Rican *señorita.* (Perhaps the sequence was the other way around.) The last we heard he was still living in Costa Rica, the father and grandfather of a large Spanish-speaking brood. Edwards, a marine engineer, hung around Puntarenas in the hope of a job. Eventually he found it, and we shall mention him again because he forms a link to another chain of events and another expedition.

The organizer of the next expedition played such a leading role in the Cocos Island melodrama of this era that we shall have to sketch his background in more detail. Early in 1932, one Captain Charles Augustus Arthur, a former aide-de-camp to Sir Hari Singh, the fabulously rich Maharajah of Kashmir, set sail from England with his wife on board his little auxiliary schooner, the *Western Queen,* bound for the West Indies and adventure. Perhaps we should say more adventure, for Captain Arthur had only a few years before figured prominently in the most famous blackmail case of the era. Not many people living today will remember this *cause célèbre,* but it filled the papers of Europe and America for months in the mid-1920's.*

As crew, Captain Arthur had a couple of seamen who became dissatisfied with conditions on board and left the ship on her arrival at Barbados. To replace them, Arthur took on two native Barbados islanders. After a lazy cruise through the Caribbean, the *Western Queen* showed up at Puerto Limón, Costa Rica. Here Captain Arthur had a narrow escape from arrest from illegal entry because he went ashore without waiting for permission. He was only able to escape the penalties by pretending that he had run short of water and had come into port "in distress."

Leaving Puerto Limón, Arthur took the *Western Queen* through the Panama Canal and thence westwards to Cocos Island, where he stayed for a short while, hobnobbing with the Canadians and meeting, incidentally, the *Vigilant* and, later, at Puntarenas, the *Southern Pearl* with their respective complements.

Captain Arthur at this time does not seem to have displayed any serious interest in the Cocos treasure, although

* See Appendix VI.

152

he did make occasional trips with his yacht between Cocos and Puntarenas, carrying, as did the *Vigilant,* provisions for the Canadians when their own ship was laid up owing to engine trouble.

Shortly after this, early in 1933, the Canadian company, its capital exhausted and with absolutely nothing to show for its many months of hard work on Cocos, decided to abandon the enterprise. Before they left, however, they renewed their concession for another twelve months, or until October, 1934. Obviously, the directors must have reasoned that if they themselves could not find the treasure, at least no one else should look for it legally without their permission. Meanwhile, they might be able to raise additional capital and renew their explorations on the island within the next year.

As for Captain Arthur, this astute gentleman left his ship at Puntarenas and with his wife journeyed up to San José, the mountain capital. There he immediately gave us the first glimpse of his charm and salesmanship. He persuaded the Costa Rican government that his craft, the *Western Queen,* was the very vessel they needed for a coastguard patrol ship, something they did not at that time possess. We can best describe his charm by mentioning that he was lavish with his drinks where government officials were concerned, and his salesmanship by the statement that he was able to sell his ship, which had cost him in England a mere 500 pounds (about $2,500), to the Costa Ricans for $10,000.

Having collected this handsome profit, Captain Arthur and his wife left immediately for England. But he forgot one important obligation. He forgot to pay off his colored crew, the Barbadians, to whom several months' wages were due and they were left stranded in Puntarenas. They subsequently lodged a complaint against Arthur with the British Consul.

The Costa Rican government, now in possession of their one and only naval vessel, renamed the *Puntarenas,* looked around for a competent captain. The very man for the job was right on the beach in Puntarenas. He was Norman Edwards, of the *Southern Pearl*. He quickly became the only naval officer in the service of the government and as such might reasonably be excused for his habit of calling himself "Admiral of the Costa Rican Fleet."

However, the job did not last very long because the *Puntarenas* was found to be far from seaworthy and she was laid up on the beach for such a long time for repairs that Edwards gave up in disgust and returned to England. However, that is not the end of our able marine engineer, as we shall see.

At the time Captain Arthur sold his yacht to the Costa Rican government, Weston, of this reporting team, happened to be staying in the same hotel, while Hancock, in covering his Caribbean beat, stopped regularly at the same place. Thus we got to know him well by sight but we never had any conversation and, in fact, it is doubtful whether he ever even noticed either of us. Newspaper correspondents are notoriously nondescript if not unobstrusive. We modestly mention this fact because, simple and unimportant as it was at the time, it was later to become one of prime importance.

When Captain Arthur arrived back in London early in 1933, flush with the funds obtained from the sale of the *Western Queen*, his thoughts turned at once to Cocos Island. Was its legendary treasure there or not? If it were . . . ? Well, let it not be said that Captain Arthur was a man without vision. An idea formed in his fertile brain. He speedily got in touch with the heads and members of various expeditions which had already been to Cocos and to them he expounded his plan.

A private company would be formed, to be called "Spanish Main Exploration, Limited," with a nominal capital of only 100 pounds. The directors should all be ex-Cocos treasure hunters who would pool their knowledge of the island as a preliminary to the formation of a much larger company which would go after the treasure in earnest.

Arthur's idea appealed to the treasure hunters and soon Spanish Main Exploration, Ltd., came into being and was duly registered under the British Companies Act as a private company. The directors included Stratford Dowker Aird Jolly, lately captain of the *Vigilant;* Captain Charles Polkinghorne, a horny-handed old son of the sea who had sailed round the Horn innumerable times and who had been to Cocos Island on treasure hunting trips time and again during the past 50 years; Captain Arthur, himself; Mrs. Arthur; Arthur's cousin, Richard Studdert, a mining engineer of uncertain experience; and one or two others.

The company immediately sought out likely candidates to constitute the rank and file if and when an expedition could be organized. Among those enlisted were Percy Howe and Commander Finnis, who had both been on the *Vigilant;* Edmund Davidson, a mining man in Costa Rica who had been on Cocos Island with the Canadian company; and Dr. J. W. Harris, a geologist who, curiously, had once worked with Weston in the Venezuelan oil fields.

These and a dozen other adventurously inclined fellows, including a radio operator and an aviator, formed the personnel of the company, and all signed contracts agreeing to go to Cocos Island on a fixed salary basis just as soon as an expedition could be arranged. It is worth mentioning that a few of these men had sufficient confidence in the enterprise to invest in it. Dr. Harris, for instance, "invested" 250 pounds.

Having thus prepared the ground, Captain Arthur's next step was to float the big public stock issue which was to finance the actual expedition to Cocos. The company was to be called "Treasure Recovery, Limited." Its capital was to be £75,000 (if they could get it) divided into 300,000 shares of five shillings each. Of these shares, 180,000 were offered to the public at par, while the remaining 120,000 were distributed free to the promoters in varying proportions, in exchange, so the company's prospectus said, for their "valuable fund of knowledge and experience of the actual task ahead." Captain Arthur retained sufficient shares to give him control of the company.

The romantic cable address "PESOVEIGHT" (piece of eight) was duly registered. And Treasure Recovery's prospectus inviting the public to subscribe to its highly speculative venture appeared in the London newspapers on March 17, 1934. Since the document is of historical significance, we shall quote from it somewhat extensively.*

The initial capital of Treasure Recovery, Ltd., was fixed at £75,000 (about $375,000). The shares, said the directors, "can be regarded as a very attractive gamble because in the event of success, a small holding will secure a very handsome return."

The directors were stated to be: Eric Norman Alers-Hankey (the Chairman); Rear-Admiral Thomas John Spence Lyne, C.B., D.S.O., R.N. (Ret.); Commander Frank Arthur Worsley, D.S.O., O.B.E., R.N.R. (Ret.), Capt. of S.Y. *Endurance*, Sir Ernest Shackleton's Antarctic Expedition, 1921, and joint leader of the British Arctic Expedition, 1925; Stratford Dowker Aird Jolly, explorer, Sacambaya Treasure Expedition, 1928, Montezuma Treasure Expedition, Guatemala, 1930, owner of the ketch *Vigilant* in Spanish Main Treasure Expedition, 1932–33; Commander Joseph Russell Stenhouse, D.S.O., O.B.E., D.S.C., R.N.R. (Ret.), Captain of S.Y. *Aurora*, Shackleton's Antarctic Expedition, 1914–16, Captain Royal Research Ships *Discovery*, 1923–28; and Captain Charles Osborn Polkinghorne, Master Mariner, owner of S.S. *Gunner*, Cocos Island Treasure Expedition, 1923.

One could hardly find a more imposing board of directors

* See also Appendix VII.

156

for a treasure hunt, but what the public did not know at the time was that the three famous naval officers had been invited to join the company solely so that the company could have the benefit of the prestige which went with such well-known names. Rear-Admiral Lyne soon discovered this and he promptly resigned after having taken little or no part in the organization.

The prospectus declared that "The task on Cocos Island is a formidable one, but the personnel composing the Field Executive which is handling it is unique. This Executive has a fund of highly valuable knowledge and experience which will be pooled and scientifically applied in the present enterprise. The Executive includes the following: Colonel J. E. Leckie, C.M.G., C.B.E., D.S.O., F.R.G.S., mining engineer, Pacific Treasure Expedition, N.Y. *Silver Wave,* 1932–33; Dr. J. W. Harris, B.Sc., Ph.D., geologist; and Commander Worsley, Commander Stenhouse, Mr. Stratford Jolly and Captain Polkinghorne, directors of the Company."

In all fairness to Colonel Leckie, it should be made clear here that the prospectus is as far as he ever got in his association with the company. At no time did he go to Cocos Island with Treasure Recovery's expeditions.

As bait for the public, the prospectus further stated:

"TREASURE ON COCOS ISLAND. The Directors rely upon the following publications, viz: Handbooks Nos. 141 and 142, prepared under the direction of the Historical Section of the Foreign Office and published by H.M. Stationery Office, 1920. These publications, inter alia, state: 'The existence of treasure concealed on the island is well established.' Further reference is made to three distinct treasures, the first 'A vast plunder obtained by rifling certain churches in Peru;' the next, 'Gold bars and specie, worth ELEVEN MILLION dollars;' and, finally, 'About TWELVE MILLION dollars worth of stolen gold coin, jewels and silver ingots.' The Handbook further

157

states: 'The main stores of treasure are still hidden, in spite of various excavations and blasting operations which have been undertaken from time to time.'

"Apart from the Foreign Office publications, other records of treasure buried on Cocos Island include 300,000 POUNDS WEIGHT in silver dollars; 733 bars of gold; 7 kegs of gold coin, reputedly buried by the pirate Davis. The treasure buried by the notorious Bonito on the island has been said to comprise THREE HUNDRED AND FIFTY TONS of bullion.

"The portion of the Island in which the treasure is likely to have been concealed is not more than 350 acres. Well authenticated clues to the hiding place of the main treasure are all in agreement as to general locality. When the presence of metal is detected, by electrical means, a sample will be obtained by means of a mining drill, and thus unproductive excavation will be avoided. Modern science having provided such highly efficient apparatus for the locating of buried metals and minerals, *clues form no part of the Company's programme.*" (The italics are ours.)

This estimate of treasure on Cocos Island was neither exaggerated nor emphasized more than in a dozen similar Cocos promotions we have seen. It merely serves as an example of the typical and to confirm the magnitude of the island's hold on the public's imagination.

The prospectus explained the methods of recovery to be employed:

"METHODS OF RECOVERY. The methods to be employed by the Company are strictly scientific. They have been subjected to many rigorous tests in the field. The geo-electric and electromagnetic methods which the Company will employ in the search for the Cocos Island treasures are today extensively and successfully employed in important surveys."

A paragraph read, "It is proposed that the Expedition will leave St. Katherine Dock, London, during the month of April.

Four weeks after sailing the Expedition should arrive at Cocos Island, when operations for the location of the treasure will start forthwith. The Company has in view a highly suitable vessel, fully equipped, which will constitute the headquarters of the Expedition."

The "highly suitable vessel" which the Company had in view, although the prospectus did not say so, was the *Queen of Scots*, the magnificent 600-ton private yacht of the late Anthony Drexel, the Philadelphia banker. Captain Arthur had somehow persuaded Drexel to "lend" his ship to the expedition for an indefinite period.

From our present perspective it is easy to see that the Company's promotion was full of sucker bait, misleading statements calculated to catch the unwary. But the usual crop of suckers was there and ready for the harvest, although in nothing like the numbers anticipated by the optimistic directors. According to a statutory statement filed by the Company at Somerset House, London, the allotment of shares up to June 15, 1934, showed 34,563 shares allotted for cash; 120,000 shares allotted to Spanish Main Exploration, Ltd. (thus giving Arthur the control of the Company); 46,579 shares to underwriters, but forfeited on account of the underwriters not taking them up; preliminary office expenses of £254; leaving an available balance of £8,514 (about $42,570).

In the prospectus there is the statement that £20,000 was required for the purchase of the ship and the equipment of the Expedition, for the preliminary expenses and for working capital. It was therefore fairly obvious that with only £8,514 in the kitty at the start of the expedition estimated to require at least £20,000, the directors were assuming great risks.

A second point worthy of comment was that although the chief promoter of the whole scheme was Captain Charles Arthur, not once in the prospectus did his name appear or was there the slightest indication that he was connected with the company in any way. His identity and connection with the enterprise were very carefully hidden under the title of Spanish Main Exploration, Ltd., with offices at the same address as Treasure Recovery, Ltd., i.e., 40 Broadway, London. The reason for this will soon become evident.

One other item worthy of attention was a statement in the prospectus concerning Cocos sovereignty: "OWNERSHIP. Since all of the treasure buried on the Island of Cocos dates back to the period of the great American Colonial Empire of Spain, which empire no longer exists, there is little risk of an individual claimant putting forward any claims to the Cocos treasures."

Nobody knew better than Captain Arthur that Cocos Island belonged unquestionably to Costa Rica. He had been on the island; he had met the Canadian treasure hunters under Colonal Leckie there; and he knew that they were working under a concession obtained from the Costa Rican government. How, then, could he pretend that Cocos Island was a sort of no man's land?

Obviously, knowing that Cocos Island is normally uninhabited, Arthur had calculated that it would be possible, perhaps easy, to land his expedition on the island, hunt for the treasure and get away with it, if found, without the Costa Rican government ever being aware that intruders were on the island.

Treasure Recovery, Ltd. rapidly went ahead with its preparations for the expedition. The big twin-screw *Queen of Scots* was filled with equipment and enough provisions to last the expedition for a year or more. Nothing was overlooked. There was lumber for huts, tents, an electric light plant, a radio, an Electrolux refrigerator, tools, an electrical metal-detecting apparatus, diamond drills, and even a small airplane.

Finally, in August, four months after the departure date announced in the prospectus, the expedition got under way. Just prior to the departure from London, each member of the party received a circular letter signed by Richard H. Studdert, Arthur's cousin and a director of the company. The following excerpts from this letter are pertinent: "With reference to the Expedition to Cocos Island which is now about to sail, I have to inform you, as one of the Members of same, that the following arrangements have been made by the Board: (1) from the time of sailing from London, all members of the Expedition will come under the instructions of Commander J. R. Stenhouse until S.Y. *Queen of Scots* arrives at Cocos Island. (2) After arrival at Cocos Island, all members will come under Mr. C. W. A. Arthur, who is in sole charge of operations." There were other instructions pertaining to pay allotments, care of the yacht, and censorship of all mail from the island,* but the item of importance was the unequivocal statement that Captain Arthur was to be in sole charge of operations. Here, for the first time, the cat is out of the bag. The expedition was Captain Arthur's enterprise and nobody else had any voice or control in it.

Furthermore, the rank and file of the expedition—the radio operator, the airplane pilot, the diggers, the cooks, the camp steward, in fact, every employee of the expedition—had been contracted for the trip, not by Treasure Recovery Limited, but by the parent company, Spanish Main Exploration Limited, which was wholly and solely Arthur's company in control.

In other words, the shareholders, who had subscribed the working capital, had unwittingly entrusted their money to Captain C. W. A. Arthur, whose name did not even appear in the prospectus or any of the promotion!

* The full text is given in Appendix VIII.

16.

THE Cocos Island expedition of Treasure Recovery Limited on the *Queen of Scots* was one of the best endowed ever to sail. Its finances were far from the budget originally proposed, but the loan of the big yacht was a tremendous help. And nobody knows how many fond hopes went with it. The humble clerks, stenographers, charwomen, pub-keepers and sundry Britons who dug into the sock and bought the shares that gave the expedition its $42,570 "working capital" were its biggest asset.

The "Executive," however, is an item we would question. Though touted as "a valuable fund of knowledge and experience," we have our doubts. And we had them then, for we had seen too many treasure hunters come and go on Cocos to view any new endeavor with anything more than skepticism. Indeed, Weston, who was soon to become a naturalized citizen of Costa Rica, was always hypercritical of his British countrymen, and any expedition that originated in England was likely to come in for a good inspection. Besides, Cocos and its legends were already a hobby with him and invariably the favorite topic of conversation when Hancock hit town. Thus, from this point on, we, and especially Weston, play important fiddles in the Cocos Island cacophony.

The *Queen of Scots* left London at the end of August, 1934, and proceeded leisurely, calling at various places on the way to Cristóbal, at the Atlantic end of the Panama Canal. On board were Captain and Mrs. Arthur; Jolly and his wife; the three retired naval commanders, Stenhouse, Worsley and Finnis; Percy Howe; Polkinghorne; and a dozen or more other treasure hunters. They all traveled as passengers, the management of the yacht being in the hands of her regular captain and crew.

The ship reached Panama about the end of September and after passing through the Canal she took out clearance papers at Balboa for Tahiti. At Balboa the expedition was joined by Edmund Davidson, the Canadian gold miner who was operating a mine at Miramar, in Costa Rica. Davidson had been a member of the original Canadian expedition to Cocos and evidently he could not pass up this further opportunity to search for the island's fabulous treasure. It was at Balboa, too, we think, that the only American in the expedition was taken aboard. He was Archie Sloan, of Hollywood, who was in some way related to Mrs. Arthur.

Weston, through his newspaper connections, got the tip on Treasure Recovery's promotion and plans soon after the expedition left London. In an interview with the Costa Rican Minister of Foreign Affairs, *don* Raúl Gurdian, he discovered that the government, too, was aware that the expedition was on its way.

Despite the superior attitude and the obvious condescension exhibited by many who have written about these little Central American republics, there was one thing we had learned in several years of covering them—never underestimate their diplomatic perspicacity. The average *tico* or

163

guatemalteco's knowledge of world affairs generally exceeds that of the man in the street in Chicago, New York or Los Angeles. Weston went from the Foreign Minister's office to the cable office and filed this report to the *New York Times:*

The government of Costa Rica, to which Cocos Island belongs, is greatly perturbed by the fact that the *Queen of Scots'* treasure seeking expedition has not applied for official permission to carry out its operations, and it may be that if the hunters are lucky enough to find the treasure they will find it taken away from them in the moment of success on the grounds that the treasure belongs to Costa Rica and not to any haphazard adventurer who digs up the island just because it happens to be uninhabited.

That Costa Rica has some faith in the existence of the treasure is demonstrated by the fact that the government is quite prepared to grant treasure hunting concessions to responsible expeditions, the usual terms being a royalty of one third the value of any treasure recovered, besides which the treasure seekers must pay the wages and board of the posse of police which the government insists must accompany all expeditions to assure that there is no cheating, if and when the treasure is found.

For every advertised expedition which visits Cocos Island in search of its treasure, at least a dozen do so clandestinely, and in view of the possibility of one of these intruders finding and carrying away the treasure without paying Costa Rica its "commission," the government is considering maintaining a permanent detachment of police on the island in order to safeguard its sovereignty.

Meanwhile, Crede Calhoun, our colleague and senior correspondent of the *New York Times'* headquarters in Balboa, had been keeping an eye on the *Queen of Scots* and her passengers as they passed through the Canal Zone. That is how we knew the ship had been cleared for Tahiti. But on September 26th, a couple of days after her departure from Balboa, the yacht anchored in Wafer Bay on Cocos Island.

Supplies and equipment started pouring ashore almost immediately, though everything had to be hauled in a small rowboat under conditions which were very difficult and dangerous because the waters around Cocos abound with sharks. However, huts and tents were rapidly put up, the electric plant was started, and in a few days everybody was as comfortably installed as one could expect on a lonely tropic island in the Pacific Ocean.

The morning after their arrival the Union Jack was hoisted to the top of a tall coconut snag and, jokingly or seriously, the expedition "took possession" of the island in the name of His Majesty King George V.

Mrs. Jolly supervised the setting out of a kitchen garden to keep the camp supplied with fresh vegetables. Fresh meat was to be had in plenty as it was an easy matter to shoot the wild pigs and deer in the jungle. Fish were plentiful everywhere. All things considered, the treasure hunters had nothing to complain about as regards food and accommodations.

Captain and Mrs. Arthur and Commanders Stenhouse and Worsley slept aboard the yacht in the bay, going ashore early each morning to supervise operations. All the members of the expedition were full of enthusiasm and anxious to start the actual search for the treasure. Here they were at last, after many months of preparation, right on the very spot where the hidden millions lay waiting for them.

At the time, it was intended that the *Queen of Scots* should remain at anchor indefinitely, or at least until the expedition had had time to get properly organized for the hunt. But just as a mere scrap of treasure information can launch a major expedition, so also may a small incident set off a chain reaction that disrupts everything. The *Queen of Scots,* could she have spoken in her own dialect, might have said: "The best laid schemes o'mice an' men gang aft a-gley." Captain Arthur's gang aft a-gley when Chief Engineer G. A. Jones of the *Queen of Scots* cracked his skull.

No one appeared to know exactly how this happened. Some said he had been fighting with members of the expedition. Others said he had fallen down an iron companionway. Whatever the cause, it got lost in the shuffle of events that followed.

Since medical facilities on the spot were inadequate, there was nothing to do but rush back to Balboa, five hundred and fifty miles, for proper hospitalization. It was a futile effort, however, for the Chief died en route, on October 7, and was buried ashore in Panama the next day.

Captain and Mrs. Arthur, with Commanders Worsley and Stenhouse, had come to Balboa on this emergency trip, and after they had buried the Chief Engineer, Arthur announced that the yacht would sign on a new engineer and return to Cocos.

At this the Canal Zone authorities picked up their ears. Where, they wanted to know, were all the men who had been on the *Queen of Scots* when she recently passed through the Canal? Where had they been landed and why? On Cocos? Then why had the ship cleared for another destination?

The Canal Zone authorities evidently considered the replies offered by Captain Arthur and his aides unsatisfactory because the *Queen of Scots* was forthwith impounded and a heavy bond demanded to guarantee the cost of repatriating the twenty or more treasure hunters who had been left on the island. Commander Worsley stated on October 13th that the bond money would be remitted promptly from the expedition's headquarters in London. However, this money failed to arrive.

Meanwhile, some of these events were beginning to figure prominently in the news. On October 6th, Weston received this query from Calhoun in Panama: "Have you any report *Queen of Scots* Cocos Island expedition?" to which Weston could only reply that he knew nothing except that the expedition was somewhere between England and Cocos Island.

Then, on the morning of October 8th, Weston received news from Calhoun about the return of the *Queen of Scots* from the island with the dead chief engineer. Weston immediately called on Señor Gurdian, the Costa Rican Foreign Minister, and asked him if he knew that a party of British treasure hunters had landed on Cocos Island and its leaders were now in Panama.

The Minister expressed no surprise but he did not know the details, for which he thanked Weston.

"What are you going to do about it?" inquired the correspondent.

"I shall consult the President," replied *don* Raúl. "Come back later in the day and I shall be glad to give you whatever information there is."

A few hours later Weston saw the Minister again. From this conversation he cabled the *New York Times* as follows:

"SAN JOSÉ, C.R. Foreign Minister Gurdian said today that the *Queen of Scots* treasure expedition to Cocos Island was unauthorized and illegal. Commenting on the return of the yacht to Balboa as a result of the death of Chief Engineer G. A. Jones, Señor Gurdian said he was requesting the British Minister to Panama to inform the yacht that it could not return to Cocos."

An Associated Press report from London, dated October 11, was received by Central American subscribers as follows:

BRITISH BAR COCOS CLAIM

REFUSE TO BACK TREASURE HUNTERS IN DISPUTE OVER ISLAND

The efforts of British treasure hunters to claim Cocos Island for their nation were rebuffed today by the government. It was officially said that Great Britain was not interested in the claim to the island in the name of this country by the expedition to the island.

Commenting on press reports that the men revealed claims at Panama yesterday, a spokesman said: "Before the expedition left London its members were informed that the status of the island never was internationally recognized, but that for some time it had been claimed by Costa Rica. It was understood that when the expedition reached Panama a message was given to them by Costa Rica saying that country did not want the expedition to land." The British government does not intend to get into any controversy with Costa Rica, regardless of the claims of the expedition.

Meanwhile, the treasure hunters left on the island had not yet got their radio working so they were blissfully unaware of the storm brewing over the horizon.

Weston saw Señor Gurdian again on the morning of the 11th, when he was informed that the government had decided to send a force of fifty soldiers to Cocos Island to arrest the intruders. The Minister appeared gravely concerned over the probability that the Britishers were armed and that they might put up some resistance. Peace-loving Costa Ricans, long proud of the fact that their country boasts more school teachers than soldiers, viewed this situation with considerable anxiety. If the treasure hunters should decide to resist arrest, all the advantages would be on their side because the landing party would be able to disembark only a few men at a time in small rowboats, it being impossible for launches to get close inshore at either of the two harbors on the island.

Weston agreed with the Minister that the treasure hunters undoubtedly had plenty of firearms, but he doubted whether they would be so foolish as to use them, since they had no means of leaving the island now that their supply ship was impounded in Balboa.

"Perhaps so," said the Minister, "but we shall take no chances. Our men will go armed."

And go armed they did. Not only did every one of the soldiers have his rifle and machete, but they took a dozen machine guns as well.

Early on the morning of October 12th, Weston cabled the *New York Times*, through Calhoun at Balboa, that two government launches with fifty soldiers under the commands of Colonels Paniagua and Valenzuela were about to leave Puntarenas for Cocos Island to evict the treasure hunters.

It was pretty serious business at the time but years later, when Colonel Valenzuela was Director General de Aviación and Hancock was director of publicity and public relations for TACA (Transportes Aereos Centro Americanos) we had many a good laugh with the Colonel as he told and retold the story of that expedition.

Later on the 12th, Weston received an airmail letter from Calhoun which read as follows:

Captain Arthur, leader of the Cocos Expedition, was in my office this morning before your cable was received. He gave me fifteen good pictures of the activities of the treasure hunters on the island. I have sent the information contained in your cable to him with request for comment, but have not heard from him yet. It looks as though this might develop into a hot story, possibly with international complications, as the Associated Press cabled from London yesterday to the effect that Britain is not interested in the claims of the treasure hunters to Cocos Island.

Keep close touch with the launches that have gone to evict the treasure hunters from Cocos. Have they any radio means of communication with San José? The expedition has a radio set on the island that now communicates with Colón. They have no boats that could make the mainland. However, Stenhouse and Worsley are expected to return from here with such a boat. I presume that the Costa Rican police could not bring the whole gang back to the mainland in their boats, but if they should, that's your story.

The government launches were the *Valle Riestra* and the

Puntarenas, the latter, remember, was the former *Western Queen*, Captain Arthur's yacht, which was hastily pressed into service after long disuse.

On October 13th, Weston cabled the *New York Times* that the soldiers had been given unequivocal orders to overcome any resistance and that they were to bring the prisoners to Puntarenas, whence they would be deported to England.

Naturally, when this news reached Panama, it caused consternation among Captain Arthur and his fellow directors. Fortunately for them, the radio on Cocos was now working and they were thus able to inform the men there what was happening. When the treasure hunters first learned that Costa Rican soldiers were on their way to the island to arrest them all, there were a few valiant souls among them who wanted to offer resistance, but wiser counsel prevailed and so they anxiously awaited the coming of their captors. All thought of continuing the recently begun search for treasure was abandoned.

Normally, the trip from Puntarenas to Cocos Island by any launch of moderate speed requires about 36 hours. The *Valle Riestra* and the *Puntarenas* left Puntarenas on the morning of October 12th, and therefore might reasonably be expected to arrive at Cocos sometime during the afternoon of the following day.

However, when night fell on October 13th, the lookouts on the island reported that there was no sign of the two launches. They reported this by radio to Captain Arthur in Panama but no great attention was paid to the delay because adverse currents sometimes make the approach to Cocos a slow one.

The following morning, the 14th, there was still no sign of the Costa Rican launches. One of them had a small radio transmitter supposedly strong enough to keep in touch with government headquarters in San José, but ever since the boats left Puntarenas not a word had been received from them.

The government was alarmed. Neither of the two launches was built or equipped for such heavy work on the open sea; they were certainly not in a good state of repair, especially the *Puntarenas;* and they were obviously overloaded because at the last minute seventy-five men had been sent instead of only fifty as originally announced. The government had taken out special insurance for the contingent (about $22,-500) but this fact, when announced, probably contributed to the fears of the relatives and friends of the soldiers who had visions of the two little craft being swamped and sunk.

Another day, the 15th of October, came and went with still no news of the Costa Rican troops. No radio message was received from the launches and the men on Cocos radioed Panama that there was still no sign of the boats on the horizon. The alarm and tension in Costa Rica increased by the hour.

On October 16th a report from Panama said that Commander Worsley was planning to fly up to San José to intercede personally with the government on behalf of his men on the island.

Weston queried Calhoun on this by cable. Meanwhile, he received an airmail letter from Calhoun posted the previous day explaining the situation. He had just read through this when he received Calhoun's reply to his cable. In this the Panama reporter merely said that Worsley had been unable to leave Panama as planned. He further cabled the *New York Times* as follows:

BALBOA, C.Z. Leaders of the Cocos Island treasure-hunting expedition are endeavoring to clear up the misunderstanding over the sovereignty of Costa Rica, which has sent armed police to evict the party now operating on the island.

Captain C. A. Arthur, leader of the expedition, explained today

171

that he had sent radio instructions to the men on the island to receive the Costa Rican police courteously and to make every effort to comply with their wishes. Commander F. A. Worsley, another leader, cabled President Ricardo Jimenez of Costa Rica today as follows:

"Commander Worsley, representing the directors of Treasure Recovery Limited, presents his compliments to His Excellency and tenders deepest regrets for his expedition's misunderstanding concerning the situation, and hopes His Excellency will grant him an audience at San José in order that this apology may be offered in person."

Captain Arthur explained the statement in the promotion prospectus regarding the ownership of Cocos Island was originated by the company's lawyer in London. The prospectus says: "In the past Costa Rica appears to have had some pretensions to ownership of the island, but at the meeting of the Boundary Commission in 1900, Costa Rica laid no claim to any territory seaward of Coiba Island, adjacent to her own coast line. Cocos Island, 300 miles seaward of Coiba, is thus definitely excluded from Costa Rican territory." Apparently the lawyer was equally uninformed as to the location and ownership of Coiba Island, which is off the coast of Panama, and belongs to that country which maintains a penal colony there. Captain Arthur said he had been in radio communication with Cocos Island all day and that all was well there. Captain Arthur and his wife are sailing for England tomorrow. He says he will return immediately with the *Veracity*, a 150-ton vessel owned by the company which will replace the *Queen of Scots*, owned by Anthony Drexel, Jr., now held here awaiting information regarding the deportation of the treasure hunters by Costa Rica.

Not only was the company's lawyer uninformed but the spokesman for the British Government, quoted in the Associated Press dispatch mentioned above, seems to have been a little hazy in his political geography. "The status of the island," he said, "never was internationally recognized." August Gissler, who was still alive at the time, took issue with these statements and wrote us from New York: "Since 1894 when I established permanent residence on the island,

172

people have asked this question. At that time the ownership of the island was still in dispute between Costa Rica and Colombia. However, by the arbitration of President Loubet of France it was granted to Costa Rica."

Came the morning of October 17th with still no news of the two launches bound for Cocos. In the afternoon Calhoun cabled from Balboa: "RADIO FROM COCOS SAYS POLICE NOT ARRIVED UP TO 4.30 P.M. TODAY. HAVE POLICE RETURNED TO PUNTARENAS? IS GOVERNMENT CONCERNED FOR THEIR SAFETY?"

Weston was drafting an answer to this message when his telephone rang. It was a government official who, obviously relieved, informed him that they had just made radio communication with the launches. Further, because the *Puntarenas* could develop a speed of only two knots, the *Valle Riestra*, a faster vessel, had had to slow down to the same speed in order not to part company. They reported all on board well, despite a lot of seasickness among the troops. They expected to reach Cocos that night.

The radio communication was broken then, and although the San José station continued its efforts, it never renewed contact. Throughout the rest of the night there was only the intermittent report from Cocos that the launches had not yet arrived. By morning the two boats had been at sea for five days on a trip that should have taken less than two.

The American Minister to Costa Rica, Mr. Leo R. Sack, had, in common with the entire population of this little country, been taking a special interest in the voyage of the government launches. He asked Weston to cable Calhoun, to report the latest news from Cocos that night (the 17th) or early the next morning, and if the launches had not arrived by then, then he would consider requesting aid from the American forces in the Canal Zone.

By 9:30 A.M., October 18th, the country was frantic. In response to the request of the Costa Rican government, the

173

United States Minister, Sack, forwarded a formal request to Washington for a squadron of naval aircraft from the Canal Zone to fly out over the route of the missing launches. Nearly everyone by now had given them up for lost.

At 10:30, with tension at the breaking point, the San José radio station made contact again with the launches. Their silence, they said, was due to another breakdown of the little radio set. "All is well," they said, "and we are about to arrive."

Simultaneously the Cocos Island radio reported that the two launches had just come into sight. Government officials and everybody else in Costa Rica breathed sighs of relief and thanksgiving, and the request for Washington aid was cancelled. The launches had taken six days to cover 350 miles. It was an adventure Colonel Valenzuela could recount with humor in later years, but at the time it was no joking matter.

So far, the *New York Times,* thanks to the combined efforts of Calhoun in Balboa and Weston in San José, had been giving its readers better coverage on the Cocos Island story than any other newspaper. Each had been cooperative and helpful with local authorities. Calhoun now thought it time they got a little benefit out of this friendly cooperation and he cabled Weston on the 18th: "GET STORY ARRIVAL LAUNCHES AND SUBSEQUENT HAPPENINGS THROUGH GOVERNMENT RADIO IF POSSIBLE. EMPHASIZE IF NECESSARY NEW YORK TIMES COOPERATION."

Thus, through Weston's contact in San José, the *New York Times* was able to give its readers exclusive coverage on the Cocos story which by now had provoked a lot of interest in both Europe and America.

During the afternoon of October 18th, the Costa Rican Foreign Minister reported that Colonel Paniagua had taken into custody 18 treasure hunters, including Mrs. Jolly, Polkinghorne, Burke, Finnis, Davidson, Dr. Harris and Archie

Sloan. The colonel also had confiscated a large quantity of stores and equipment, including the radio set, electric refrigerator, electric plant, firearms, etc. The latter were 12 rifles and 19 revolvers with "unlimited" ammunition.

But now the government had another problem. The colonel reported further that owing to the large amount of stores captured, the number of prisoners, and the lack of space on the launches, it would be impossible to bring everything and everyone back in one trip. The government replied that it would send a larger and faster vessel to help him.

However, there was no larger or faster launch available in Puntarenas and Weston communicated this fact to Calhoun, who passed the news on to Captain Arthur, who instantly perceived that here was a chance to get his men off the island in his own way and perhaps even evade the penalties awaiting them in Costa Rica. He got Commanders Worsley and Stenhouse to cable *don* Ricardo Jimenez, the President of Costa Rica, offering the use of the *Queen of Scots* for the evacuation of the men and equipment on Cocos.

But the old president was as crafty as they were. He agreed to the proposal—provided that the *Queen of Scots* came to Puntarenas in the custody of the Costa Rican police.

Worsley countered this proposal with the statement that he would cable the company in London for instructions.

In all this exchange of cables between the President of Costa Rica and Treasure Recovery Limited's directors, it is curious that not once did Captain Arthur put his own name to a message. He delegated Stenhouse and Worsley to try to get the expedition out of the hole. Why was Arthur, although he was "Controller of Operations," so anxious to remain anonymous? The answer was soon to become apparent.

Arthur was tipped off that if the *Queen of Scots* went to Cocos and thence to Puntarenas, she would probably be seized by the Costa Ricans for smuggling. Even the San José afternoon newspapers of the same day mentioned that possibility, and it seems to have also occurred to Anthony Drexel, Jr., the owner of the vessel, for he cabled Arthur that under no circumstances was his yacht to go to Cocos again and that, in any event, he would be glad to have her returned to him as quickly as possible.

Arthur's reaction to this state of affairs was curious. He and his wife hopped a departing steamer bound for England and left Commanders Worsley and Stenhouse to hold the fort (or was it the bag?) in Panama. While he was still in Panama, Arthur sold the expedition's small amphibian airplane which there had not been time to unload during the *Queen's* brief stay at Cocos.

Meanwhile, Colonels Paniagua and Valenzuela reported from Cocos Island that they were busy packing up the captured stores and equipment and that the arrested Britishers were giving no trouble. Then came another spell of silence, all efforts of the San José radio station to contact the island being unsuccessful. The expeditionaries' radio had now gone kaputt.

On October 19th, Commander Worsley again cabled the president, this time to say that the *Queen of Scots* was unable to proceed to Cocos but that if the president would grant the company a last minute concession to search for the treasure, and allow the treasure hunters to remain on the island, they would charter a new supply ship in England. This request was promptly refused by the president on the grounds that the concession of the Canadian company was still in force. Actually, it was due to expire the very next day, October 20th, and Worsley must have known this when he made his request.

Throughout the past few weeks it had been a matter of surprise to everyone that so far neither the British Consul, Mr. Frank Cox, nor the Vice Consul, Mr. Alex Murray, had made any representations to the Costa Rican government on behalf of their countrymen. On the other hand, acting on instructions from the Canadian company in Vancouver, which had been kept informed of local developments, Messrs. Cox and Murray asked the Costa Rican government to renew the Canadian company's concession for another 12 months as from October 20th. This the government promptly did and thereby cut off all chances of Treasure Recovery Limited obtaining any rights.

It was also reported that the Canadian company was annoyed to find that one of its own directors, Colonel Leckie, had become associated with the rival company, since the Canadians were themselves planning to renew their explorations on the island in November. We later discovered they had passed a resolution back in May protesting and deprecating Colonel Leckie's defection.

The Costa Rican government, scouting for a way to get the expedition to Puntarenas, instructed their consul in Cristóbal, Señor Enrique Pucci, to charter in Panama a vessel suitable for the job. Señor Pucci, energetic and anything but a *mañana* man, raced around Panama and in a few hours had chartered the 200-ton motor ship *Nuevo Panama*.

Weston just had time to flash this news to Crede Calhoun —the negotiations had been kept secret by the government— and he in turn just managed to obtain permission from President Jimenez in time to send a newspaperman along on the *Nuevo Panama* for the *New York Times*. For this special assignment Calhoun picked our old friend Ted Scott of the *Panama-American* who was also Reuter's correspondent in the area. Thus we smugly thought we still had an exclusive beat on the Cocos story, but—alas!—there's many a scoop 'twixt cup and lip.

17.

IT took Ted Scott nearly four years to get around to a write-up in his regular column of his adventures on the *Nuevo Panama*. As a record of events in connection with the Cocos Island story and Treasure Recovery's fiasco, it is probably not very important, but it illustrates how a great many people can become involved in one treasure hunt. It was also Ted's contribution to the obituary of a great news reporter. Here it is as it appeared in the *Panama-American* April 18th, 1938:

Back in 1934, when Jimmy Ryan was representing Hearst and some newsreel outfits on the Isthmus, he and I were thrown together with considerable violence on what is perhaps the most famous of all Cocos Island treasure hunting stories.

A couple of English naval officers, Commander Worsley and Commander Stenhouse, both well-known Arctic explorers who had been to the South Pole with Sir Ernest Shackleton, had taken a party down to Cocos on the Drexel yacht *Queen of Scots*. They had every imaginable kind of device for metal detection and generally were well equipped. Before they got properly started on their excavations, however, the Costa Rican government sent over a party of eighty policemen under Colonel Paniagua to place the Britishers under arrest and bring them back to the mainland.

Now after landing the party, Worsley and Stenhouse had come back in the *Queen of Scots* to the Isthmus and they were in Cristóbal when they received the sad news about the impending arrest of their compatriots. The police should have arrived at Cocos in three or four days but they took something like a week and a half.*

In the interim we had plenty of time to get in touch with them from the shore to warn them that the cops were on their way and to instruct them not to resist arrest. These Englishmen were well armed and I really believe they could have prevented the seasick policemen from making a landing had they felt disposed to fight it out. They would have been aided by the formidable nature of the rocky shore and the fact that the cops had had a great deal of the belligerence pounded out of them by the heavy seas they had encountered in the small launches in which they made the 300 mile trip from Puntarenas.

All of this was before the criminal assault on Ethiopia and the rape of Austria, so you can imagine that the papers throughout the world gave the story considerable attention. There were no headlines on China or Spain in those days and the time when the democratic nations would have to beat hell out of the fascists seemed too far away for that problem to attract much public notice.

Stenhouse and Worsley were using an amateur radio station in New Cristóbal and a smart local operator named Pincus did some sterling work in contacting the Englishmen on Cocos, who were also equipped with a ham receiving and transmitting set.

In view of the fact that I had been of some assistance to the Britishers, the Commanders let me sit in with them while they were working the island and I secured some pretty good exclusive stories. They were so good, in fact, that my cable tolls to London alone were something like $700 for three days and I was also filing heavily to the United Press in New York.

When Jimmy Ryan found out what was going on, he developed

* Ted was exaggerating, of course.

a big mad and denounced the station to the Colón authorities as being clandestine, unlicensed, illegal and irregular in a score of other ways. He and I then came to grips in print and the fight was at its height (with no punches barred) when Crede Calhoun borrowed me from the *Panama-American* to go down to Cocos on the *Nuevo Panama* for the *New York Times*. This ship had been chartered from the Elliot Company by the Costa Rican Consul, Enrique Pucci, to evacuate the soldiers and their prisoners from the island. The fact that the vessel was sailing had been kept secret and Crede Calhoun and I figured that we had a complete steal.

What was my surprise, however, on boarding the ship just before sailing time, to have Captain Osterberg take me down to my cabin for the purpose of introducing me to my room mate, "another newspaperman."

He opened the stateroom door and you could have knocked me down with a belaying pin. There, lying on the bunk as large as life, was my old pal Jimmy Ryan.

Jimmy spoke first: "I can stand you if you can stand me," he said, with that wry grin which he could turn on with pretty good effect.

We were going to be together on that tiny ship for three or four weeks, sharing the same room, and I had just made up my mind that it was going to be too much of a job to stay mad at a fellow for that long when Captain Osterberg broke in on my meditations:

"Shake hands, you damn fools," he commanded.

We did—and Jimmy and I had a swell trip together.*

The *Nuevo Panama* sailed from Balboa the night of October 20th. Besides the two rival newspapermen aboard, there was the energetic Señor Pucci in his role as diplomatic representative of the Costa Rican government. Ryan also carried a movie outfit for International Newsreel and he obtained the only newsreel pictures of the Cocos Island evacuation. Weston was delegated to meet the ship in Puntarenas and

* It was not the last great news assignment for Jimmy Ryan. He was drowned a couple of years later in British Guiana while searching for the missing aviator, Paul Redfearn.

take over the story from Ted Scott who would return to Panama on the same ship. Meanwhile, Weston kept in touch with Ted Scott over the government radio and relayed his stories to the *New York Times*. With this hook-up the *Times* was able to beat International News and all other services.

The *Nuevo Panama* had to make a stop at Puerto Armuelles to discharge some cargo, and this and the contrary currents stretched the trip to Cocos to five or six days. When she arrived at the island on the morning of October 26th, the Costa Rican soldiers immediately began the embarkation of their prisoners and the confiscated material and stores. This was not an easy operation because everything and everybody had to be carried from the shore to the ship in small rowboats, with swarms of sharks swimming around them all the time. Ted Scott practically monopolized the island radio and Weston relayed to New York whole reams of copy, but the *Times* boiled the story down to this:

TREASURE HUNTERS QUIT COCOS ISLAND

COSTA RICAN POLICE TRANSFER EIGHTEEN BRITONS AND

EQUIPMENT TO STEAMER IN ROWBOATS

PRISONERS ASSAIL LEADER

ARE IRKED BY CAPTAIN ARTHUR'S RETURN TO ENGLAND,

LEAVING THEM UNDER ARREST

COCOS ISLAND (By Radio to San José, C.R.) Oct. 26.

Costa Rican police on the steamer *Nuevo Panama* reached Cocos Island this morning and immediately began loading the equipment of the British expedition, eighteen of whose members were arrested while preparing to search for the island's legendary buried treasure.

Members of the British party expressed appreciation of their treatment at the hands of Colonels Paniagua and Valenzuela, who led the party of Costa Rican police that took them into custody. They criticized Captain C. A. Arthur, leader of the expedition, for returning to England and leaving them in their predicament.

It was expected that the evacuation of the expedition would

181

be completed by night. The *Nuevo Panama* will carry the Britons and their equipment to Puntarenas, where they are due Sunday. It is not proposed to leave a garrison here.

Wafer Bay, usually a solitary place, was a scene of animation as the Costa Rican police broke up the treasure-hunters' camp. The equipment was transferred to the steamer in rowboats, riding the breakers over dangerous reefs. Sharks clustered around the frail craft.

More than 500 packages had been loaded by 3 P.M. There remained only the lighting plant and the radio, over which President Ricardo Jimenez was personally directing operations from San José.

The British prisoners were a picturesque group after days of exposure to the tropical sun. They were visibly perturbed as they assisted in dismantling the camp they had expected to occupy for two years.

"We are all employes of Treasure Recovery Limited," explained S. D. A. Jolly, who headed the group that landed here. "We believed the questions of permission and a concession had been arranged before we left England. We never made any claim to Cocos Island, but were interested only in finding treasure."

He denied that they had received instructions from the British Legation in Panama not to proceed to the island.

Radio Operator J. Sancho sent his last message at 4:55 P.M., stating that the radio was about to be dismantled for installation on the *Nuevo Panama*.

The loading proceeded smoothly in spite of sharks and frequent heavy showers, and consequently they were able to leave Cocos that night. They arrived in Puntarenas about four o'clock Sunday afternoon, October 27th. Weston was on the dock, and so were some two thousand others who had been gathering since morning.

But it was Sunday and too late anyway to do anything with the prisoners that day, so they were kept on the *Nuevo Panama* under custody of the local police. The two colonels and their 75 men were put aboard a special train for a heroes' return to the capital. Mr. and Mrs. Jolly, as a special concession, were permitted to spend the night in a local hotel. There, in an interview with Weston, Mrs. Jolly voiced confidence that there was treasure on Cocos Island and said that, despite the present contretemps, she hoped to return there one day and find it.

Among the captured stores and equipment which were landed and placed in the custom house was an item which caused considerable conjecture among those who could read English. It was a large wood sign which read:

DO NOT MOLEST THE CHICKENS, RABBITS, GOATS, DUCKS, CATS AND OTHER ANIMALS WHICH HAVE BEEN PLACED ON THIS ISLAND FOR EXPERIMENTAL PURPOSES. COMMUNICATE ANY OBSERVATIONS ON THESE ANIMALS TO JULIUS FLEISCHMANN, CINCINNATI, U.S.A.

The livestock referred to had apparently been placed on the island by the Yeast King during a brief visit, but the fact that his visit was unauthorized and unknown to the Costa Rican government, and thus as illegal as the British expedition, sort of got lost in the ensuing shuffle. The only "observations" we could communicate to Mr. Fleischmann are these: One of the cats, a magnificent big, tigerlike animal, was caught and brought back as a gift for President Jimenez. It probably would have become a champion ratter (and San José's rats are notoriously large) had it not succumbed to civilization and became instead the palace pet. The other observation is that Mr. Fleischmann's notice board eventually came to rest in the city museum at Alajuela.*

Neither Weston or Scott got much rest that night. Ted came ashore and shared Weston's room at the Hotel Imperial, but they spent the night discussing the story. Weston was sure the trial next day would "blow the lid off a very smelly intrigue. If my suspicions are correct we are going to find

* For another result of Mr. Fleischmann's visit to Cocos see Appendix IX.

that some people in very high places have been doing some curious string-pulling in this affair."

As it turned out his suspicions were absolutely correct.

The trial of the British adventurers started early the next morning. The prisoners were kept under armed guard in a large room at the Port Captain's headquarters near the pier, and from there they went in batches to another large office in the same building which had been converted into a courtroom. Here the judge, a court interpreter, and other functionaries in a typical Costa Rican court system, heard the case. The press was not admitted at first, which surprised Weston, used to the open doors of democratic Costa Rica. Only after he showed a press-pass signed by Dr. Fernando Muñoz, the president's private secretary, was he admitted, and, on the strength of this, all the local reporters as well.

Curiously, Mr. Murray, the British vice-consul, was present, admitted on account of his diplomatic position, but, according to him, "unofficially" just to be on hand in case he were needed. The evening before, when the Port Captain's launch went out to meet the *Nuevo Panama*, Weston had asked permission to go along in the one available spare seat but was informed that Vice-Consul Murray had already claimed it in "his capacity as British Vice-Consul." Therefore, when Murray announced himself to the prisoners as their British vice-consul, everyone, including Weston, assumed he would act officially to protect the interests of the treasure hunters.

Mr. Jolly was the first to give evidence. He produced his contract with Spanish Main Exploration Limited and declared that the expedition had been from start to finish promoted and organized by Captain Charles Augustus Arthur. Arthur, he said, was not a director of Treasure Recovery Limited owing to his bad reputation, which he was anxious to conceal. Jolly said he had personally invested 500 pounds in the enterprise and that although they had no written permission to land on Cocos, Arthur had assured them in Panama that he had everything properly arranged.

Captain Polkinghorne, looking like an old-time pirate with his tufted beard and squinting eyes, followed Jolly and similarly testified that Captain Arthur was responsible for the whole affair and that he, Polkinghorne, had invested most of his savings in the company. He displayed considerable resentment at Arthur's hurried flight from Panama.

In the course of the trial, Vice-Consul Murray intervened from time to time in an apparently official status, interrogating the men, prompting them, telling them not to answer certain questions, and so on.

But Weston was still suspicious. "I've got a hunch," he whispered to Ted Scott, "and I'm going to put it to the test."

Stepping forward he asked the judge for permission to ask Mr. Murray a few questions. The judge readily consented.

Then in a loud voice so all could hear, Weston asked Murray whether he was acting in his official capacity as British vice-consul on behalf of the British prisoners. The vice-consul answered unequivocally that he was not and that he was present merely as an interested observer.

Weston thereupon pointed out that all the prisoners were under the impression that he was intervening in the case officially on their behalf and suggested that he had better put them clear on the subject at once.

This was obviously astonishing news to the treasure hunters. When Jolly taxed Murray with this, the vice-consul admitted that he was not acting on their behalf, giving the very weak reason that nobody had asked him to. Mr. Jolly then asked Murray formally to act on their behalf, but the vice-consul replied lamely that he could not do this without instructions from Consul Cox in San José. Then the treasure hunters realized they had been deliberately misled by the vice-consul's actions, and there was a tremendous uproar among them.

When the judge finally got silence in the courtroom again, Weston continued his questions. He asked Murray whether it was true that he was a stockholder in the rival Canadian company. Somewhat to everyone's surprise, Murray admitted that he held several thousand shares in company with his partner Consul Cox, and that they also held power of attorney for the Canadian company.

"O.K.," said Scott, now getting into the act. "Since you have stated that you are not here officially as British vice-consul, kindly answer my questions in your capacity as attorney for the Canadian company. Isn't it a fact that the removal of these Britishers from the island was instigated by the Canadian company, through their attorneys in Costa Rica, Messrs. Cox and Murray, who in such capacity prompted the Costa Rican government to take the action they have?"

"I cannot answer that question," Murray replied, "because it is treading on consular ground."

The reporters then turned their interest to Edmund Davidson, who had gone from Costa Rica to join the expedition in Panama. They already knew he had had the forethought (through the agency of Messrs. Cox and Murray) to provide himself with legal re-entry papers for Costa Rica and a properly visaed passport. Due to his possession of these, the court intimated that he would be allowed to remain free in Costa Rica. In other words, of all the treasure hunters Davidson was the only one who had been acting within the law throughout.

In response to Weston's questioning, Davidson admitted that he was a shareholder in the Canadian company—a fact which was not until that moment known to the others!

One can imagine the anger of the other treasure hunters

186

when they realized the import of this. The only logical conclusion was that Davidson had gone to Panama to join the expedition as an agent of the Canadian company with the help and probably the direction of Cox and Murray. Further, it was obvious that even if the consuls had been prepared to act officially on behalf of the prisoners, they could not have done so impartially because they were at the same time agents of the rival Canadian company. Weston then threw the final punch when he informed the court that the Canadian company had, at its directors' meeting in Vancouver on May 4th, resolved to take whatever steps necessary to protect their interests in Cocos Island.

The Canadian company had already announced its intention to return to Cocos within a couple of months. But the news correspondents refrained from adding fuel to the flames by any surmise that the Canadian company, through their agents, Cox and Murray, would offer to buy, at their own figure, from the Costa Rican government all the stuff confiscated from Treasure Recovery Limited. The booty was enormous. There were hundreds of barrels of flour, bacon, dried foods, canned goods, and all the utensils needed to prepare it. There were tents, camp beds, furniture, an electric refrigerator, an electric plant, firearms, drums of gasoline, kerosene and oils, diamond drills, a radio plant, wire netting, spades and picks, and a hundred other useful items. The value was calculated at $40,000 by the treasure hunters but actually it was about $25,000. It was useful loot, and if the Canadian company could obtain it cheaply then they would be the chief beneficiary of the present disaster.

Shortly after noon on the 29th, the judge pronounced his verdict. (There is no jury system in Costa Rica.) He was satisfied, he said, that the treasure hunters had all been victimized by Captain Arthur (who had persuaded them to invest an average of $1000 each in the venture, as their testi-

187

mony disclosed), and he alone was responsible. The judge therefore considered that any penalties should fall on Arthur and not on his innocent victims, and he would leave it to the government in San José to take the necessary steps to bring the captain to book, if that were at all possible. The prisoners were ordered released and returned to Panama on the *Nuevo Panama*, if the Canal Zone authorities would have them, and all the expedition's supplies were ordered impounded. The men would be permitted to retain all their personal effects with the exception of their firearms. Davidson would be allowed to remain in Costa Rica because his papers were in order (mutterings of disapproval came from the rest of the treasure hunters).

Glad to get out of their immediate difficulties so easily after having for days contemplated a spell in a Costa Rican prison, the treasure hunters to a man voiced their appreciation of the courtesy and consideration with which they had been treated by the Costa Rican officials. Before they left on the *Nuevo Panama*, however, they declared their intention of suing Captain Arthur as soon as they reached home, and there were several who threatened to wreak their vengeance on the captain personally.

Back in Panama they were eventually permitted to sail on the *Queen of Scots*, and they returned to England toward the end of November. This was the end of the first Treasure Recovery Limited expedition to Cocos Island, which had set out from London so jubilantly and confidently only two short months before.

Back in Costa Rica, the government announced that it would in due course auction the confiscated stores and equipment to the highest bidder. An exception was made of the electric plant, capable of lighting 200 lamps, which was to be installed in the penal settlement on the island of San Lucas in the Gulf of Nicoya. The colony has long been famous for the fact that no wall or barricade surrounds it. The waters around the island are alive with enough sharks to discourage any would-be escapees. The new light plant was a further great improvement.

On November 5th, the *Panama-American* ran a scathing two column article by-lined by Ted Scott denouncing British Consul Cox and Vice-Consul Murray for the unmeritorious part they had played behind the scenes in this most recent Cocos Island controversy. The article duly came to the attention of both these gentlemen but neither did anything about it.

Yes, it was the end of the *Queen of Scots* expedition, but it was not the end of Treasure Recovery Limited. As August Gissler once said, "Once you get the bug, you're hooked for life."

18.

A FACTUAL story should not be encumbered with the author's opinions or colored by any flights of his imagination. Facts alone should be enough and the reader left to do his own coloring and imagining as his background and his personal experience will enable him. Thus, if we have been more laconic than customary, understand that it is the result of our attempt to be objective and report the story as we find it. This portion, for instance, being a highly significant episode in one expedition's experience, offers opportunity for innumerable lines of pure imagination but we shall forego all such and hold the account to a handful of letters, eyewitness accounts and clippings stacked and offered in their chronological order.

When the *Queen of Scots* was nearing England about the middle of December, 1934, the ire of the treasure hunters against their "controller of operations," Captain Charles Arthur, had not diminished in the least. If anything, their wrath had increased considerably as they exchanged the pleasant, comfortable warmth of the tropics for the cold, wintry winds of the English Channel. Many of the returning adventurers had invested their life's savings in Treasure Recovery Limited and the future looked far from rosy.

Yet, when the yacht docked in the Thames, who should be waiting alongside the dock to receive them but the suave Captain Arthur himself, his round, red face wreathed in smiles. Arthur greeted the despondent treasure hunters like long lost children.

"Now, boys," he said, when they eventually got ashore and he had bought them all a good stiff drink, "I know what you are going to say, but hold your horses for a moment. Let me speak and then you can have your say." There was a lot of grumbling, but they let him talk.

"I admit," he said, "that appearances are very much against me. It looks as though I ran out on you all. Nothing of the sort. I rushed back here to protect your own interests. I knew that most of you had invested all your spare cash in Treasure Recovery Limited and I didn't want any of you to be let down on my account.

"I made a mistake in going to Cocos Island without first obtaining the permission of the Costa Rican government. But mistakes can be rectified and that's exactly what I have been doing since I arrived back here a few weeks ago. Not only have I rectified all the mistakes previously made, but we are still going through with our original proposition in spite of the present setback.

"Listen carefully, while I tell you the present set-up. We have appointed Venus Trust Limited, of Carlton House in Regent Street,* our sole authorized agents, and the Trust has been able to sell to the public a large block of our un-issued shares which the underwriters had failed to take up

* A brokerage concern which dealt only in stocks which could not obtain an official listing on the London Stock Exchange.

and had therefore forfeited. Therefore, we now have sufficient capital in our treasury to go ahead with our new plans.

"While you fellows have been on your way home, I have had my own yacht, the converted North Sea trawler *Veracity*, refitted at considerable expense and I have chartered her to Treasure Recovery Limited on terms very advantageous for the Company. We are starting for Cocos Island again in the very near future.

"And before you ask me how all this is possible without a concession from the Costa Rican government, let me give you another piece of news. We have been in communication with the Clayton Metalphone Company of Vancouver, who, incidentally, have no funds of their own, and we have made a deal with them whereby they will allow us to seach for treasure on Cocos under their concession. Naturally, we have to pay the Canadian company for this sublet deal, but we have been able to come to terms which are mutually satisfactory."

Captain Arthur went on to explain in some detail the arrangement with the Canadian company and his agreement to include some of the Canadians in the next expedition—to protect the Canadians' share of the treasure when, and if, found.

"There remains," he admitted, "just one fly in the honey. We still have to square ourselves with the Costa Rican government and obtain their consent to our taking over the rights and privileges of the Canadian company. However, I do not anticipate any difficulties in this connection. To take care of these negotiations, the chairman of our Board of Directors, Mr. Eric Norman Alers-Hankey, will be leaving here for Costa Rica, via New York, on February 13th. As soon as he arrives in Costa Rica he will make the best possible deal with the Costa Rican government. In fact, he will try to recover all the stores and equipment which they took from us—even if we have to pay a ransom—to get the stuff back.

"We are so confident that Mr. Alers-Hankey will be able to fix matters satisfactorily that we are not going to lose any time waiting on this side. The *Veracity* will leave here within a few weeks and proceed leisurely to Panama where she will wait for Mr. Alers-Hankey's green light to Puntarenas en route to Cocos."

He followed this with a sales talk about the continued enthusiasm of the Board of Directors and their willingness to "risk everything" they had on another try for the treasure. "As before, it is going to be a strictly scientific search—no following of personal clues or old documents or anything like that. That's a sucker's way of searching for treasure. No, we are going to tackle this job scientifically."

Anyone who wanted to quit, he said, could do so, but if he did, "let him remember that he has no right to kick about the failure of the last expedition," because the Company was willing to let him continue with the enterprise and return to Cocos.

We have often thought that Captain Arthur was cut out for bigger things. He could have sold snowballs to the Eskimos, for instance, or swayed multitudes in a political campaign. Long before he finished talking, the faces of his listeners underwent a radical change. The scowls that greeted him turned to smiles and by the end they were enthusiastically discussing the new project.

A few days later Finnis, Worsley, Harris and Atkinson announced their intention to return to Cocos; Polkinghorne and Stenhouse agreed to remain with the Company; and Norman Edwards, after renouncing his job as "Admiral" of the Costa Rican Navy, also joined the group. Percy Howe dropped out and, in partnership with other venturesome Britons, went to Trinidad to search for a sunken galleon.

193

Later they operated a successful freighting service between Port-of-Spain and British Guiana, but in February, 1936, Howe, then only twenty-four years old, blew his brains out with a revolver. It was a strange end for a treasure hunter, for this is a breed that almost never gives up hope.

Back in London, the usual publicity which treasure hunting expeditions never fail to get, especially when the treasure sought is on Cocos Island, appeared in the English newspapers and once again the offices of Treasure Recovery Limited swarmed with smiling, enthusiastic people as everybody with a shilling invested in the company and looked forward with eager anticipation to the coming expedition.

The yacht *Veracity* left Lowestoft on February 11th 1935. On board were Captain and Mrs. Arthur; Commander Finnis, listed as captain of the yacht; Commander and Mrs. Worsley, he as paymaster of the expedition; Edwards, chief engineer; Dr. Harris, of whom great things were expected as the geologist of the group; Atkinson, radio operator, nicknamed "Lightning" because of his inability to do anything quickly; Lieutenant Loughnan, mate; Paynter, a relation of Arthur's, steward; Tucker and Leighton, seamen; and Cedric Mallabey, motion picture cameraman.

Although no one aboard knew it, the *Veracity* was registered under Mrs. Arthur's name. Mallabey, a skinny, pipe-smoking Englishman, had made a deal with Arthur for exclusive motion pictures of the discovery of the treasure, if found.

We heard the news of the *Veracity's* departure over the London radio that same night and Weston made a mental note to be on hand when they unearthed the famous treasure, whether they liked it or not. Meanwhile, their "advance" man, Mr. Alers-Hankey, arrived in San José on March 2nd and checked into the Gran Hotel Costa Rica. Half an hour later he checked out and departed hurriedly, explaining to the surprised clerk that he had unexpectedly run into some old friends who had invited him to stay with them at their house. He told the taxi driver, however, to take him across town to the Hotel Europa, but to tell no one where he had gone.

Weston arrived at the Hotel Europa about two minutes later—taxis were scarce at that hour—and sent up his card, asking for an interview.

"How did you find out I was here?" snapped Mr. Alers-Hankey, coming out into the hall.

"I heard you were here in connection with the Cocos Island treasure hunt, so I'd like to know whether you have anything to say about the expedition?"

"I have nothing to say," said Hankey, "and please don't bother to ask me again because I shall still have nothing to say. Newspaper publicity was what wrecked our last expedition and we are going to take care not to get any publicity this time."

"Tsk, tsk, Mr. Hankey," clucked Weston. "A million readers of the *New York Times* are anxiously waiting for news of your expedition. If you find the treasure your discovery will rank with the great discoveries of Egyptian tombs. Surely you would not want to deprive the public of such a thrill!"

"I've said all I have to say," barked Mr. Hankey, and slammed the door.

What did Mr. Alers-Hankey do in Costa Rica? He wouldn't "talk" to Weston, but let him tell it in his own words as he reported it to his fellow directors in London a few days later:

The Chairman & Directors,
Treasure Recovery Ltd.,
40 Broadway, London, S.W.I.

Gentlemen:

The following is a brief report of my activities since leaving
London on February 13th.

I arrived in New York on the evening of February 20th after
four days of extremely heavy weather. I sailed again at noon
on Saturday, Feb. 23rd, by the Grace Line *Santa Barbara* and
arrived at Cristóbal, 6 A.M. on Friday, March 1st.

Having wired to Mr. Dagnall of Payne & Wardlaw from New
York that I was arriving, he was very kindly there to meet
me and assist me through the Customs, etc. As there was a
United Fruit Co. steamer leaving that night for Puerto Limón,
I booked on her in preference to waiting till the next morning to
catch the air mail.

Mr. Dagnall was extremely helpful and kind but gave me very
clearly to understand that under no circumstances would their
firm act as agents for or have anything to do with any further
expedition that was going treasure hunting, and that it was
Captain Payne's definite instructions and ruling.

As I had the whole day to put in at Cristóbal I decided to take
advantage of the opportunity to find out if Captain Arthur was
definitely *persona grata* with the Canal Zone authorities. I asked
Mr. Dagnall to introduce me to the Chief Immigration and
Quarantine Officer, which he very kindly did and then I asked
the Doctor if he could confirm that Captain Arthur, formerly of
the *Western Queen*, had a clean sheet so far as they were concerned.

He replied that Captain Arthur was a gentleman for whom
they had been on the lookout for a considerable time and that
if they caught him in the Canal Zone he would be arrested, and
in addition to having to pay the amount due to the Government,
which, speaking from memory, was some $150 to $200, he would
be liable to a year's imprisonment and a fine of $500 for a de-

liberate breach of the laws. He outlined the case against Arthur but the details are of no concern of ours.

Leaving Cristóbal that night I arrived at Puerto Limón at 6 A.M. Saturday, March 2nd, and after completing all the necessary formalities, left by train at 10:30 for San José where I arrived at 5 P.M. and found our lawyer's son there to meet me and drive me to my hotel.

On Monday, our lawyer took me round to meet Cox and Murray, and in the afternoon Cox took me round to pay an official call on the Minister of Foreign Relations. The next two days I was expecting any minute to get word to go and present my respects to His Excellency but things have not panned out as expected and the President has instructed the two Ministers to go ahead and fix things up, so I shall probably see the President at the end instead of at the beginning.

I found on my arrival that the missing assignment from Vancouver had arrived two weeks previously and had been handed by Cox to the Minister of Foreign Relations, but up to the time of my arrival, nothing had transpired, but on my official visit to the gentleman in question the document was eventually dug out and was sent to the President for his approval that afternoon which was about the quickest bit of work that had ever been done in San José.

The official approval of the Government to our agreement with the Canadian concern only awaits the settlement of the indemnity and stores question as the President insisted that the two had to be fixed at the same time.

I was hoping for an appointment for this afternoon in which to get our final negotiations well under way, but just before lunch our lawyer came round to see me to say that the Minister of the Interior had cabled last night to their consul in London to find out the financial status of the Company and whether they were in a position to carry out their obligations—such obligations, as far as I can see, consisting of paying the police and making provision for repatriation.

I cabled you immediately to get in touch with the Consul and to give him every assurance that the Company were fully able to carry out all their commitments and obligations. The success of all, EVERYTHING, hangs on a satisfactory report being received and I hope I made this clear to you.

While this was going on our lawyer has had a number of conversations with me in regard to Arthur and he was very much perturbed when he learned that Arthur was coming out in charge. He states that he, personally, has nothing against him, but that as he is acting for the Company, the Company's interest is the only thing with which he is concerned and it was his strong recommendation that I cabled you as I did—in fact, the cable was almost made out by him. I asked Cox his views about it and whilst on account of his official position he did not want to say anything, he privately assured me that he entirely agreed with our lawyer.

I have really found MOST EMBARRASSING the questions I have been asked about Arthur and whether he is coming out, and although there is nothing official against him up here, everybody knows about him and, to put it bluntly, he is not liked nor is he trusted. His connection with the "A" case was published *in extenso* in the local Press * which is the worst possible thing that could have happened for him and for us, and our lawyer is quite sure that when it is known that he is coming out with the expedition, it will all be raked up again with most damaging results to the Company. It was very unpleasant for me to have to cable as I did but I endeavored to be as impersonal and impartial as I possibly could and nothing but actual facts were stated, and I refrained from expressing my personal opinion. I felt it was my duty to inform the Board exactly what the position was and to leave the matter in their hands.

As regards Puntarenas, Cox takes a very much more serious view of this as Arthur's colored ex-cook is still down there and as recently as three or four weeks ago stated he heard Arthur was coming out, and he and his lawyer were just waiting for him. Cox warned me that besides being extremely unpleasant for Arthur, it might result in the holding up of the expedition in Puntarenas for an indefinite period—another bad reflection on the Company.

Since writing the above, I have had a further interview with our lawyer and he has further explained that whilst the Minister of Foreign Affairs is quite satisfied and ready to go ahead, it is the Minister of the Interior who is more anxious to get outside assurance that the Company is really a serious affair and that

* See Appendix VI.

the Directors are men of good standing and repute, and that in the event of the treasure being found, the party would not be just a bunch of buccaneers and try to make off with it. With a whimsical smile he added that "if Arthur's name had not cropped up we should never have heard anything about this little hitch."

Everything now is at a standstill until the Government receive a satisfactory reply from their Consul-General and I shall feel mighty relieved when I know it is O.K.

With regard to a possible vessel to replace *Veracity*, I have made pretty full inquiries and have got on to an engineer who is in close touch with the position in Panama as regards small vessels, and he told me that at the present time there are quite a few really good Chinese-owned Diesel-engined craft that are laid up there owing to the bad times, and that the owners would be only too glad to charter them for a very reasonable sum. He had no hesitation in saying that he could get a suitable vessel on a bare ship charter basis for £50 to £60 per month, and fully expected he could get it down to £40. If we did anything on these lines he would be O.K. as engineer at £10 per month. He is an Englishman and has been out here many years and I have received excellent reports about him.

I was hoping to be able to catch the steamer from Cristóbal to New York on March 11th, but that is impossible as nothing but a Mills bomb would awaken these officials into any sign of activity and I now plan to leave on the 20th, arriving New York 26th, and sail for home on the *Berengaria* March 30th, due April 6th.

I mentioned in my cable for Polky [Polkinghorne] to be on tap ready to leave for here. There is a good two weeks hard work here sorting out the stores and chucking out bad stuff and checking what is left in readiness for shipment to Puntarenas, and as all this should be done and in readiness by the time the party arrives in Puntarenas, the natural thing would be for Polky to take charge of it once everything is settled and I can give the "all clear."

With regard to the indemnity, I don't think it will be possible to cut it down much, but I have a plan in mind which, if I can pull it off, will be almost as good as a fifty per cent cut. It will be time enough, however, when it is accomplished.

In regard to the matter of cables. I did not include them in

199

my estimate of expenses and as I did not want to find myself running short, started cabling you "collect," as I hoped that by this time Venus Trust would have you fairly well in funds. However, I got a polite note from the cable office to the effect that you would be glad if I would pay for my own cables from which I gather that you consider there is no limit to the depths of my pocket or else my hopes about Venus Trust have not materialized. I have not heard if you have cabled that £25 I advanced to Worsley out of my expense money, to New York or not. I sincerely hope so as I have cabled our New York man to transfer it here and if it is not forthcoming, well, Costa Rica will be just so much poorer by that amount. There is no exclamation mark on this machine which I have borrowed from the proprietor of this "Pub" so I cannot quite complete the finesse that is intended.

I think I have posted you up to date as far as I can, so will close with the wish that if it should fall to my lot to visit San José again, it will only be en route to Cocos.

E. Alers-Hankey

One may conclude from this that Mr. Hankey is concerned about Captain Arthur's connection with the Company. Certainly the case he builds against him is strong.

Mr. Hankey arrived in Costa Rica confident that he would be able to complete his negotiations with the government in a week or two, but, considering his inexperience in *mañana* land, he may be forgiven this little idiosyncracy. Five weeks passed before Hankey had completed his task and during those five weeks Weston shadowed him day and night.

"Whom do you represent, anyhow?" he asked the reporter one day, visibly annoyed at Weston's persistence.

"The public," responded Weston meekly.

Shortly before he left Costa Rica in the first week of April, Hankey wrote a long letter to Commander Worsley giving full details as to how the *Veracity* expedition was to be handled. This letter, which he sent to Panama to await the arrival of the *Veracity*, advances our story so we shall quote from it in detail. (Should you question why Hankey did not address this to Captain Arthur, the commander-in-chief, the reason will become apparent shortly.) Written from the Hotel Europa in San José and dated April 4th, the letter said:

My dear old Wuz,

My mission here which I figured would take me five days to complete has taken me just five weeks and I am leaving here on Sunday next for home, having eventually completed everything to my entire satisfaction.

On two or three occasions I thought everything was going to be a washout and, positively, I could not see a ray of daylight anywhere, and I damned nearly went demented. However, we stuck to it like grim death and I am now delighted to say that everything in the garden is lovely and the Government are now eating out of my hand.

CORRESPONDENCE: For your information, I enclose a complete file of my correspondence with the Government which will give you in concise form the result of my five weeks negotiations with our lawyer and Cox and the Government. The only point on which the Government are absolutely adamant is that the ship is to proceed to Puntarenas direct BEFORE going to the Island, and as they have met us in practically everything else, we have not done too badly, so you will have to bear this proviso specially in mind.

PASSPORTS AND VISAS: Please see that every member of your party is provided with these, otherwise it will cause trouble on arrival at Puntarenas. They can be obtained from the British and Costa Rican consuls at Colón.

PUBLICITY: Please do your utmost to avoid any interviews with the Press anywhere in the Canal Zone. They are sure to be on your track the same way as they were on mine as soon as I arrived in Cristóbal, but I told them point-blank that I had no news or any statement to make to them other than that I was proceeding to Costa Rica and what might happen there I was not in a position to say. For your guidance, I enclose a copy of a considered statement which, in consultation with our lawyer and Cox, I am going to give to the Press here and which they will get after my departure, and if you find yourself obliged to give

201

those damned rats in Cristóbal or Balboa any statement, I would suggest you merely repeat or just hand them a copy of my statement. If they want any details of your plans or anything, plead absolute ignorance, explaining that you will not know what has been arranged until you arrive at Puntarenas where your instructions are awaiting you.

STORES: I have got the Government to agree to deliver these f.o.b. Puntarenas. They are all in store in the Barracks here, and as far as I can judge from outside appearances, they appear to be in pretty good shape. The electric light plant has been installed in the penal island off Puntarenas, but the Government has agreed to send it over to Puntarenas with the rest of the stuff.

IMPORTANT: Please do not fail to telegraph Cox from Cristóbal advising him the date you will arrive at Puntarenas. This is most important as arrangements are being made for the Police and Stores to arrive at Puntarenas to coincide with your arrival so as to avoid any unnecessary delay.

POLICE: At the moment, these are to number eight and two officers. The officer in charge will be Colonel Valenzuela, who was second in command during the "ousting" operations. He is a damned nice chap, talks English very well indeed, and was desperately keen to go, and as I made a personal application for him and he has been officially appointed, he will do anything for me and you will find him a very big asset to you. He is dining with me tonight, and when I have got him well oiled, I am going to try and get the number of police reduced to one officer and three others. He will be in charge of the police and stores between here and Puntarenas. The police have got to be on board when the ship first arrives at the Island. That is one of the laws of the Medes and Persians which nothing can change.

IMPORTANT: When sending the ship to the mainland for supplies or anything, take special care not to arrive at Puntarenas on a Sunday or a holiday as it will cost money.

There were other instructions concerning landing and loading in Puntarenas but no mention of Captain Arthur. The press release he mentioned was published in the *La Tribuna* of San José, the morning of the day he left Costa Rica. We translate it here:

202

THE "VERACITY" EXPEDITION WILL BRING NEW DOCU-
MENTS REGARDING THE LOCATION OF THE COCOS ISLAND
TREASURE. THE EXPEDITION WILL ARRIVE AT PUNTARENAS
IN THE EARLY PART OF MAY.

MR. ALERS-HANKEY, WHO RETURNS TO ENGLAND TODAY,
DELIVERED TO THE GOVERNMENT THE SUM OF 24,784
COLONES FOR THE PURCHASE OF THE EQUIPMENT CON-
FISCATED FROM THE LAST EXPEDITION.

Mr. E. Alers-Hankey, President of Treasure Recovery Limited,
the English company to which our government has ceded the
rights of exploration on Cocos Island, in accordance with the
terms of the concession granted to the Clayton Metalphone
Company of Vancouver about three years ago, returns to England today on board the United Fruit Company's steamer *Peten*
which leaves Puerto Limón this afternoon.

Mr. Hankey was able to arrive at a complete understanding
with the Minister of the Interior, Don Santos Leon Herrera,
who had been commissioned by the President of the Republic
to take charge of the negotiations. The English company has acquired all the stores and equipment confiscated from the previous expedition for the sum of 24,794 colones [about $5,000]
which has already been paid by Mr. Alers-Hankey.

Apart from this transaction, Mr. Alers-Hankey undertook not
to include among the expeditionaries who will soon arrive at
Puntarenas, certain individuals who had taken part in the
previous expedition, one of these being Captain Arthur, who
in days gone by sold to the government the auxiliary sailboat
Western Queen, and who was also commander of the yacht
Queen of Scots which conveyed the treasure hunters of the last
expedition to Cocos Island.

According to the statements which Mr. Hankey made to us,
the new expedition will arrive at Puntarenas early in May on
board a small fishing boat called the *Veracity,* in order to embark the stores and equipment which the company has just
acquired. Besides this, the yacht is bringing a complete outfit
of the most modern instruments capable of indicating the presence of buried metals, and he is practically certain of the success of the expedition.

In a recent conversation, Mr. Hankey informed us that the

company was in possession of certain clues which had been submitted to the company by their respective owners after having satisfied themselves of the seriousness of the enterprise.

One of these clues, probably the most authentic was obtained only a few days before the expedition left England; consequently the treasure hunters are coming out full of enthusiasm and with a complete belief in their ultimate success.

Mr. Hankey explained to us that the "Metalphone" treasure-detecting apparatus, which the Canadian company used on Cocos Island some three years ago, was not exactly satisfactory and that he expected much better results with the new instruments they were going to use.

Mr. Hankey further went on to say that they would not look for the treasure on the tops of inaccessible mountains because, according to the information in his possession, the treasure was not buried in any such place. "Do you think," he asked, "that the pirates who buried the treasure had the necessary time to carry treasure chests weighing many tons right into the interior of the island? I think not, because they were probably being pursued at the time they buried the treasure, either by men-of-war or by rival pirates. We believe that the treasure is buried somewhere near the beaches, perhaps under high-water mark, which would serve as an added protection against possible haphazard discovery.

"Our electrical apparatus consists of a small box which encases a delicate electrical instrument which can be carried anywhere without difficulty. The instrument is used in conjunction with a radiolike antenna suspended between two poles, and if the instrument should indicate the presence of metals, it is possible to determine the exact spot by a simple geometric calculation."

Mr. Alers-Hankey expressed himself as highly contented with the courtesies extended to him by our government officials, and he reiterated his faith in the success of the expedition. He emphasized the fact that his company would at all times cooperate loyally with the government, seeing that they were both interested in finding the treasure.

By now it is pretty obvious who was trying to double-cross who. Hankey's reports all show a deliberate attempt to

204

get rid of Captain Arthur, in spite of the fact that Arthur (notwithstanding Hankey's frequent denials to the contrary) controlled Treasure Recovery Limited and the expedition's supply ship, the *Veracity*, was Arthur's property.

The small clique of correspondents and local reporters who gathered in the "tea room" of the Gran Hotel Costa Rica for afternoon coffee and refreshments could talk of little else than the island intrigue. Serious trouble was in store for "somebody" and as yet he didn't even suspect it. For the *Veracity* and Captain Arthur were in the middle of the Atlantic, blissfully unaware of Hankey's hanky-panky in Costa Rica. Indeed, he had other troubles to occupy his mind at the moment. The *Veracity* had suffered a series of delays due to bad weather and engine faults ever since she left England. She had put in at Poole harbor, and later at Vigo, Spain, for repairs; and there were long periods of calm weather when the sails could not be used and other times when they encountered heavy seas. Thus it was not until April 23rd, two and a half months after her departure from Lowestoft that she reached the island of Barbados in the West Indies.

Upon Hankey's departure from Costa Rica, Weston summed up the situation in this cable to the *New York Times:*

As a condition of its approving the transfer to Treasure Recovery Limited of the concession to search for buried treasure on Cocos Island previously held by the Clayton Metalphone Company of Vancouver, the Costa Rican government stipulated that Captain Charles Arthur, who is understood to be on board the steam drifter *Veracity*, now on its way to Cocos from England, should not be included in the list of treasure hunters.

Captain Arthur's exclusion is due to the fact that he was the promoter of the ill-fated expedition which was evicted from Cocos Island by Costa Rican troops last October. He is also on the Costa Rican government's black list on account of his having left the crew of his former yacht, the *Western Queen,* stranded in Costa Rica some two and a half years ago. He sold the yacht to the Costa Rican government and then left with the money without paying off his crew who have had a claim pending against him in the courts ever since.

The stranded crew, who are beachcombing in Puntarenas, threatened to have Captain Arthur arrested if he ever set foot in Costa Rica again and it was in order to avoid any complications in this respect that the promoters of the new expedition to Cocos consented to the government's demand that Captain Arthur be excluded.

It is understood that Captain Arthur will leave the expedition's ship *Veracity* when she arrives in Panama.

Meanwhile trouble was also brewing in London. Arthur's private company, Spanish Main Exploration Limited, was under fire from Mr. and Mrs. Jolly and a few other disgruntled treasure hunters who had not swallowed all of Captain Arthur's revival pitch. They had petitioned the courts to declare the company (which was Arthur) as bankrupt.

The *Diario de Costa Rica,* chief competitor of *La Tribuna* in San José, reported:

We recently published information received from London to the effect that the creditors of Spanish Main Exploration Limited had petitioned the Court to declare the company in a state of bankruptcy. The company, however, informed the judge that they expected to find the treasure on Cocos Island very soon; therefore the judge postponed the bankruptcy proceedings until June 25th, saying that if the treasure was not found by that date he would order the company to be liquidated.

The *Diario de Costa Rica,* acting upon well-founded information, informed its readers that the affairs of Spanish Main Exploration Limited were very closely related to Treasure Recovery Limited. Against this assertion, Mr. Eric Alers-Hankey, the representative of Treasure Recovery Limited, who at that time was in San José for the purpose of obtaining the approval of the government to the transfer of the Cocos Island concession from the Clayton Metalphone Company to his own company, protested very strongly and he stated emphatically that the affairs of Spanish Main Exploration Limited had nothing to do with Treasure Recovery Limited, and that the former company was simply a shareholder in the second company.

The *Diario de Costa Rica* has since obtained from Somerset House, London, which is the British government's office where all public companies are obliged to file statements of their constitution and finances, exclusive information which proves two things: first, that Mr. Eric Alers-Hankey was incorrect in stating that his company was not connected with Spanish Main Exploration Limited, and, second, that Treasure Recovery is purely a speculative company whose shares were not received with confidence by the British investors.

According to the British government records, *120,000 shares of Treasure Recovery Limited were given to Spanish Main Exploration Limited* FREE in exchange for the information which they were supposed to have about the treasure on Cocos Island.

The record showed, continued the news account, that Spanish Main owned about 75 per cent of the issued capital, despite Hankey's denial that it had anything to do with Treasure Recovery. The account continued:

The company's prospectus states that: "most of the directors and members of the executive have studied the Cocos Island problem on the island" and that four of them have visited the island and carried out prolonged investigations there. The *Diario de Costa Rica* thinks it proper to inquire whether these visits were made with the consent and knowledge of the Costa Rican government.

The paper pointed out that the offices of both companies were at the same address. Concluding its detail of the information received from London, it asked its readers to form their own opinions as to the standing of the company which "the government has just authorized to proceed to Cocos Island to search for the legendary treasure."

One thing the *Diario* pointed out was certain, and that was that unless the treasure was found before June 25th, the British court would declare Spanish Main Exploration Limited in a state of bankruptcy, which would inevitably create difficulties for Treasure Recovery Limited.

It is not difficult to imagine the situation in London. What with all the publicity the two companies were getting, the shareholders were beginning to have second thoughts. The company's offices were inundated with requests for information as to the progress of the expedition. Finally, as tension mounted, the Venus Trust (which, meanwhile was still trying to unload Treasury Recovery Ltd.'s shares) decided it was time to issue a "Special Progress Report." Here it is:

Dear Sir (or Madam),

The Ship *Veracity,* conveying the personnel of the second Expedition to Cocos Island, under the leadership of Commander Worsley, duly arrived at Barbados in the West Indies on the 23rd April, a few days after their scheduled time, the delay being due to engine trouble whilst crossing the Atlantic. The necessary repairs have been effected at Barbados, and the ship is now making for the Panama Canal, a few days' journey only from its ultimate destination.

We have previously hinted at certain very definite and important information which the Treasure Recovery Company have in their possession regarding the location of the principal treasure hidden on the island. It will be readily appreciated that we, as the Company's publicity agents, are still unable, for obvious reasons, to disclose generally details of that information, but Shareholders may draw their own conclusions from the significant moves that are now taking place in London, the principal of which is the departure tomorrow, the 15th [of May], of the Managing Director of Treasure Recovery Limited for Cocos Island. He is making the journey by ordinary steamship lines, and is taking the most direct and quickest route to the island. His presence on the island is considered essential in anticipation of developments of the highest importance during the next few weeks.

There was more, all couched in language intended to allay the fears, increase the hopes and inspire confidence and support among the shareholders. And it wasn't all dreamed up by the Venus Trust's publicity department. The company really did have "definite and important information," or so its "executive" believed, for there seem to have been no skeptics among them.

19.

CONSIDERING the wide difference between science and supposition it may be a little difficult to understand how the original premise of the Treasure Recovery company could have changed. This treasure hunt began on a high plane, a scientific approach to the problem, said its directors; no "clues" or suppositions were to be considered. How, then, could its policy have degenerated into the credulous, its "executive" exhibit gullibility typical of the most unlettered bumpkin? We cannot explain it, unless treasure hunting is something like love, which, Shakespeare said, "is blind, and lovers cannot see the pretty follies that themselves commit."

The directors of Treasure Recovery Limited were preparing to commit some pretty foolish follies. One might say the first was Hankey's handout to the Costa Rican press, and the next was in the Venus Trust's "progress report."

Hankey said: "The company is in possession of certain clues. . . . One of these, probably the most authentic, was obtained only a few days before the expedition left England." The Venus Trust hinted at "certain very definite important information which the Treasure Recovery Company have in their possession regarding the location of the principal treasure hidden on Cocos Island."

What was this important clue that the company had got hold of? What clue could be so important that men—normal, highly educated men—would be inspired to follow it like schoolboys after a will-o'-the-wisp?

One day early in February, while Treasure Recovery leaders were busy fitting out the *Veracity* expedition, due to leave in two weeks, an elderly man of seafaring appearance walked into the offices of the company and asked to speak to the directors. His name was George Lane, he said, and he refused to talk to anyone but the T. R. leaders. Significantly, they were easily persuaded to humor him, and behind locked doors he proceeded to tell them a remarkable story.

He had been, Lane told them, a stoker in the Royal Navy. A few years ago, the British Admiralty had offered to lend to the Colombian government the necessary officers and crews to operate the four destroyers which Colombia had purchased in England, until such time as they could train their own men, and Lane had been one of the Royal Navy reservists who had volunteered for the job in Colombia. He had only recently finished serving his time on this hitch, had been paid off and repatriated to England, and was now living at Southend-on-Sea, not far from London.

He had returned home on the *Caribea* of the Hamburg-American Line, he said, and on board that ship he had met and befriended a down-and-out Belgian marine engineer named Petrus Bergmans who was returning to Belgium from Panama. Lane had given Bergmans money and the latter seemed to appreciate Lane's friendship and kindness. He told Lane that one day he would be able to repay his favors a thousandfold; and from time to time during the voyage, he hinted that he knew where an enormous treasure was buried and that he was the only living man who knew where it was. Later he revealed to Lane that the treasure was on Cocos Island and all he needed to obtain it was enough money to organize a small expedition to the island.

Lane's cupidity was aroused and he showed it. Bergmans, however, was sufficiently cautious that he gave away none of the vital details. He described the island in detail and once he said that the treasure was buried in a big cave near a certain creek, but that was all he would say.

Lane told Bergmans that he had read in an English newspaper that a London company was organizing a treasure hunting expedition to Cocos Island and suggested that he, Bergmans, should get in touch with them. Bergmans, however, said he wanted to go to Belgium first, but since Lane was going to London perhaps he could stop off and visit the company and tell them about Bergmans. If Lane would do this and Bergmans thereby made a tie-up with the company, then Lane should have a share of the profits. Lane accepted the proposition, and since Bergmans was jobless and penniless, he agreed to pay Bergmans' expenses while he was in Belgium awaiting word from Lane.

Since his return to England, Lane had been in frequent communication with Bergmans who, unfortunately, had been arrested on arrival on an old charge as a deserter from the Belgian army. At the moment, said Lane, he was lodged in Antwerp prison, located at 42 Rue des Beguines. Bergmans had engaged a lawyer, M. Verboet, of 191 Belgie Lei, Antwerp, who demanded one thousand gold francs to cover his fee and Bergmans' fine. This Lane could not pay, having only his small Navy pension, but he had been buying some small comforts for Bergmans, such as tobacco and magazines, while he was in prison. He was sure, he said, that Bergmans could lead them to the treasure if the directors would pay

212

Bergmans' expenses and give him a fair share of the treasure found.

The directors told Lane to come back the next day when they would let him know whether or not they were interested in his proposition.

The reaction of some of the directors was to turn down Lane's story as being too utterly fantastic. It was, they said, simply a stunt to get some easy money out of the company. There were a few, however, especially Hankey, Arthur and Studdert, who thought there might be something in Lane's story. And, in any event, Lane had been able to give them only the barest details. It would not cost much to investigate the matter further by getting in touch with Bergmans himself and see whether he could furnish some proof of his story.

Thus a group of serious-minded men, who had announced that their treasure hunting expedition would be conducted on nothing but "strictly scientific lines," were now not only ready and willing but obviously anxious to turn to one of those vague "personal clues" they had so often condemned.

The *Veracity* was due to sail within a couple of weeks and someone suggested that she be delayed until Bergmans' story had been properly checked. On the other hand, it was pointed out, Bergmans was in prison and there was no knowing how long it might take to get him out, even if his story were true. The directors decided, therefore, to let the *Veracity* sail on schedule on February 11th, and send Alers-Hankey on to Costa Rica to assuage the Costa Rican government as already arranged, before some other outfit queered the deal.

Meanwhile, it was agreed to treat the Bergmans' story with the strictest secrecy. Neither the men about to leave on the *Veracity*, the shareholders, the Costa Rican government, or the press (especially the press!) should have the slightest inkling that Bergmans was involved. They agreed that if there should be anything in Bergmans' story, the utmost secrecy would be necessary right up to the moment of unearthing the treasure.

When George Lane returned to T. R.'s offices the next day, he was told that the company was willing to investigate Petrus Bergmans and his story of the Cocos Island treasure. They had decided, therefore, to send Captain Polkinghorne over to Belgium on the next steamer to interview Bergmans in the Antwerp jail. Their future actions in the matter would depend on that interview. In the meantime, Lane would be given some expense money and he was to keep himself available but quiet.

Captain Polkinghorne caught the next boat to Antwerp where he had no difficulty locating the lawyer, M. Verboet, who readily confirmed Lane's story. The lawyer took him to the jail where the warden's consent to an interview with Bergmans was easily obtained.

Polkinghorne introduced himself to Bergmans as a director of Treasure Recovery Ltd., a responsible London company, and said he was interested in hearing Bergmans' version of the Cocos Island treasure story which George Lane had briefly related to the company.

Petrus Bergmans seemed willing to talk as soon as he realized that Polkinghorne represented a company which held a valid sub-concession to search for treasure on Cocos Island. (At least, Polkinghorne was telling part of the truth—they did have an agreement with the Canadian company although Hankey had not yet fixed it with the Costa Rican government.) But Bergmans' story was so fantastic that we hesitate to include it here in association with a factual account. However, it caused some important action so we give it here in Bergmans' own words as we got it from four different sources: George Lane, Captain Arthur, a Treasure Recovery circular, and from Petrus Bergmans himself. Here it is as Bergmans told it to us in Costa Rica, late in 1935:

My name is Petrus A. Bergmans, but I am more usually called Peter or Pete. I am 41 years old. In the summer of 1929 I sailed out of San Pedro, California, in the yacht *Westward*. This ship had belonged to a Mr. C. W. Young, of Seattle, and it may be that she was renamed. She was chartered by a party from the movie colony, and on their business they visited a number of places in Lower California, and then continued south towards Panama. The date of the charter was July 28th, 1929. The captain of the *Westward* was H. Peterson, of Portland, Oregon. Peterson had two daughters, now both married.

Coming down the Nicaraguan coast, the *Westward* was caught in a hurricane and she foundered with all hands with the exception of Captain Peterson and myself. This disaster took place on September 25th, 1929, which is in the season when strong squalls, known locally as *papagayos*, come down from the Andes.* The *papagayo* comes after sundown and without warning, at least to those without local knowledge, and even a well-built sailing vessel, caught unprepared, is liable to founder. The *Westward* was in none too seaworthy condition.

Peterson and I got away in a small boat and we drifted for three days, when we sighted an island. This was on September 28th, but we did not make the land until the 30th, and then only with great difficulty on account of the variable currents around the island, which Peterson said was none other than Cocos Island.

When we got ashore, we found and occupied the ruins of the settlement abandoned by the German, Gissler, many years before. Unfortunately, Peterson fell ill and I had to leave him in the hut while I wandered about the island searching for food. One day, about two weeks after we had landed on the island, while I was prowling about in the undergrowth, I happened to set my foot down on a spot which gave way under my weight, leaving what appeared to be a bottomless hole.

This strange occurrence aroused my curiosity, so I examined

* Authors' note: Pete was a little mixed up in his mountains. He meant the Sierra Madre (of Mexico) or the Cordillera (of Central America).

the hole and then I got down on my knees and shouted through the hole made by my foot. To my surprise my voice echoed back at me. Naturally, I became still more curious, so I enlarged the hole and then I found that it was the entrance to what appeared to be a tunnel or a natural cave. I entered this cave and found that it was evidently the hiding place of long-buried treasure.

I saw stacks of gold and silver, bars and coins piled loosely on the floor, large quantities of golden ornaments such as are used in churches, numbers of gold statues resembling those found in Roman Catholic churches, large chests full of jewelry and precious stones, two large unopened chests, and the skull and bones of a man.

The floor of the cave measured approximately 40 paces by 15. I also found some parchment documents on which I recognized the name of "Bonito." I took some of these documents away with me and placed them in a safe deposit in San Francisco after I left the island.

In company with Peterson, I later removed about half a sackful of the treasure and secreted it in two selected spots on the island. We then resealed and covered up the entrance to the cave.

On October 16th, 1929, a derelict ship's boat drifted ashore, and on November 30th we set out in this boat in an endeavor to make the mainland. Four days later, on December 4th, we were sighted and picked up by the German steamer *Nachwezeld*. The captain's name was Carl Heinrecht or Heinrich and from him we learned that the ship was going through the Panama Canal to Boston.

We decided to take the captain into our confidence, so we showed him the jewels we had brought away with us from the island and asked him if he could help us to dispose of them. The captain said he would, and when we got to Boston at the end of December, he took us to New York where he introduced us to an underworld firm named Strauss Brothers. He told them that we had some jewelry to sell and after they had looked it over, they paid us $56,000 for it.

This was only about one quarter of its real value, but we were quite satisfied and we split three ways with the captain. Peterson then went to his home in Portland, where he continued to suffer bad health and eventually he died in a hospital there in 1932.

The captain gave up his job and settled down to enjoy his share of our sale to Strauss Brothers, while I sailed for Europe on the S.S. *Cleveland* in April, 1930.

In March, 1934, I returned to the United States and for a time I was connected with the Belgian section at the World's Fair in Chicago. While there, I made the acquaintance of a Colonel Hunter who was a prominent Chicago lawyer, to whom I told the story of the treasure cave which I had found on Cocos Island. Colonel Hunter spent five months checking my story and then he decided that we would go to Cocos Island to take away the treasure.

I sailed in his yacht, the *Nautilus*, from Seattle to Panama, where Colonel Hunter and five of his friends, who had come by air from Chicago, joined us. We then set out for Cocos Island, ostensibly on a pearl-fishing expedition. However, on the way over, the yacht's cook, with whom I had become friendly, warned me that my life was in great danger. Therefore, when we reached the island I decided to pretend that I could not identify the proper landmarks to relocate the site of the treasure cave.

The *Nautilus* therefore returned to Panama, but Hunter and his friends were so mad with me for not revealing the treasure cave to them that they beat me up badly, and as a result I had to spend a long time in a hospital in the Canal Zone. Under the Canal Zone regulations, the yacht was not permitted to sail without me, and it was detained until I was discharged from the hospital. I was then taken on to Trinidad and put ashore there.

It was here that I made the acquaintance of an English seaman named George Lane who befriended me. Lane had been serving in the Colombian Navy and had just been discharged and was returning to England. He paid my passage to Europe and we came home together.

Ever since I disposed of the jewelry to the Strauss people in New York, they have had agents shadowing me, figuring that I had a lot more stuff available. Hunter's men have also been watching my movements to make sure that I do not disclose the whereabouts of the treasure to anybody but themselves.

To be on the safe side, I have given Lane certain information regarding the site of the treasure, but he is not to make use of it except in the event of my death.

This, essentially, was the amazing narrative Bergmans gave Captain Polkinghorne in the Antwerp prison. The Englishman's first reaction was disbelief. He wanted to reject the entire story as being nothing more than the product of a fertile imagination, utterly without foundation and altogether too fantastic to warrant any further waste of time. But the captain had a duty to perform. He was there to check Bergmans' story whether he personally believed it or not.

Polkinghorne, as we mentioned before, had several times visited Cocos Island to search for its treasure so he knew the island intimately. He knew every hill, beach, creek, waterfall and practically every tree. He doubted whether Bergmans had ever been on or even near Cocos Island, much less that he had found any treasure on it, so he began to cross-examine Bergmans. There were several questions about the topography of the island: how did one get to Chatham Bay overland from Wafer Bay: where was the largest waterfall; where were the remains of Gissler's main house; in which direction did Wafer Creek run; what were the positions of the islets around Cocos, and so on. And as the questions continued, Polkinghorne gradually became amazed at the way Bergmans answered every question correctly and without the slightest hesitation. He then and there made up his mind that whether Bergmans' story of finding the treasure was true or not, he certainly knew Cocos Island.

Bergmans said he would lead the expedition to the treasure for a paltry ten per cent, if Treasure Recovery would pay his fine and give him transportation and some spending money. He also wanted Lane included for a cut of the treasure and he wanted Lane to go along as his bodyguard because he was afraid of the Hunter people.

Back in London, Polkinghorne gave a full account of his interview. We shall not pretend to know by what mental processes the directors of Treasure Recovery Limited arrived

218

at their ultimate decision, but it was complete belief in Peter Bergmans' story. Perhaps it was sheer avarice, simple cupidity or just plain stupidity that prompted their decision. We do not know. What is obvious, however, looking back on it, is that their hitherto steadfastly maintained intention to conduct a scientific search for the Cocos treasure was abandoned. In its place was the dream of untold millions in gold, silver and jewels just waiting for Petrus Bergmans to point a finger and say "There it is, pick it up."

Polkinghorne was promptly commissioned to return at once to Belgium with sufficient funds to get Bergmans out of prison, buy him some presentable clothes, and bring him back to London with all speed.

The plot thickened rapidly after that. The *Veracity* got on her way, with Arthur in high spirits. Two days later Mr. Alers-Hankey left for Costa Rica via New York. And in those two short days, with Arthur safely out of the way, Alers-Hankey and some of the other directors of Treasure Recovery Ltd., concocted a plot to drop Captain Arthur from the company and bar him from sharing in Bergmans' assist.

Now arose the question of how to get Bergmans over to Cocos Island without the knowledge of anyone outside the Board. The directors had already adopted a policy of strict silence, as we said, and not even the company's shareholders were to be told about Bergmans until after he had delivered the goods. After all, the shareholders had invested their money in what was claimed to be a "scientific treasure hunt," and some of them might ask awkward questions if they knew their money was being used to support something more like a fairy story.

The directors decided that Bergmans should be sent out to Costa Rica in the guise of a mining engineer. Once there he was to follow through and actually inspect certain gold properties. As part of the act, some special letterheads were printed with the name of a nonexistent gold mining company, and on these various letters of authorization were written for Bergmans. He was to show these "credentials" to anyone in Costa Rica who questioned him about his business in the country. (He showed them to us.)

Polkinghorne persuaded Bergmans to leave Lane behind and write Lane at Southend-on-Sea explaining the plan. Lane was suspicious but Bergmans assured him he would get his share of the treasure.

After considerable discussion, it was finally decided to delay Bergmans' departure until Alers-Hankey returned from Costa Rica. They did not want the Belgian loafing around Costa Rica indefinitely, waiting for the *Veracity*, and they thought it best to keep a watchful eye on him.

But Hankey did not return to England until the end of April, as we said, or about the time the *Veracity* reached Barbados. And what Hankey told his fellow directors on his return convinced them that no harm was done in deferring Bergmans' departure. Hankey had taken effective steps to prevent Arthur's going to Cocos on the *Veracity*, or even entering Costa Rica. He would have no alternative but to abandon the expedition and return home. The company, Hankey suggested, should select a new field manager for the expedition and send him to Costa Rica prepared to take over the expedition after they got rid of Captain Arthur. The directors agreed and, accordingly, Richard Studdert, a professional mining man and the only one among them who knew about prospecting, was selected to go.

This arrangement fitted in well with the plan for Bergmans because Studdert and Bergmans could arrange to meet in Costa Rica and secretly keep in touch. No one wanted the public to know that Bergmans was connected with Treasure Recovery Ltd. They arrived in Costa Rica by separate routes but at nearly the same time. Bergmans carried out his pretense and even visited briefly the Miramar goldmine operated by our old acquaintance, Edmund Davidson of the Canadian company.

Cedric Mallabey, the cameraman aboard the *Veracity* when she sailed from Lowestoft, suffered so from seasickness that he abandoned the ship when she put in at Poole and returned to London. There he booked passage on a regular steamer and so arrived in Costa Rica long before the *Veracity* reached Panama. Since photography was an adjunct to our profession and we used cameras as part of our daily routine, we naturally found much in common with Cedric Mallabey. It was a friendship that paid dividends in more ways than one. It was Mallabey who gave us the first tip that Studdert had come out to be Managing Director of Treasure Recovery's second expedition to Cocos.

Weston was introduced to Studdert at a dance in the Gran Hotel Costa Rica and the reporter tried to find out when the *Veracity* was expected, but Studdert had been cautioned by Hankey to watch out for newspapermen and he was wary. Later Weston went to interview him at his hotel and when the door opened he got a glimpse of a short, red-faced, bespectacled man with curly, blond hair, sitting inside. It was weeks later before he learned his name was Peter Bergmans.

20.

The *Veracity* reached Barbados on April 23rd. Up to that time the people on the yacht had somehow managed to get along doing their own cooking, but the increasing heat of the tropics and the rather arduous voyage made galley work too much for the women of the party, so Arthur hired at Barbados a colored cook, Hubert Casey, who was a U. S. citizen, and a pantry-boy, Saunders, a native of that island. He gave them each the usual Treasure Recovery contract, promise of a small salary and a minute fraction of the treasure when found.

The *Veracity* called at Curaçao, then reached Cristóbal, and passed through the Panama Canal in the latter part of May. At Balboa they found a considerable amount of mail waiting for them. Worsley received Hankey's final letter of instructions, written in San José on April 4th, which he showed to Arthur. Captain Arthur also received, from someone loyal to him in London, a copy of Hankey's report to the directors wherein he stated that Arthur was liable to arrest if he set foot in the Canal Zone.

The British Legation in Panama City informed Arthur that the British Consul in San José had informed them that the Costa Rican government had definitely barred Arthur from going to Cocos Island or even entering Costa Rica.

One can imagine Captain Arthur's indignation. He sensed at once that Hankey's handiwork was aimed at preventing his taking part in the Cocos hunt and his first impulse was to turn the *Veracity* on her heels and sail back to England. But as Commanders Finnis and Worsley took pains to point out to him, the *Veracity* might be his property (albeit in his wife's name) but she happened to be legally chartered to Treasury Recovery Ltd. (for £100 per month) and until that charter expired it was the company who would decide the movements of the vessel.

Arthur realized there was nothing he could do but acquiesce, so he and Mrs. Arthur got off the *Veracity*, leaving Worsley in command of the expedition, just as Hankey had intended. And thus the first round went to Hankey.

But Captain Arthur still held controlling interest in the company and he figured he could put Hankey & Co. in their place in any showdown. Furthermore, he would return to London prepared with other documents. He wrote this letter to the Chief Immigration and Quarantine Officer of the Canal Zone:

The Chairman of Treasure Recovery Ltd., in an endeavor to bring about my removal as an official of that Company, has reported to the Directors in London, giving the Chief Immigration and Quarantine Office of the Panama Canal as his authority, that should I enter the Canal Zone I would be arrested and liable to one year's imprisonment for a deliberate breach of the laws.

As I am unaware of ever having committed any breach of the U. S. Laws, I would much appreciate the Chief Immigration and Quarantine Officer's comments on the above statement attributed by the Chairman of Treasure Recovery to him.

223

This is the reply which Arthur received to his letter:

. . . please be advised that no such statement has at any time been made by the Chief Quarantine Officer of the Panama Canal to any officer of your company.

At the present time there are no charges of violations of the Quarantine and Immigration Regulations held against you and you are therefore free to enter the Canal Zone on any business connection with the transit and sailing of your vessel, the M. Y. *Veracity*. (This reply was signed by C. V. Akin, Chief Quarantine Officer.)

Arthur had this letter properly authenticated and sealed by the British Consul in Panama and other officials of the Zone. Then he and Mrs. Arthur caught the next steamer for London.

The *Veracity*, meanwhile, continued on to Puntarenas, arriving on June 6th. Weston flew down on the morning plane and checked in at the Hotel Imperial, where Richard Studdert was staying. He noticed hovering about the hotel the same red-faced, curly-haired stranger he had seen in San José but although this man and Studdert several times passed each other, Weston never saw the slightest sign of recognition pass between them.

The *Veracity* docked at the small wharf in the estuary backwater and Weston went aboard to greet his acquaintances, Commander Finnis, Doctor "Jock" Harris and Norman Edwards. They introduced him to the others whom he had not met, but the reception was notable for its coolness. Obviously, they had already been told to beware the press and this member of it in particular. Worsley and Studdert especially were annoyed at Weston and his prolonged conversation with his old friend Harris, though the two were merely exchanging reminiscences of the days they had been together in Venezuela years before.

Once, when Weston slipped back to his hotel for a change of film, he glimpsed a man sneaking out of his room. Coming into the dim hallway from the brightness of the street he was unable to trust his eyes, but he was pretty sure the intruder was the same mysterious stranger he had seen in Studdert's room in San José. Perturbed and no little annoyed, the reporter scolded the maid for leaving his door ajar and inquired of the manager who the man was. The manager said he was a mining man by the name of Bergmans and that he had probably entered Weston's room by mistake.

With this explanation the reporter had to appear content, but the affair, trivial though it was, worried him. But he did not see the mysterious Mr. Bergmans again that day or the next, and it was not until nearly three months later that he encountered him again.

The loading of the ransomed supplies from the first expedition got under way with typical British despatch, but there was such a quantity that it took them nearly two days to get everything aboard. Meanwhile, some delay may have been caused by the importunities of another potential treasure hunter who wanted to join the expedition. This was a Miss Isabel Elmore, a comely, romantically inclined young lady who said she would do almost anything to get over to Cocos Island. All day long she hung around the *Veracity* trying every line of persuasion—in the end even attempting to bribe Casey, the cook, to hide her aboard as a stowaway. Finally, when she had apparently convinced Mrs. Worsley she needed a companion to replace Mrs. Arthur, she cabled her stepfather, a Mr. Beresford, manager of the Panama Gold Corporation in Panama, for permission. She got a stern "No." (We were sorry too. Miss Elmore's contribution to our story could have been much more. Ah, yes!)

Late in the afternoon of the 7th, the *Veracity* was loaded and ready to sail but no effort was made to cast off. Looking on and ready to bid her *bon voyage, buen viaje* and good hunting, we became curious. The detachment of ten soldiers (Hankey hadn't succeeded in getting the complement reduced despite the "oil" he had used on the Colonel) under the command of Colonel Valenzuela, detailed to protect the government's share of the booty, was aboard. Also aboard were three deer, a magnificent stag and two does, which President Jimenez had requested the *Veracity* people to take to Cocos and release on the island.

The president's idea, perhaps originating with Mr. Fleischmann's notice board, was that left to themselves on the island the three deer would multiply and in a few years Cocos Island would become a sportsman's paradise. We shall hear more of this later, for although we have no desire to complicate our story with the addition of animal characters, the fate of the president's stag, tethered on the *Veracity*, and the destiny of Mr. George Lane, ex-stoker of the Royal Navy, sleeping soundly in his humble cottage in Southend-on-Sea, six thousand miles away, were from this moment inextricably woven together.

It was noticed that both Studdert and Worsley had disappeared from the wharf just before the *Veracity* finished loading. Now there was a subdued murmuring among the men on board. Something was in the wind. But what? Had there been a last minute hitch of some kind?

Two hours passed and then Studdert and Worsley came hurrying along the wharf. They jumped aboard the ship, the order to shove off was given, and the *Veracity* turned and pointed her prow into the setting sun, a great golden ball that seemed somehow prophetic. Her departure for Cocos Island and its fabulous treasure was watched by a curious crowd of several hundred *ticos*.

And what of the mysterious Mr. Bergmans? If he were connected with the expedition, which we suspected, we were pretty sure he was not aboard the *Veracity*. In fact, as we found out later, it was his absence which had delayed the departure. While we were watching the loading of the ship and waiting for her to depart, Studdert and Worsley had been frantically searching Puntarenas from end to end. Bergmans was missing. Police and local detectives were asked to help but Bergmans, the man who was to guide the expedition to the treasure cache on Cocos, had disappeared.

Looking back on it now, we know that Studdert was in a spot, and he knew it then. The *Veracity* was loaded, the Costa Rican soldiers were aboard, everybody was anxious to be off, and other ships were standing by waiting for the wharf space. Studdert dared not stall for another hour, or put off departure for another day, in the hope of finding the missing Belgian. Perhaps Bergmans would never show up again! Anyway, any appearance of indecision or unnecessary delay at this stage might queer everything. The Costa Rican government had agreed to the subconcession without any great enthusiasm. It might still call the whole thing off. There was no time, either, to cable London for instructions. Everybody in London was in bed at this hour, anyhow. And it would look funny if any remark or action of Studdert's should make it appear that the success of the treasure hunt depended on locating a mining man named Bergmans who was supposed to have nothing at all to do with the expedition! Studdert, poor fellow, had to make up his mind and do it quickly. He did. "Shove off!" he said.

As the *Veracity* headed into the setting sun, Weston remained standing on the pier, preoccupied in speculation on the strange and mysterious events of the past couple of days. As the crowd dispersed, a ragged old man made his way across the pier and sidled up to the reporter.

"You're a newspaper feller, ain't you?" he said, and Weston admitted he was, recognizing the old fellow as a local beach-

227

comber, and one who, from the sound of his voice, was probably a New England whaler.

"Not much of a story in the *Veracity*, is there?" he said, gazing out to sea.

"Not much," answered Weston, "unless they find the treasure."

"I could give you a story," said the old man, "a good one."

"That so?" asked Weston, only a little curious. This port has always been full of such characters and he knew it. He knew, too, what the old man's next words would be.

"I'll tell it to you if you'll buy me a drink," he said, and then as he saw the grin on the newsman's face he added, "maybe two."

Two drinks, that is, and it was worth it. Here's the story:

"Don't ask me how I know it but I swear it's true. When the *Veracity* reaches Cocos two days from now, the people on her are going to have the surprise of their lives. They are going to find four Americans on the island.

"These Americans were shipwrecked on the island several months ago, or so they will say, and they have been living all alone there ever since. Between you and me, though, I think they've been digging for the treasure."

"Never mind," said the old man, when Weston asked him how he knew all this. (The correspondent was dubious, knowing quite well that no one had been over to the island from Costa Rica since the eviction of the *Queen of Scots* expedition.) "It's true. You can take my word for it."

After mulling it over, Weston decided to take the old whaler's word and shot a brief cable to the *New York Times* announcing the departure of the *Veracity* to Cocos with yet another treasure hunting expedition. He added: "It is reported that four American castaways are on Cocos Island. If the *Veracity* expedition finds them, they will probably be brought back to Puntarenas at once."

The *Times* printed the story the next morning, June 8th. The *Veracity* arrived at Cocos on Saturday night, the 9th. It was Sunday afternoon, however, before the island's radio was installed and communication established with San José.

Colonel Valenzuela's first message, sent at 3:50 P.M., Sunday, June 10th, was directed to President Jimenez and laconically stated: "*Veracity* had a good trip. We are already comfortably installed on the island. On arrival we found four shipwrecked Americans suffering from exposure and hunger. But for our timely arrival they would probably have died."

The message was picked up by radio sets in Costa Rica and Panama. Associated Press and United Press correspondents in the area immediately relayed the story to their American headquarters and the story appeared throughout the country in the morning papers of the 11th.

Then it was that the *New York Times*, perturbed about the supposed scoop, queried Calhoun in Panama as to why they had missed this story. The Timesman's reply must have knocked the ears off the Latin American "desk." In effect it said: "What are you worrying about? Weston filed that story two days before the castaways were even discovered. What more do you expect?" The *Times* had in fact printed the story three days before any other paper!

21.

THE story of the four castaways on Cocos Island got such a build-up in the press that every news service and publication with representation in Central America was clamoring for news. All the correspondents from Guatemala to Panama and every part-time stringer in the area was being hounded by editors with a flow of cable queries. Who, where, what, when they asked. Fortunately, we were sitting on the story with a ringside seat, for we had a direct pipeline to all the reports from the island as they came in to the presidential office. A quick translation and they were on the wires to those services and papers we represented.

Briefly, this is the story as Colonel Valenzuela reported it on June 12th: When the *Veracity* was still a long way from the island, the people on it saw the four castaways on the beach in Chatham Bay, making desperate signals of distress.

On landing, the expedition found the men in a rough shelter made from sailcloth, "with only enough provisions left for

four days." The men, who gave their names as Theo H. Freeman and P. M. Freeman, brothers, Morris W. Burd and Frank
M. Saxer, told Valenzuela they had left San Diego, California, in the auxiliary sloop *Skukum* owned by Theo Freeman,
on December 19th, 1934 (six months before), bound "on a
pleasure cruise" for New York via the Panama Canal.

On January 30th, when about 30 miles off the Mexican
coast, they ran into a terrible storm. They rode the heavy
seas for eight days and nights and when at last the tempest
subsided, they rigged a jury rudder and made other repairs.
After fighting another storm and several days of adverse
currents, they were picked up by the motor-ship *Europa*,
which towed them as far as Chatham Bay on Cocos Island,
where they arrived on April 6th.

The four men managed to get their boat into shallow water
and make a cursory inspection. The heavy buffeting had almost completely wrecked the little ship. She would need a
complete overhaul before she could be made seaworthy
again. They rested on the beach for several days and then
they carried ashore everything movable. The work of repair
began at once, but for want of the proper tools and materials
it was two weeks before the *Skukum* was shipshape again.
Then, on the night of April 23rd, just as they were about
ready to leave the island, an oil lamp on the boat overturned
and set the ship on fire.

All their efforts to save the yacht were in vain, though
they fought the blaze until the boat sank under them. They
then swam ashore and on April 26th the tuna fisher *San
Rafael*, out of San Diego, came into the bay. They asked the
captain to inform the United States Navy in the Canal Zone
of their presence on the island, which the captain promised
to do, but they had had no further communication with any
ship until June 8th, when the crew of another tuna boat, the

Rajah, also from San Diego, told them they had heard about the *Skukum's* mishap while the *Rajah* was in the Galapagos Islands.

When Colonel Valenzuela questioned the men as to whether they had refused the offer of a fishing boat to take them off the island, they flatly denied it. The only ships they had spoken to, they said, were the *San Rafael* and the *Rajah.* The latter offered to send a message to the officials at Balboa, but Freeman said he had declined the offer because he believed that his earlier message via the *San Rafael* had got through.

Theo Freeman, reported the Colonel, was 37 and the oldest of the four, and they all appeared to be "decent, educated and hardworking fellows. If I had any doubts about their story, they vanished when I saw the sunken remains of their burned ship."

Colonel Valenzuela concluded his report to the President with the name and address of the Freeman brothers' mother. President Jimenez immediately sent her the following cable: "DO NOT WORRY ABOUT YOUR SON THEO H. FREEMAN, BROTHER AND PARTNERS WHO ARE SAFE IN COCOS ISLAND UNDER THE PROTECTION OF GOVERNMENT FORCES." It was signed, "Ricardo Jimenez President of the Republic of Costa Rica."

When we had translated and filed Colonel Valenzuela's report we thought we had covered this little newsbreak and wrung from it every possible line. Maybe we were so close to the Cocos Island jungle we couldn't see the trees, but later that same day we got a tip that opened up a whole new train of thought. The North American Newspaper Alliance sent us an authorization to radio Theo Freeman on Cocos and make him a substantial cash offer for the exclusive story about his experiences.

This offer was immediately passed on to Freeman but he didn't make the expected jump at this opportunity. Obviously, he wasn't interested in a little easy money. His answer came back, "Not interested."

The *Veracity* remained at Cocos for a few days until the treasure hunters and the police were properly installed. The huts which the *Queen of Scots* party had erected were still standing and these were converted into dormitories, storerooms, a mess hall and a kitchen. The Costa Ricans occupied tents near the other buildings. When they were settled, the *Veracity* returned to Puntarenas, but it didn't bring off all the castaways. Burd and Saxer left on the *Veracity* but the Freeman brothers elected to remain on the island, "to give the Britishers a helping hand."

Burd and Saxer came up to San José and took a room in a cheap *pension*. We interviewed them there and they admitted they were broke, but they both looked pretty husky and well fed for a couple of castaways reported on the verge of starvation only a few days before. Furthermore, any attempt to get them to talk about their experiences on the island met with the same statement: "What Freeman said is the truth and we have nothing to add." They did admit, however, that they had made a compact with the Freeman brothers not to talk or write about their adventures on Cocos Island. And on our cross-questioning they said that several tuna fishing boats had put in to the island while they were there and that the crews had come ashore in rowboats to get fresh water and bathe in the creeks.

The United States consul in Costa Rica took them in tow and when, a few days later, a U. S. destroyer put in at Cocos, he managed to get them all repatriated to San Diego, though, we learned later, the Freeman brothers did not seem overanxious to leave the island. After they left, we discovered other curious things about these "castaways," and it wasn't long before we had a completely new twist to the story.

They had several guns and plenty of ammunition and it

was evident that they had shot a lot of wild pigs and other animals and were never at any time short of food. Furthermore, the British treasure hunters later reported that before Freeman left the island he disclosed to them a big store of canned provisions and that they had bought these stores from the castaways because they were American products and superior to their own. There were also several picks and shovels and plenty of evidence that these had been used at a number of places on the island.

Another thing which puzzled everyone was why Freeman & Co. should elect to live in a miserable sailcloth shelter in Chatham Bay—a shelter scarcely big enough to hold four men and which certainly afforded no protection from the heavy Cocos rains—when just around the corner in Wafer Bay were the substantial wooden buildings left by the *Queen of Scots* expedition. The bays were connected at that time by a fairly well defined trail through the forest, and it was not difficult to go back and forth between them.

When we thought about it, we discovered some discrepancy in their timetable too. The rescued men said they left San Diego on December 19th, but they did not land on Cocos until April 6th, three and a half months later, during which time they did not touch at any other port. Is it possible, one asked, that a small boat (the *Skukum* was only 35 feet long) could carry sufficient food and water for four men for four months? Food, perhaps, but not water.

An acquaintance of ours in the United States Legation in San José summed it up for us this way: The four men had really been on the island for much longer than they would admit. They had gone to Cocos intentionally to search for treasure; and they hadn't been in any storms en route, or, at least, they weren't delayed by any. They had deliberately burned their boat, which probably wasn't worth much anyway, knowing full well that the island was frequently visited by fishing boats so that they could always get off when they wanted to. Meanwhile, they could appear as castaways should anyone from Costa Rica come snooping around.

Finally, it was pretty obvious that the brothers Freeman, after spending several months on the lonely island, were not a bit anxious to leave it after they had been "rescued from almost certain death."

Every Costa Rican we talked to believed Freeman & Co. had left San Diego with the specific intention of going to Cocos Island in search of treasure and that they had been comfortably installed on the island for at least five months before they were discovered by the *Veracity* party.

But whether they were on the island for a long time or a short time, the most significant fact our investigations turned up was that these illegal treasure hunters had some communication with Puntarenas. Otherwise how could the old beachcomber have known that "four Americans" were on the island long before the *Veracity* got there?

Whatever the truth about the wreck of the *Skukum* and the intentions of her crew, it must be left to conjecture as just another minor mystery among Cocos chronicles.* We uncovered only one more suspicious story that we could tie to this jig-saw narrative.

Shortly after the *Veracity* arrived back in Puntarenas with the two castaways, Burd and Saxer, it was boarded by two detectives who had between them a man who identified himself as Petrus Bergmans. Commander Finnis, captain of the yacht, to whom Studdert and Worsley had confided the whole story of Bergmans and his importance to the expedition, was both surprised and relieved.

The detectives told Finnis how Studdert had hired them to continue searching for Bergmans and how, after three or

---

* Freeman & Co. set no precedent; see Appendix IX for a previous example.

four days of looking high and low, they had finally run him to ground in a local brothel. Bergmans, they said, was in a state of stupor when they found him. He also had a big bump on his head, a cut over one eye, and, in sum, he bore all the signs of having been severely beaten up. The detectives had taken Bergmans to a hotel and when he had sobered up sufficiently, he told them an amazing story, which he now repeated for the benefit of Finnis.

Just before the *Veracity* was due to leave, he said, he was on his way to board her as he had arranged with Studdert. He was only about a block or two from the pier when he suddenly sensed that he was being shadowed by three tough-looking strangers. To throw his pursuers off, he slipped through the first open door he came to only to find himself in an open lumber yard.

The three men came in after him, collared him, and then frog-marched him to a house he would not recognize again. There they kept him a prisoner for several days, bound hand and foot and gagged. Several times he heard his captors talking about Cocos and something they called "Skukum," and he got the impression his captors had collaborators on the island. From all this Bergmans decided his attackers were agents of Colonel Hunter, whose men had beaten him once before in Panama. They were down here to prevent him from revealing the whereabouts of the treasure to Treasure Recovery's people.

One night, on the third day of his captivity, during which he had been given very little to eat or drink, two men came into the room and started to beat him up. He lost consciousness and the next thing he knew he was in the brothel without the slightest idea of how he got there. Bergmans thought he might have been drugged as well as beaten up.

The Puntarenas detectives did not appear to have much interest in Mr. Bergmans' story, but having found the gentleman they had been paid to look for, they had been keeping a close watch on him ever since. They turned him over to Commander Finnis with obvious relief.

And Finnis, pleased to get Treasure Recovery's key man back in *any* shape, turned the *Veracity* around and immediately departed for Cocos.

22.

IT WAS pretty obvious that Peter Bergmans had been to Cocos Island before. When he was put ashore he readily found his way around without having to ask anybody where the principal features of the island were. He was as much at home there as the other treasure hunters who had had time to familiarize themselves with the island.

So great was the faith in the Belgian that Worsley and Studdert, the two directors, really believed that all Bergmans had to do was walk over to the right spot and point a finger. There they would find the fabulous Cocos treasure with no more effort than lifting a hand. But Mr. Bergmans didn't work like that. He loafed and wandered aimlessly for several days, "taking his bearings," as he put it. Then one morning at the breakfast table he showed unmistakable signs of jubilation.

"I've got it, Mr. Studdert," he exclaimed. "You remember how I told you in London that when I first found the treasure in 1929, I took away a small part of the main treasure and cached it on the beach where I could lay my hands on it quickly at some future date? Well, I recall now that in order to be sure of the spot I buried a beer bottle under a nearby palm tree on the beach right here in Wafer Bay. In the bottle I put a long piece of string. All I have to do is put one end of the string against the tree, run the string out in a certain direction, and right at the other end of it we'll find my cache!"

It is not hard to imagine the sudden enthusiasm of all the treasure hunters (by now everyone had been let in on the secret) as they trooped along the beach after Bergmans. Studdert, especially, was elated and relieved that Bergmans was finally showing signs of promise.

About halfway around the bay, Bergmans stopped, turned on his heels a couple of times, stared for a moment in deep concentration, and then pointed to a palm tree 50 yards away. "That's the tree," he said triumphantly.

Someone with a shovel started digging immediately. "Go easy!" cautioned Studdert. "Don't break the bottle."

About 18 inches down and half-a-dozen careful shovels full later the bottle came to light. It was sealed with a mouldy cork. The bottle was handed reverently to Bergmans who equally carefully removed the stopper with his jackknife, then proceeded to extract from it a long piece of thin, damp, knotted string.

"What did I tell you?" exclaimed Bergmans, with a note of triumph in his voice.

There followed several moments of silence while everyone stood patiently waiting for Mr. Bergmans' next move. He looked first one way and then the other, squinting as his eyes roved along the beach. "Somebody hold the end of the string against the palm," he finally said. "The rest, follow me!"

Taking the string in his hand and carefully paying it out

as he went along, Bergmans walked to the water's edge. Fifty yards from the palm tree the string gave out. Bergmans stamped his foot in the wet sand from which the tide had only just receded.

"Here's the spot," he said. "All you have to do is dig!"

Shovels were quickly brought into action as everyone began to dig. And how they dug! But it didn't seem to do much good. As fast as they took out a shovelful the hole filled up again with the tide-soaked sand.

But Dick Studdert was no fool. As a mining engineer his analytical mind sized up the situation at once. "Wait a minute!" he commanded. "Let's get this clear. This place is under high-water mark; in fact, practically at low-water mark, and the sand here never gets dry. We'll never be able to dig a hole in this sloppy stuff." Then, looking straight at Bergmans, he asked:

"Do you mean to tell us this is the spot where you cached some of the treasure six years ago?"

"I've already told you this is the place," snapped Bergmans, his triumphant tone suddenly turned to petulance.

"All right," said Studdert. "Continue digging, boys!"

But it was no use. The hole never seemed to get any bigger, however much they dug, and finally the returning tide came in, erasing the shallow hole and making further work impossible for that day.

"Never mind," said Studdert. "We'll start again tomorrow morning when the tide is out. Meanwhile, we'll prepare some timbers and have some empty oil drums on hand to use as shoring. If we have to dig a hole in this stuff, we'll do it properly."

And properly they did, the next morning. They shored up the four sides of a hole about ten feet square, but at a depth of three or four feet Studdert again called a halt. Water was rapidly seeping into the hole.

Bergmans, meanwhile, having indicated the spot where "X" appears on treasure maps, evidently considered his job done and his presence no longer necessary. At the moment he was taking a nap in one of the huts.

"Wait, fellows," said Studdert. "Let's use our heads. We're digging a hole big enough to put a house in, to find a handful of treasure buried in the sand six years ago by a man who says he scooped out the hole with his bare hands. If that handful of treasure was ever put here, countless tides have long since washed it away to hell and gone!"

They returned to camp, silent with disappointment.

Bergmans, nonchalant, greeted them.

"Any luck?" he asked.

"No!" growled Studdert. "Are you quite sure you told us to dig in the right place?"

"Oh, sure," replied Bergmans carelessly.

"Well," said Studdert, passing it off, "what's the use of digging for a little private cache? It's the main treasure we're after. Suppose you show us where the cave is."

"Tomorrow," replied Bergmans, returning to his cot.

But when tomorrow came, Mr. Bergmans had other excuses. He complained about the niggardly ten per cent he was to get for revealing the treasure. He thought he ought to have more, he said, perhaps 25 per cent.

"Ten per cent was your proposition," Studdert reminded him.

"Well, anyhow, I'm a sick man. I ought to rest up a bit."

"What have you been doing but resting?" asked Studdert.

"My memory is bad," said Bergmans.

"It rather looks that way," agreed Studdert. "Do you think your memory might be better tomorrow?"

"Maybe," replied Bergmans peevishly.

But Bergmans' memory was no better the next morning, or the next. Then one morning he said that during the night he had suffered a paralytic attack and, look, his left arm was now useless! The arm certainly looked limp. It dangled at his side, and from that day until Bergmans left the island no one ever saw him use that left arm again. That is, no one except Colonel Valenzuela, who once saw Bergmans when the latter thought he was alone in the forest. The colonel, recounting this whole sequence to us later, said he caught Bergmans climbing a steep hillside, using both arms with equal dexterity.

One day one of the colonel's men told him of a very curious incident. It occurred, the soldier said, a few nights before the bottle was dug up. The man had to get up during the night and in the moonlight he saw Bergmans prowling cautiously along the beach. He followed him and saw Bergmans bury the bottle they dug up a few days later.

Colonel Valenzuela decided it was time he told all this to Studdert. He did, and added, "I think Bergmans is a fraud."

"Maybe you're right," replied Studdert, "but I can't help thinking he really knows something and, for some reason or other, he is afraid to show us where the treasure is." Obviously Studdert's faith in the Belgian was still strong. They discussed the pros and cons of the situation for a while and then Colonel Valenzuela said, "By the way, do you still have that bottle?"

Studdert fetched the bottle from his cabin and gave it to the colonel, who turned it slowly in his hands, studying it intently. Then he broke into a loud laugh.

"*Amigo*," he said, "you've really been 'taken.' Look at the brewer's name embossed on this bottle!" He handed it back to Studdert. "See that name 'Gambrinus'? You wouldn't know this, but the Gambrinus Brewery has been in existence only about three years. Bergmans claims to have buried this bottle in 1929, or at least three years before the Gambrinus

Brewery existed. Why, this is just like the bottles you have in the ice box right now!"

"I'm beginning to think you're right," admitted Studdert, ruefully. "Even so, I still believe Bergmans knows something and all this is simply a stall."

"There's one sure way to get him to tell if he really knows," said the colonel, and when Studdert asked him how, the colonel suggested sterner measures. "Beat him up!" he said. "I have a hunch he is more afraid of that than anything, and that's why he pretends to have a paralyzed arm."

Studdert, however, did not like the suggestion. "No," he said, "if we did that we might never get the information we want. I think I know a better way."

Studdert called all his men together and told them that Bergmans, for reasons best known to himself, had evidently decided not to live up to the terms of his agreement with the company. "But don't worry," he said. "Treasure Recovery has another card up its sleeve. We'll find the treasure without the aid of Mr. Bergmans."

The extra card, as it turned out, was the "scientific" approach. With no personal clues to follow, the treasure hunters fell back on the method so loudly proclaimed in the company's original prospectus. The electric metal-detecting apparatus was rigged up and "Doc" Harris and "Lightning" Atkinson spent hours testing likely spots—but with no luck. Once the pointer of the dial vibrated sharply as the detector was carried along the beach and hopes flamed high, only to wane a few minutes later when their shovels unearthed a few rusty links of an old ship's cable.

Meanwhile, Bergmans became an outcast on the island. Ostracized and shunned by all, he wandered off by himself for hours at a time. Whenever anybody was near, his left arm hung lifeless at his side. Daily he demanded to be taken off the island and returned to London, where, he said, he would talk to the directors, and one day he told Worsley that the reason he would not disclose the location of the treasure cave was because he objected to Captain Arthur's association with the company.

Bergmans was taken to Cocos at the end of June. The events just related took place during the first half of July, and by the middle of that month, Studdert was convinced of the futility of persuading Bergmans to cooperate. Something had to be done. He sent Captain Arthur, who was now back in London, a long cablegram, relayed in the first place over the island radio to San José. In this he expressed his opinion that Bergmans had double-crossed them, and suggested that he be immediately removed from the picture.

Cameraman Mallabey also wanted to come off the island. His patience, too, had given out. He had come to get a picture of the discovery of the treasure—not just scenes of Pete Bergmans sauntering half-naked along the beach.

Meanwhile, though Mallabey and Bergmans might be itching to get away from Cocos, there were three newcomers to the island who seemed perfectly contented with the idyllic life. These were the stag and his "wives" brought over on the *Veracity's* first trip.

The deer had thrived on the lush vegetation and already blessed events were in the offing. And they had become quite tame. At least the two does had, for they would frequently come into camp and take morsels from the hands of the men. But not the stag. He remained aloof and alone in the forest for days without anyone getting a glimpse of him. And when he did emerge for a brief visit with his wives, woe betide any hapless treasure hunter or *tico* soldier who happened to be near. The stag would leap forward and in one lightning-like stroke of his great antlers rip the pants right off his victim. The bruises that went with these encounters were soon

244

seen on nearly everyone in camp. Even "Lightning" Atkinson, who ordinarily moved quickly only when mess call sounded, was observed to cover a hundred yards in nothing flat one morning when the stag challenged his stroll along the shore.

Some, who had experienced particularly painful encounters with the animal, threatened to shoot him, but Colonel Valenzuela waved an admonishing finger. "No, señor," he said. "That's the president's stag. If anything happens to him the president, likely as not, would cancel your concession. Better grin and bear it!"

Meanwhile, we should look in on Captain Arthur, who left Panama to return to England on May 26th. Once back in London he confronted his partners with accusations of treachery and deceit. Alers-Hankey, Commander Stenhouse, and Captain Polkinghorne, he said, had deliberately maneuvered to prevent his being on the scene when the treasure was discovered. Furthermore, he said, they had tried to jockey him out of his position of command in the company.

Alers-Hankey pointed out that the fault lay in circumstances beyond their control, which could only be attributed to Arthur himself. And he pointed out Captain Arthur's previous dealings with the Costa Rican government and the disastrous *Queen of Scots* expedition.

At the insistence of his fellow directors, Arthur was forced to resign as "controller of operations," in order to comply with the Costa Rican government's stipulation to Hankey that Arthur should have nothing to do with the present expedition. Arthur connived to offset this by appointing a friend, his lawyer, as director in his place, and this man immediately called a meeting of the directors on June 19th. Arthur did not attend this meeting, but his lawyer friend (a Mr. Thorp) put up a good fight for him, as the following excerpt from the minutes of that meeting shows:

245

At this juncture Mr. Arthur was asked to join the meeting and Mr. Thorp raised the question of Mr. Arthur's position in the Company, stating that in his opinion, judging from certain facts in his possession, every step should be taken by the Board to reinstate him in his original office as Controller of Operations.

Mr. Thorp read a copy of an official document from the Chief Immigration Officer at Panama stating that there was no embargo upon Mr. Arthur's landing in the Canal Zone. It was noted that this document contradicted the previous information reported by the Chairman [Alers-Hankey].

Mr. Thorp stated that Mr. Arthur had also taken great exception to the action of the British Vice-consul at Panama, who had personally informed the ship's company that Mr. Arthur was not persona grata in Costa Rica and would be refused entrance into the country. He further stated that he fully intended to follow up this matter on behalf of Mr. Arthur.

After a long discussion on the matter, it was RESOLVED that the Company's Managing Director, Mr. R. H. Studdert, be instructed to open up diplomatic inquiries through the President of Costa Rica with a view of eliminating the Government's alleged reasons for forbidding Mr. Arthur's entry into Costa Rica and/or employing him in the Expedition, in order to expedite as much as possible his resumption of duties with a view to relieving Mr. Studdert, and that the wording of the cable should be edited by Mr. Thorp before dispatch.

In compliance with this resolution, a cable, duly "edited" by Thorp and Arthur, was sent to Studdert, who consulted immediately with the company's lawyer in San José. Studdert's reply, on the advice of the lawyer, was to the effect that if the truth in the "Mr. A" case * could be explained to the Costa Ricans, and if Arthur could prove he was not responsible for dispatching the *Queen of Scots* expedition without Costa Rican authority, then there might be a chance; but if these things were proved, then the entire board of directors who were responsible at that time (during the

* See Appendix VI.

246

Queen of Scots expedition) would be rated by the government as undesirables, which would probably result in the cancellation of the concession and the inevitable liquidation of Treasure Recovery Limited. The present great injustice to Arthur was fully realized, etc., etc., but unfortunately no other solution was possible.

The wily Captain Arthur was worried. Then, while the Venus Trust was issuing further "Progress Reports" that painted in glowing terms the progress of the expedition, predicting the early discovery of the treasure though carefully omitting all mention of Bergmans and urging shareholders to buy more shares "before it got too late to get in on the ground floor," another cable came from Studdert. This was the one reporting Bergmans' default. Arthur decided then that it was time for him to do something on his own and let Hankey & Co. shift for themselves.

And when the foxy captain made up his mind to do anything he could work fast, especially if he were cornered. We saw him once drive off in a taxi without a cent in his pocket, figuring that before he arrived at his destination he could devise an "out" and get away with it. His first step now was to arrange a secret meeting with George Lane, Bergmans' old partner.

"Lane," said Arthur, as they sat together in a London pub, "your pal Bergmans has let us down. He refused to show us where the treasure is. That means you lose your share too. You told us Bergmans had given you certain information as to the locality of the cave. I know you've never been on Cocos Island, but can't you think what the place ought to look like?"

"Well, sir," answered Lane, " 'e told me that the cave were concealed by big ferns, so ter speak, and that it were on the right bank of the Wafer Bay creek, just afore yer come ter some kind of a waterfall. I've often pitchered wot the place must look like. Nah yer come to arsk me, sir, I really believe if I were on the island, I could idintify the place."

"Lane," said Captain Arthur, with a grin of satisfaction, "you're going to Cocos Island with me. Go home and pack your bag."

23.

CAPTAIN and Mrs. Arthur and George Lane sailed on the first boat going to Panama. Before leaving London, Arthur cabled Studdert to be prepared for any emergency and to have Bergmans ready to leave Cocos about three weeks hence. In the meantime, his London lawyers got busy in an attempt to grease Arthur's entry into Costa Rican territory. A letter was written to the British Foreign Secretary in Whitehall, asking this high personage to intercede through diplomatic channels with the Costa Rican government in Arthur's behalf. This letter was referred as a matter of routine to the British Legation in Panama which, after consultation with the British consular officers in Costa Rica, Messrs. Cox and Murray, decided to refuse to take any action on behalf of Arthur.

Since we now have copies of most of the letters, cables and other documents that figured in Treasure Recovery's great fiasco in Costa Rica, we are now able to tell the story in some chronological order, but at the time we were completely in the dark about as often as we were able to uncover a bit of news. We must, therefore, admit that up to this point Treasure Recovery Limited had successfully kept Peter Bergmans a strict secret. His presence on the island was known only to the directors, to the people actually on the island, to George Lane, and to the company's lawyer in San José. Neither the public, the press, nor the company's shareholders knew anything about Bergmans and his fantastic story of having discovered the Cocos treasure back in 1929. But when Captain Arthur reached Balboa on the morning of August 11th, he found, to his intense surprise and chagrin, that Mr. Bergmans was no longer a secret. The news break had occurred three days before his arrival, thanks to cameraman Mallabey.

By the end of July, Mallabey was fed up with the expedition. His contract with the company called for the making of a film depicting the search for and discovery of the treasure. Nearly six months had passed since he joined the expedition and all he had to show for it was a few feet of film, a shot or two of Cocos jungle. Very little effort had been made to find the treasure and the chances of this expedition's finding it now seemed remote indeed. Mallabey, an ambitious fellow and a first-rate photographer, had other things to do besides twiddle his thumbs while the treasure hunters fished, hunted wild pigs, or simply loafed in the shade of the palm trees. He demanded to be taken off the island, and Studdert's continued refusal resulted in a lot of ill feeling between them.

Into this hiatus came Captain Arthur's order to Commander Finnis, captain of the *Veracity*, to take the boat to Balboa to meet him on the 11th of August. Mallabey jumped at this unexpected opportunity to leave the island, and Finnis, to avoid unforeseen delays en route, left Cocos a few days earlier than necessary. Thus the *Veracity*, with Mallabey aboard, arrived in Balboa three days ahead of Arthur.

Every newsman in Panama and the Zone immediately pounced on the captain and crew for news of the Cocos treasure hunt. Finnis and his men refused to talk, but not Mallabey. He had a grievance and he was glad to have an opportunity to talk about it. With little prompting from the reporters he spilled the whole story: the delays, the fruitless efforts, his difficulty getting off the island, and—richest tidbit of all—the story of Pete Bergmans and his connection with Treasure Recovery Limited. The Belgian, said Mallabey, was being kept virtually a prisoner on the island because he would not reveal the hiding place of the Cocos booty.

The story as Mallabey told it appeared in the Panama City papers of August 9th, and Crede Calhoun, our *Times* colleague in Balboa, airmailed us all the clippings with the request to check. Mallabey's story was reprinted in San José's *Diario de Costa Rica* on August 11th under the screaming headline: "BELGIAN SUBJECT A PRISONER ON COCOS ISLAND."

When Captain Arthur arrived, Commander Finnis informed him that Mallabey had spilled the beans, and Arthur realized at once that mischief would result if he did not immediately try to counteract the bad impression given by Mallabey of affairs on the island. He decided to call on Crede Calhoun and make a clean breast of the Bergmans story. Calhoun recounted the interview in a letter to Weston dated August 12th, from which we quote the following:

Capt. C. A. Arthur arrived yesterday . . . when he filled me full of a cock and bull story about one Bergmans' knowledge of the location of the Cocos treasure. It is patently a share selling scheme but, of course, I accepted his story without question. . . . Arthur invited me to go to Cocos with him and his wife on the *Veracity*, and when I found it impossible, he offered to take you.

He hinted that he would like you to intercede with President Jimenez to gain permission for him to visit the island. I gave no encouragement. It appears now that there is a conflict between him and Hankey, with Treasure Recovery's lawyer in San José and Hankey pulling against Arthur. This may be all cooked up to lend a shade of verisimilitude to the Bergmans story.

Arthur claims Bergmans is under contract to Treasure Recovery to reveal the hiding place of the treasure, but is stalling off, because he has joined up with Hankey and the lawyer to arrange a new concession and get the treasure. I told Arthur I was only interested in news and am not concerned in the controversy except in the form of news. . . .

There followed several days during which Captain Arthur and Treasure Recovery's lawyer in San José exchanged salvos by cable, the lawyer emphatically refusing to attempt to change the government's mind, yet pointing out that Arthur must not go to Cocos without special consent. Arthur threatened that if the government still withheld its consent, then he would be compelled to call off the search and withdraw the men from the island owing to lack of funds to carry on.

The lawyer finally contrived to settle the argument by cabling T. R.'s directors in London. They promptly replied repudiating Arthur's application, and the lawyer thereupon informed Arthur that in order not to prejudice the company's present good standing with the government, he would take no further action in the matter.

Arthur was intent upon making a last desperate effort to go to Cocos. To the puzzled old sea dog, Commander Finnis, he related in detail how Alers-Hankey and the other directors had tried to double-cross him. He even gave the commander a satisfactory explanation of the "Mr. A" case and in the end convinced Finnis he should fly up to San José and intercede for him.

Finnis interviewed the company's lawyer who listened carefully to him as he narrated Arthur's story as Arthur had told it to him. But the lawyer could hold out no hope for Arthur. He explained to Finnis how all along Captain Arthur had violated Costa Rica's laws in his management of the *Queen of Scots* expedition. He explained how when Hankey came, practically on his knees, to beseech the government to grant T. R. a proper concession, the price to be paid—apart from the simple ransoming of the stores and equipment—was the absolute exclusion of Captain Arthur from the expedition. The one *sine qua non,* said the lawyer, reading from the Minister of Interior's note on the subject, was that: "The government cannot allow in any form that Captain Arthur may form part of the said expedition, neither that he arrives in Puntarenas with the expedition, nor that he lands on the island. The armed force which goes to the island has instructions to capture him."

Finnis, like the dutiful ex-officer of the Royal Navy he was, flew back to Panama and reported all to Captain Arthur. So what was there now left for Arthur to do? Nothing, except to send Lane over to the island in the care of Finnis.

The *Veracity* left Balboa on August 22nd, carrying George Lane, who was going to do what Pete Bergmans had failed to do. He was going to unearth the Cocos Island treasure. But we suspect that Captain Arthur was more sure of this than was Lane himself.

That night Arthur sat down and typed out a letter to Weston. In it he said, "Lane has disclosed to me what he claims to be Bergmans' locations, and all I can say is that they are very likely ones. Lane will not face Bergmans; he stipulates that he must be secretly landed on the island, and Bergmans taken aboard and then to the mainland, and only on those conditions would he leave Balboa. . . . The *Veracity* will only make a short stay at the island as she has to get back here for engine repairs. If treasure is discovered and you wish to get to the island, you are welcome to go in the *Veracity* next trip."

With the letter was enclosed a formal invitation to go to Cocos on the *Veracity.*

Finnis headed the *Veracity* straight for Cocos Island, although he well knew that in going direct he was committing an unlawful act. But such was his loyalty to Captain Arthur, as he later confessed to us, that he was prepared to take a chance in order to help Arthur with his plans, and hope that he would be able to get away with it.

Fortunately for him, he did get away with it. When he was subsequently called to task by Puntarenas authorities, he pleaded that he had done so merely to save time without realizing the gravity of the offence. He got off with a mere caution.

When the *Veracity* was well out to sea, Finnis called Lane into the chart room and told him Arthur's instructions. It was important, and Lane agreed, that Bergmans should not know that Arthur had brought Lane out from England. The problem, then, was how to get Bergmans off the island and Lane on it in one stroke. Obviously this could not be done if the *Veracity* came into either Chatham or Wafer Bay with Lane aboard, because his presence would immediately be known by Bergmans and then the fat *would* be in the fire.

Not only that, but Lane knew quite well that he was, in effect, double-crossing his own partner by coming out to make use of the information he had got from Bergmans. Thus Lane was afraid to meet Bergmans and it was only on Arthur's assurance that "matters would be arranged," that he consented to go at all.

The "matters arranged" were these: Finnis began by showing Lane a large map of the island. He explained that instead of going directly to Wafer Bay on the north of the island, they would approach it from the south.

"We shall go close inshore," he said, "to a small beach near Mule Bay and put you and your kitbag ashore in the dinghy. Here's the spot on the map. Make yourself comfortable on the beach for a couple of hours and then take off along the trail—it's marked here—which goes due north through the forest to the camp at Wafer Bay. You can't miss it because some of the boys from the camp have used it often of late and it's quite well defined all the way. Take your time. Don't hurry, and while you are on your way to Wafer Bay overland, I shall go round the island and then approach the camp from the north as though I have just arrived from Puntarenas.

"I'll take Bergmans off immediately and we'll be on our way to Puntarenas long before you can cross the island on foot. Don't worry about the trail. There are no wild animals and no snakes. If the ants bite you, bite 'em back."

Lane, his heart thumping loudly at the mere thought of being about to set foot on Bergmans' treasure island, swallowed his instructions with a gulp.

"Doncher worry abaht me, Commander," he said in his broad Cockney. "I'll find me way acrorst the blarsted island orlright. An' wot's more, I'll find the swag when I git there. 'Ow long d'yer say it'd tike me ter git over?"

"Oh, about ten or twelve hours from the time we land you. You ought to be at the camp long before nightfall easily, seeing that we'll be putting you ashore at daybreak."

Everything worked out as planned without a hitch. Lane was dumped ashore on the lonely south side of the island. The *Veracity* sailed out and around and approached the island again, this time from the north, dropping her anchor in Wafer Bay. Commander Finnis went ashore immediately, gave Studdert the gist of the plan, and summoned Bergmans.

It didn't take Bergmans long to pack his bag and within the hour the *Veracity* was at sea again, on its way to Puntarenas. There was one other passenger. Commander Worsley, disgusted with the discord in camp and fed up with Treasure Recovery's inept approach to treasure hunting, was leaving the island and the company. Mrs. Worsley had already returned to the mainland on a previous trip of the *Veracity*

255

The yacht pulled out of Wafer Bay about three in the afternoon and the camp settled down to await Lane's coming. But at six o'clock, with night already closing in, there was no sign of Mr. Lane.

"No need to worry," observed Studdert. "Finnis said Lane has a flashlight. He'll be in soon."

At ten o'clock Lane still had not arrived. At midnight nobody really cared whether he came or not because everybody in camp was asleep. But when daylight came and woke the camp, and it was discovered that Lane was still not there, Studdert began to worry. Could Lane somehow have missed the trail and got lost in the jungle?

"If he doesn't show up by the time we've finished breakfast," he said, "we'll send out a search party."

Accordingly, after breakfast, Studdert sent three men out on the trail to the south coast. About half way across they found Mr. Lane. He was safe, though a little groggy from lack of sleep, for he had spent the night, the past 24 hours in fact, high up in the crotch of a tree. Why? All the evidence was there to see. Pawing the ground, in a well-trod circle around the base of the tree, was the president's stag!

Later Mr. Lane explained how it happened. He was coming slowly along the muddy trail, whistling an old sea chanty to keep his spirits up, he said, when he chanced to lift his eyes in time to see a "big wild hanimal wit' 'orns on 'is 'ead" charging down upon him. Mr. Lane, who had climbed many a ship's rigging in his day, had lost none of his quondam agility. He was up the nearest tree long before the stag got there.

C
O
C
O
S

I
S
L
A
N
D

24.

PETE BERGMANS slipped out of the country and the next we heard of him was through a cable from Calhoun in Panama: "BERGMANS HERE REPORTED TRYING CHARTER SHIP FOR TRIP COCOS. SAYS HE ONLY WANTS ONE HOUR ASHORE."

There could be two interpretations of this, we figured. The first was that Bergmans *really* knew where the treasure was and that he wanted to get to the island quickly, land on it at some spot without the people in the T. R. expedition being aware of it, lift the treasure, and beat it back to Panama. The other was that the whole thing was just another stunt of Bergmans to convince some other sucker that he knew where the treasure lay, and so make another haul of expense money.

As it turned out, this latter is exactly what he did, and we know that he pulled the trick several other times before he finally faded from the Cocos scene. Pete Bergmans may or may not have known where the Cocos Island treasure was hidden, but he got money out of it just the same. As George

Lane said in an interview with Weston, "If yer arsk me, Bergman is nuthin' but a perfessional racketeer like. . . . Th' man's a fraud, if yer arsk me. I'm sorry I hever met 'im."

As to Lane's own experiences on the island, they were enough to make him sorry he ever saw the place. As Lane expressed it: "Gor'blimey! I 'ad no ideer th' island were as big as she be. I thought I were acomin' to a small island a few acres big. Instead I finds a island as big as th' Isle o' Wight, halmost. I've orlready sin a dozen criks an' waterfalls thet's th' sime wot Bergmans told me. I were lorst from th' very start, an' I told 'em so. They was disappointed orlright but thet weren't my fault. I done me best."

Before Treasure Recovery Limited gasped its last breath (early in 1936) and its expeditions gave up the hunt for Cocos treasure, it had used up $125,000 in shareholders' money and inveigled over 1,500 Britons to foot the bill. Even so, the company left a long list of unpaid accounts in Costa Rica. At the last, several of the expedition members were left stranded, the police on the island were not paid, several hotels in San José were left to "charge it" to Treasure Recovery's offices in London, and even the company's lawyer in San José put in a bill for several hundred pounds which he never got. In London, too, there were many unpaid bills, and in the end it was pronounced the biggest stock swindle ever to use Cocos Island's treasure as the come-on.

All that is left today is a pile of carbon copies of company letters and cables, "progress reports," the various brochures used to inveigle the public to part with its money, and a formidable file of newspaper clippings. Even these would not be in existence were it not that a couple of news correspondents covering the Central Americas kept them as the foundation for a book. The whole got condensed into these half-dozen chapters because that's the way it balanced out with the rest of the Cocos story—and because other expeditions were looming on the horizon, which from the looks of things promised to be even more newsworthy than this one. One of these had this advance notice in San José's *La Tribuna* on November 13th, 1935:

ANOTHER EXPEDITION TO LOOK FOR COCOS ISLAND TREAS-URE IS BEING ORGANIZED IN VANCOUVER, BRITISH COLUM-BIA. ERSKINE (SLIM) NICHOLS WILL BE THE CHIEF AND THE "WINDWARD" THE YACHT WHICH WILL CONVEY THE EXPEDITIONARIES TO THE SCENE OF THEIR ADVENTURE.

A United Press dispatch from Vancouver, B.C., states that a new expedition is being prepared there to look for the legendary treasures of Cocos Island where the expedition of Treasure Recovery Ltd. is still at work.

This new expedition will be under the command of Erskine (Slim) Nichols, owner of the auxiliary yacht *Windward* * which is already well known in Central American waters. Nichols will be accompanied by five men, one of whom is the representative of the Cocos Island treasure company which in 1932 financed the expedition commanded by Colonel J. E. Leckie, which was nine months on Cocos Island without being able to find the slightest trace of the treasure, although they were using the well-known electrical metal detecting apparatus known as the "Metalphone."

The expedition has been organized as a result of information furnished by one "Bugs" Bellamy, a soldier of fortune and an adventurer who arrived in Vancouver some months ago claiming to have found thirty-three old Spanish gold coins on the beach at Cocos Island. Nichols was naturally very interested in Bellamy's story and for the last month he has been busy preparing his yacht to set out in search of the Cocos treasure.

"Bugs" Bellamy? And where had we heard that story before? One could not avoid comparing his yarn with that of Pete Bergmans. At least Mr. Bellamy did not seem to be

* This name struck us as being suspiciously similar to the *Westward*, from which Pete Bergmans claimed to have been wrecked on Cocos Island in 1929.

making quite such extravagant claims. One could hardly compare a handful of old coins with Pete's whole cave full of treasure.

Yet another thought struck us. This man Bellamy was claiming to have found his gold coins *on the beach* at Cocos. Was it possible that by some queer coincidence he had stumbled on Pete Bergmans' cache on the beach, thus explaining why Treasure Recovery's men had failed to find it? But any such hypothesis, we reasoned, would require as a corollary the one hundred per cent acceptance of Bergmans' story and that would be asking too much. Or wouldn't it?

If this sounds like "lunatic fringe" thinking, remember that a lot of highly respected people had been convinced of Bergmans' integrity. Besides, there were still a few echoes of the expedition to keep alive both sides of the question.

One notable echo occurred on February 29th, when a reporter from the *Diario de Costa Rica* interviewed Casey, the cook on the *Veracity,* who had come up to San José to put in a claim for back wages. Among other things, this is a part of the curious story he told:

Some time ago, when I was on Cocos, I went ashore with my assistant, Saunders, to wash clothes in the creek at Chatham Bay. While thus quietly occupied, we suddenly saw Bergmans prowling about in the forest. He was alone and we followed him without his being aware of it.

We saw Bergmans scrape around near a rock on which is inscribed the name "Morgan" and afterwards he went into a sort of cavern at the foot of the cliffs, without suspecting that Saunders and I were watching him all the time. Knowing Bergmans to be a man of violent temper, and fearing that he might kill us if he knew we were spying on him, we returned to the *Veracity,* but the very next day, when Bergmans had gone back to the Wafer Bay camp, Saunders and I returned to the spot where we had seen Bergmans prowling around.

We entered the cave, and inside, with my own eyes, I saw the remains of a dead man. The bones were so old they looked as though they might have been there for at least a century.

However, owing to the sharp rocks scattered about, it was too difficult for us to get right inside the cave, but from the little I saw, I feel sure that the treasure is in that cave.

If the Costa Rican government will give me one thousand dollars, I will lead their representative to the cave. . . .

When we asked Casey if this were a true story, he assured us that everything was just as he had said. "I was scared stiff to enter that cave," he further explained, "when I saw that skeleton lying there. Not if all the money in the world was alying inside that cave, would I have walked over them bones to get to it. No, sir! I'se a good Christian, and I don't want no truck with murdered men's bones!" But he did mark on our "master" map the location of the cave.

Then we acquired some more information on "Bugs" Bellamy. It seemed that "some time ago" Mr. Bellamy and a companion were shipwrecked on Cocos Island (just like Bergmans), and that shortly afterwards, his companion came down with fever and died. Bellamy buried him, and a few days later while wandering along the beach he discovered a hole with a lot of ancient gold coins in it (just like Bergmans). He gathered up 33 of these gold coins and put them in an empty tin can which he found on the beach.* He then hid the can in a safe place under a palm tree, and for several days thereafter he kept looking for the main treasure which he judged could not be far from where he had found the small cache.

But, alas! "Bugs" fell ill with the fever too. He had no

* In a long letter written in 1927 by August Gissler to Lieutenant George Williams who was planning a treasure hunt to Cocos Island, Gissler unequivocally stated: "It was near this hollow tree that I found a gold gauntlet and thirty-three gold coins minted between 1773 and 1799." Seeing that Gissler's discovery was made long before he abandoned the island in 1907, Bellamy's finding of identically the same number of gold coins many years later is really a most amazing coincidence.

medicine and he almost died. For days he lay unconscious, and when finally he came to, he was (extraordinary!) no longer on Cocos Island but in bed in a little village on the west coast of Mexico. Not till then did he find out that while he was ill and lying unconscious on Cocos Island, a Mexican fishing vessel had put in to the island and rescued him from almost certain death.

Mr. Bellamy, naturally, was grateful for being rescued and restored to health by the kindly Mexicans, but he went almost crazy when he realized that his can full of gold coins was still on Cocos Island where he had hidden it. However, he eventually made his way back to Vancouver, his home town, and there he met Lieutenant Colonel J. E. Leckie, to whom he related his strange adventure. Colonel Leckie, believing Bellamy's story to be true, immediately put him in touch with Treasure Recovery Ltd.

The company, which had swallowed whole Pete Bergmans' story about a big cave crammed full with treasure, was not going to choke on Bugs' story about a little tin can full of gold coins.

How Erskine (Slim) Nichols and his *Windward* (nee *Westward?*) got mixed up in the deal, we were, by now, too tired to find out.

There were other news items to color the Cocos picture this year. They occurred before the actual expiration date of Treasure Recovery's concession and while some of the expedition members were still on the island. At the moment the expedition was not making its usual headlines in the papers because its protagonists were literally at sea in one of their many crossings of the Atlantic bent on double-crossing each other. But the island radio was still in operation, and that is how the *Times* came to scoop all other papers on the most important Cocos visitor of the year. This was the visit of Franklin D. Roosevelt, President of the United States.

Through the cooperation of the island's radio operator, Weston was able to relay the only legitimate Cocos Island dateline on the president's visit there.

The Cruisers *Houston* and *Portland* anchored in Chatham Bay on Wednesday, October 9th, 1935. Roosevelt's first act was to request the island radio to transmit his personal greetings to President Ricardo Jimenez in San José, and to request formal permission for the battleships to enter Costa Rican waters. President Jimenez replied: "I cordially wish you an agreeable visit to Cocos and I hope it will bring you a welcome rest after so much hard work."

President Roosevelt went ashore the following morning and for once the weather on Cocos was propitious. During the afternoon about a dozen boats were lowered from the cruisers and many officers and members of the president's staff went fishing in the bay, or landed on the rocky beach. It was a gala scene, what with the going and coming of boats, the picnics ashore and the dinners aboard ship, and several of the *Houston's* planes roaring overhead on routine patrol. The President himself landed a ten-foot, 110-pound sailfish (which went in ice to Washington, where it was mounted and placed on display).

This visit was appreciated most of all by the British treasure hunters who by this time were down to "beans and rice for breakfast and rice and beans for lunch." President Roosevelt contributed quantities of fresh meat, vegetables, fruits and tobacco from the cruisers' stores, while the treasure hunters in turn filled him in on the latest Cocos legends, and thus it was discovered that the president was himself an old Cocos fan and had his own ideas about how and where the treasures lay buried. He even voiced the hope that someday he would have time to put his "clues" to the test. We have always been sorry he never got that opportunity (though he did revisit the island in 1937 and again in 1940).

The only thing we didn't like about this visit was the shock we got when we checked publication of our stories in the *Times*. We had reported simply that the British treasure hunters and the Costa Rican police had attended a movie show on the *U. S. S. Portland,* but an imaginative rewrite man rendered this as "The inhabitants of the island saw movies for the first time in their lives when the President invited them to attend a show on one of the ships last night." Fortunately, for our local reputations, the *Times'* circulation in Central America was limited at that time to a few dozen subscriptions.

The news of greatest international significance, however, occurred on January 29th, 1936, when Costa Rica issued the first postage stamps to bear a map of Cocos Island. These stamps created unprecedented interest among philatelists (including President Roosevelt) the world over, and solved a problem that had plagued Costa Rica for years. A lot of nonsense has been written and said about the circumstances under which the stamps came into existence, and here, for the first time, is the true story:

About the middle of 1935, while some people were still discussing whether Cocos Island really belonged to Costa Rica or not, Weston (who dabbled in commercial philately on the side) got the idea that the government could very effectively assert its sovereignty over the lonely island by issuing a set of postage stamps bearing a map of Cocos Island under the name of the Republic of Costa Rica.

Without saying anything to anybody, he wrote to the firm of Perkins, Bacon & Co. Ltd., in London, and asked them whether they would authorize him to solicit on their behalf an order from the Costa Rican government for a set of Cocos Island stamps. They agreed at once and sent Weston a specimen stamp with a map of Cocos Island, based on a British Admiralty chart, as the central design.

With this sample in hand, Weston approached the Minister of Finance, *don* Carlos Brenes, who was immediately enthusiastic. The idea of announcing to the world at large, through the simple medium of a legitimate postage stamp, that Cocos Island belonged to Costa Rica would settle the question once and for all. And there was no better time than the present to do it.

The minister told Weston that he would obtain the president's formal consent and place the order at once for a million stamps. "But to which firm shall I give the order?" he asked, knowing very well that up to that time only the American Banknote Company and Waterlows of London had printed stamps for Costa Rica.

"Why not give it to me for the firm of Perkins, Bacon & Company?" prompted Weston. "After all, the whole idea was mine."

"Fair enough!" replied the minister, and true to his word Weston got the order for Perkins, Bacon & Co., notwithstanding the protests of the agents of the two rival firms.

The original order which the minister placed with Perkins, Bacon & Co. through Weston was as follows:

    150,000 — 4 céntimos stamps — light brown
    100,000 — 8 céntimos stamps — violet
    150,000 — 25 céntimos stamps — orange
    150,000 — 35 céntimos stamps — pale purple
    150,000 — 40 céntimos stamps — chocolate brown
    150,000 — 50 céntimos stamps — yellow
    100,000 — 2 colons stamps   — light green
     50,000 — 5 colons stamps   — dark green

Not only did this transaction help a lot of people (there are more ways to make a buck than writing the news) and establish Costa Rica's claim to Cocos Island, it also marked another historic milestone in postage stamps. Curiously, this was the last stamp order to be executed by Perkins, Bacon

& Co. Ltd. before they went into liquidation, thus terminating almost a century of printing postage stamps, for it was this company which printed the first postage stamps ever issued, namely, the original famous British "penny blacks" of 1840, whose centenary the philatelic world commemorated in May, 1940.

What with all the publicity Costa Rica and Cocos Island were getting in those days, the sale of the Cocos stamps to stamp dealers and collectors was an immediate success throughout the world. The United States Minister to Costa Rica, Leo R. Sack, was one of the first buyers of the new stamps. He sent a complete set to President Roosevelt as a memento of his recent visit to Cocos Island, and, considering the President's interest in the island, these later formed an important item in the President's famous collection which was sold after his death.

Still, Cocos Island's buried treasures and the search for them provided a continuing source of news, and, as we said, bigger and better (and much more newsworthy though not necessarily more successful) expeditions were already on the horizon. One of them was to bring full circle the story of the Lima treasure and the infamous *Mary Dear*. It would, we boast, provide us with the greatest scoop in the long history of Cocos Island legends.

25.

IMMIGRANTS and pioneers generally are a breed apart. The characteristics common to both are not found in the average man. Perhaps this is a good thing—good for the growth and advancement of civilization, that is—for if the majority of us were not good solid citizens, willing to remain in one place and build stable, well-rooted communities, we might have a land of nomads. And rolling stones not only gather no moss but they pick up little else that can be accredited to social progress.

Nevertheless, the opening wedge in any new territory is made up of people willing to give up the comforts and the security of established patterns for the hardships and the unknowns of other lands. The promise of greener pastures, the promise of various freedoms, have no charm for the timid, the weak, the fainthearted. The pioneer, however, is something more than a simple gambler. He is a man with more fortitude than fortune, more resolve than resource, more wit than wisdom, but these are the characteristics that make him most adaptable in new environments.

The first immigrants to California and the West were unique in this respect. Subsequent pioneering efforts, up to and including our present probing of outer space, can hardly compare with the Argonauts of '49. There is only one class that exceeds the forty-niners in pioneering characteristics: The trail blazers who went before them. These were the few wandering trappers, scouts and "mountain men" who were first to travel the ancient Indian trails, and the occasional itinerant traders who came by sea. The latter, of course, were first, for it was the ships of the inquisitive and acquisitive Spanish that explored the coast and opened the way for the first overland expeditions and the establishment of the first civilized communities.

Father Junípero Serra established the mission outposts in the Californias around 1770, and by 1820 the Spanish *rancheros* were approaching the heyday of their bucolic era. Their vast domains supported great herds of cattle and horses, and these and their sprawling adobe haciendas were tended by countless Indian slaves. No more idyllic land was to be found anywhere on earth. We have come to take with a grain of salt the present-day effusions of Western chambers of commerce, but there was a time when such praise would hardly have been adequate to describe the West that was seen by the first white men to follow the Spanish *conquistadores*.

The first English and American traders who rounded the Horn and bartered manufactured products for California cowhides, tallow and wool prospered beyond their fondest hopes. And the few "foreigners" who jumped ship or dared wander into this paradise from beyond the mountains—to marry the *señoritas* and settle down—usually found themselves the wealthy masters of lordly estates or prosperous commercial enterprises. These were the real pioneers who set the pattern and opened the land to the Argonauts and the waves of immigration that came later. They came in the 1820's and the two decades before the 49ers.

But there weren't many. In the whole of California there were less than a dozen, and of these only sparse and infrequent records give any reliable account of their lives. Furthermore, the descendants of these pioneers are of little help to the modern researcher, for their knowledge of their ancestors is based on word-of-mouth family legends and the same fictional histories available to everyone else.

We consider ourselves fortunate, therefore, in having stumbled upon certain information and official records which enable us to give a fairly accurate account of one of those intrepid early pioneers, while disclosing for the first time the source of a whole new sequence of events connected with Cocos Island.

Sometime in 1822, barely a year after the Lima treasure was buried on Cocos Island, a stranger arrived in the little adobe settlement of Yerba Buena in Alta California. (The pueblo was not to be called San Francisco until many years later.) His name: James Alexander Forbes; his nationality: Scotch; his age: about 28; his profession: a doctor of medicine, he admitted but never practiced; his last place of residence: he never said and the native courtesy of the *californios* made them refrain from asking.

There are various stories about James Alexander Forbes and how he made his first appearance in California. One of his descendants told us that he came from the East in a covered wagon, but he arrived 25 years before the first covered wagon made it overland to California. Some say that he suddenly appeared on the scene overnight and they avoid any details of his arrival; others simply say that he came by sea around the Horn. Strangely, the most fantastic story of them all happens to be the true one: He drifted through the Golden Gate one dark night in a full-rigged ship with only one other man besides himself aboard, a deaf and dumb sailor.

Where was the rest of the crew? The record does not say. If the deaf-mute knew, he couldn't say, and Forbes, if he knew, never volunteered the information. Remember that California in those days was still under Mexican rule; there was no overland communication with the faraway American states; and there was little law and order. A man could come and go in any manner he pleased without any questions being asked.

James Alexander Forbes apparently remained in California for a few years, and then he disappeared for three years. When he returned, he casually dropped a hint or two that he had been visiting his family in Scotland, but it was noticeable that he seemed to be well provided with ready cash. The only explanation he ever gave was that he had found a gold mine "down south" en route to California. Stranger still, James Alexander Forbes, though admitting that he had graduated from medical school in Scotland, appears never to have practiced that profession in California and was never known as "Doctor" Forbes.

Forbes was a man of considerable education and intelligence, but in the application of his talents there was a definite trait of shrewdness that was a little sharper than natural Scottish canniness. Contrary to this, however, many historians and most of Forbes' descendants attribute to him certain honors and noteworthy accomplishments.

We take no particular pleasure in dragging into the bright light of research the family skeletons of the Forbes family in California (and it is extensive, as you shall see), or in bursting the bubbles of California historians, but the plain fact is that the members of the family and the historians who have had anything to say about Jame Alexander Forbes have been talking about two different men!

The confusion, we discovered, all derives from one simple error in identity:

In 1839 there was published in London a book entitled *California: A History of Upper and Lower California from their first discovery to the present time, comprising an account of the Climate, Soil, Natural Productions, Agriculture, Commerce, &c.* The book is described today as "important as the first book in English relating wholly to California, or better said The Californias; and it presents a foreigner's estimate of the old Spanish colony and Mexican province as it was on the eve of the American seizure." It is today one of the rarest items of Californiana. The author's name? Alexander Forbes.

Before the reader questions our long detour or grows impatient with these details, let us sketch briefly the other things we know about James Alexander Forbes. Soon after the return to California from his mysterious three-year absence, he married Anita María Galindo, the daughter of one of California's best-known Spanish families and owner of the large rancho that once encompassed the cities of Santa Clara and San Jose. They had twelve children, among them the late Judge Alonzo Forbes, a well-known agriculturist and soil conservation expert in Monterrey County. During his early days in California James Alexander Forbes was named vice-consul for the British government at a trading post where the Mission Church of the University of Santa Clara is located. Forbes' home was where the present church now stands. He acquired large land holdings through purchase and by marriage for he helped finance the beginnings of the University of Santa Clara by giving both property and funds. He also served for a time as a language instructor at the University.

271

But this James Alexander Forbes was not the author of the first book in English on California mentioned above.

Alexander Forbes (the author) was born in Scotland. His brother, John Forbes, M. D., F.R.S., to whom he dedicated his book, was a prominent doctor in London at the time and was instrumental in finding a publisher and getting the book on the press. Alexander Forbes was in business in Buenos Aires before 1825. There the rugged Scotchman joined Eustace Barron, a veteran of the wars against Napoleon in Spain, and by 1828 they had transferred their business to Tepic, Mexico. There Barron was British vice-consul for a number of years, and Forbes succeeded him in the office. Their principal business interests, however, were in mining, cotton mills and foreign trade. Theirs was one of the most important firms of foreign merchants on the west coast of Mexico and traces of the company remain today.

Barron, Forbes & Co. were on the alert for any new development in mining, and since Tepic was a popular way station on the road between Mexico City and the Californias, they learned that deposits of quicksilver had been discovered in Alta California. In 1845, Captain Andrés Castellero, sent from Mexico to California to oust the Russians, happened to notice that the Indians near San Jose painted themselves with vermilion. The captain had the good sense to discern that the paint was red cinnabar, the chief ore of mercury. He found the source and immediately made legal denouncement of a claim. Shares were sold to Barron, Forbes & Co., and this was the beginning of the famous New Almaden quicksilver mines.

This investment was so important to the company that Alexander Forbes himself came to California in October, 1847, to act as *habilitador* (technical engineer) at the mine. He returned to Tepic in July, 1848, and this was his last and only visit to Alta California, for at that time he was said to be "a very old man."

This Alexander Forbes, mining engineer, businessman, and author, of Tepic, Mexico, was associated with James Alexander Forbes, British vice-consul in California, financier, and man of mystery, of San Jose and Santa Clara. There is a large correspondence between the two which shows that they were interested jointly in a number of enterprises from 1843 to 1851, but there is no indication that they were related. They always addressed each other formally as "Dear Sir," while author Forbes always addressed his brother in London informally and affectionately.

These two Forbes pioneers were also different in age. Though James Alexander Forbes was middle-aged in 1848, he could hardly be called "a very old man." When the United States came into possession of California they both became involved with the new government in a long litigation over their ownership of the New Almaden properties. In that suit it was alleged, and in some degree accepted by the court, and upon appeal by the Supreme Court of the United States, that Alexander Forbes and James Alexander Forbes had connived, as shown by the correspondence between the two, in "securing fraud, forgeries, interpolations, and antedating of the documents [of ownership]" before American occupation of California. The Supreme Court later reversed its decision to favor the Scotsmen in 1863, the year in which Alexander Forbes (author) died, but not until Abraham Lincoln had intervened.

And while we are at it, perhaps we should expose one more misconception believed by many descendants of James Alexander Forbes. There are some who claim relationship with another well-known California writer, Mrs. A. S. C. Forbes (Harrie Rebecca Piper Forbes), who wrote articles and books on the mission and rancho past, erected plaques, raised flags, and variously decorated historic spots. (It was she who evolved the ubiquitous mission bells once used to mark the horse-and-buggy El Camino Real.) But this Forbes was a California immigrant from Pennsylvania by way of Kansas, and to our knowledge was in no way related to James Alexander Forbes of Santa Clara, California, or the Alexander Forbes of Tepic, Mexico.

James Alexander Forbes, besides siring a large family, left a strong impression on the history of Santa Clara Valley. He was one of the original owners of the New Almaden Mines and was treasurer of the corporation for many years. He also built the flour mill near Los Gatos at a cost of approximately $200,000. It was built at the peak of the California gold rush, when wages were high, and it ran for some time under his management before it passed into other hands. An historical marker today calls attention to the site.

This, in brief, was the life of one of California's first pioneers, at least insofar as the California part of it is known. But what of the other years? What of the mysterious source of his fortune? Perhaps the answer lay in the extraordinary bequest he made to his eldest son.

When Forbes died, he left to his oldest son, also named James Alexander, a chart and several documents, all in his own handwriting. *This chart was a map of Cocos Island, of Chatham Bay to be precise. The documents described in detail how the Mary Dear's treasure was buried on the island and gave full instructions for finding it!*

Of course, our chain of evidence, both circumstantial and factual, provided the answer we long had sought, but the reader, too, should ask the same questions we did and arrive at his own assumptions. For instance, why should such documents be in the possession of this James Alexander Forbes? Where had Forbes been during his three years' absence from

California? Whence did he obtain the wealth which he later invested in California real estate and industry? We ask the reader to draw his own conclusions. We can only add that James Alexander Forbes, before he died, urged his children to fit out an expedition to go to Cocos Island to find the treasure which, he said, would make them millionaires several times over.

There is one other fact which may add weight to what we have said above. James Alexander Forbes "got religion" shortly before he died, and it was pretty obvious that he suffered occasional pangs of remorse. But remorse for what? Our conclusion is obvious: James Alexander Forbes was the young Scotch doctor turned mate of the *Mary Dear!*

Time and public opinion have an erosive effect on historical fact. Forbes was a wise and intelligent man and he knew that with the passing of the years some doubt would eventually be cast on the most authentic documents. He determined that those he bequeathed to his son should never be questioned. He had all his Cocos Island treasure maps, charts and papers duly authenticated by a notary public. And the same public witness in turn confirmed their genuineness when they passed to the son.

Thus began the sequence of events, the treasure expeditions and the promotion of treasure expeditions, which continue to this day.

What did James Alexander Forbes, Jr., do with these documents? Apparently nothing. As one of the heirs of a comfortable fortune in real estate and other holdings, he felt no necessity to extend his interests beyond the Santa Clara Valley. Lacking the bold spirit of his father, the Cocos documents never had more than casual interest to him. He kept them in a safe all his life and, when he died, he passed them on to his son, again named James Alexander.

Like his father, the original Forbes, James Alexander

Forbes, Jr., had married a girl of Spanish-Mexican descent, so James Alexander Forbes III was more Mexican than Scotch. Perhaps it was this combination that inspired the first interest in Cocos documents.

James Alexander Forbes III was much like his paternal grandfather, and he had inherited some of the old man's restless spirit and adventurous nature. By this generation the family fortune had been split up into so many pieces (all Forbes families were large) that there was the added incentive of need. James III moved to Southern California with the hope that he could better his fortune in the booming citrus development of the southland. He prospered and gradually acquired some acreage in oranges around Riverside and Corona, but the great Depression of the 1930's crippled the citrus industry as it did everything else and Forbes was badly hit.

By the spring of 1937 James Alexander Forbes III (by then 65 years old) was convinced that his only chance to gain a fortune lay in the legacy left to him by his grandfather, and one day he showed all the documents to Douglas Narron, an insurance broker of Corona, California. Narron was immediately interested and after careful study convinced himself that the papers were, without question, absolutely authentic. He based his opinion on the length of time the documents had been in the possession of the Forbes family—that is, through three generations—and the obvious sincerity of the letters written by the elder Forbes in his advanced years to his son, urging him to go to Cocos Island and recover the treasure. No father, reasoned Narron, would knowingly send his son off on a fool's errand.

Narron asked Forbes why neither he nor any other member of the family had gone after the treasure, and Forbes replied that the family had never had sufficient money to organize a proper expedition. And, in any event, they were afraid that even if they did succeed in finding the treasure, they would not be allowed to keep it.

Douglas Narron, however, was anxious to organize an expedition and so he made a deal with Forbes whereby Narron was to organize and provide the financing for a properly equipped expedition to Cocos. At the proper time Forbes would turn over his documents to the expedition, in consideration of which the Forbes family was to receive a percentage of the treasure.

Thus authorized, Narron entered into partnership with a friend, one George Bosley, of Balboa Island, California, and the two partners immediately set about finding some sort of transportation for the expedition. They haunted the waterfront and searched every anchorage along the California coast in an attempt to find the owner of a suitable ship who would provide transportation to Cocos in exchange for a share of the treasure, and they spent the whole of that summer on what seemed to be a fruitless quest. Boat owners simply laughed at their story of $60,000,000 just waiting for them to go and get it.

It began to look as though they would have to call the whole thing off when they stumbled upon a prospect practically in their own backyard. They were about ready to give up when they met Captain Hugh M. Davenport, owner of the 65-foot ketch *Spindrift*, of Newport Beach, California. (Newport Beach and Balboa Island are adjoining communities.)

The two promoters were in luck, for when they started to give Davenport their sales pitch they discovered that the captain had already made a study of the Cocos Island treasure legends and was, therefore, very much in sympathy with their project. After all their disappointments during the summer of searching, it is no wonder that Captain Davenport seemed heaven sent. It was soon agreed that the captain would provide his yacht for the expedition and the two promoters would put up the cash for the provisions and equipment, everybody to share in the treasure in agreed percentages.

A few insignificant complications developed, but to meet the convenience of all concerned, the expedition was scheduled to get away sometime in 1939. Throughout 1938 the treasure hunters were busy with plans for the expedition and in arranging their individual personal affairs for the trip. Everything was progressing according to schedule when it was brought to an abrupt halt by the sudden death of Forbes in early 1939.

Forbes' estate and his Cocos documents now passed into the hands of his three sons, Charles, James Alexander IV and Robert, and two daughters, which meant that Narron and Bosley had to start all over again and try to persuade the sons to go through with the arrangement their father had made.

The sons, however, were easily interested. The financial problems of the expedition were already settled and this was satisfactory to the Forbes family. Further, the expedition was reorganized so that two of the boys, Charles and James Alexander, who were married and lived with their families in Riverside, should accompany the expedition to Cocos.

And so, on the 26th of October, 1939, the good ship *Spindrift* sailed from Newport Beach, bound for the one small spot on tiny Cocos Island where everyone concerned felt confident they had only to scoop out a little sand and uncover $60,000,000 (or more)!

The expedition consisted of eight men and one woman. They were: Captain Davenport, nominally in command, and his wife, Bernice; Captain Harris, the navigator; "Bennie" Finnerman, boatswain; Bill Ensley, engineer; Jimmy and Charlie Forbes, in possession of the treasure charts and original clues; Doctor F. Robert Johnston, President of the Archeological Society of Southern California, whose interest in the expedition was, he said, mainly academic; and, finally, insurance man Douglas Narron, on land the promoter of the hunt but at sea merely the cook. Bosley, for some reason, was not included.

Hugh M. ("Cappie") Davenport, we recall, was an example of the salty-looking, sea-going type popularized by the publicity men of the spinach industry; second in command was Harris, a capable navigator who had spent most of his life at sea. Boatswain Bennie was a husky, tattooed young seaman who knew sailing ships as well as the best of them. He was equally at home whether rolling about the deck at sea under a stiff nor'wester, or on land under a breeze of Scotch. Bennie was a quiet, unassuming guy with a heart about the size of his ship.

Young Bill Ensley was barely 19 years old so his title of "engineer" was probably a little presumptuous. But Bill had curly blonde hair, a physique like Adonis, and an appetite not matched by anyone else aboard. Needless to mention, when he arrived in Costa Rica he had half the *ticas* of that little republic convalescing with heart trouble.

The Forbes brothers were landlubbers but generally agreeable and able to take whatever came along in the way of work. They were the only "common seamen," aboard. Mrs. Davenport occupied a deck chair for most of the trip, except when she had to go below to eat. "Doc" Johnston served in a number of capacities, not the least of which was the proper administration of castor oil. He massaged strained backs and was the photographer for the expedition. He was the boy-scout type, and never passed an ant or a beetle without picking it up in the faint hope of discovering a new species.

Narron, the insurance man turned cook, said when we interviewed him after the Cocos sojourn: "I could go into considerable detail about the cook and the hell of a time he had. Obviously, he tried to do something he had never done before, in a galley right over the ship's engine, which was running all the time, making it almost hot enough to cook without bothering about the stove. However, it was all his own fault. Hadn't he promoted the jaunt in the first place?"

After considerable effort, however, and a lot of cookbook reading, he did manage to serve the first dinner. From what the others said, it was highly commendable. Afterwards, the captain went topside and in his best deck voice commanded: "All hands on deck, and damn quick about it!"

Everybody thought that a good joke, nothing like seamanship on the sea and all that, but when they finally did show topside they could see the skipper was not joking. This was serious business with him, and for the rest of the trip he let no one forget that he was in command of his ship in every respect. The "crew" figured it was a case of one or the other—let him have his way or throw him overboard—so they decided to take it and say nothing.

This was the season of the *chubascos*, those fierce and erratic winds off the Mexican coast so well known to all who have any knowledge of these waters, so the expedition had a pretty rough trip.

The weather for most of the cruise was stiflingly hot and when they entered the Gulf of Tehuantepec they ran into a severe storm which almost put an end to the expedition. It probably would have, had it not been for the capable Mr. Harris, who was in control of the ship at the time. Cappie Davenport rode it out in his bunk, with a bottle or two to sustain his courage.

From all reports it was an extraordinary voyage. It lasted 28 days, and the *Spindrift* and her badly shaken crew arrived at Puntarenas on November 23. By that time everybody was pretty well fed up with Cappie Davenport, and not entirely because of his conduct en route. When they arrived in Puntarenas, he informed them that he had run out of cash and that they would have to cable back to California for additional funds with which to purchase the necessary fuel to make the trip from Puntarenas to Cocos Island. The Forbes boys called Riverside and got an additional $350.

James Forbes, by inheritance, spoke Spanish with some fluency and appeared to take command once the expedition arrived in Costa Rica. Up in the capital, San José, the government's permit to go to Cocos was obtained without difficulty. The usual conditions were stipulated: The government was to get one third of any treasure found, and, to protect the government's interests, ten policemen were to be taken to the island at the expedition's expense.

The *Spindrift* left Puntarenas on December 10th, and arrived at Cocos three days later.

And then the trouble started! Right from the beginning there was disagreement between the Forbes brothers and Captain Davenport as to the correct interpretation of great-grandfather Forbes' chart. Jimmy and Charlie thought the treasure must be in *this* spot, and Davenport thought it must be in *that*. Jimmy and Charlie, as owners of the chart, had their way, and the digging operations with spades and shovels were carried out under their direction.

Captain Davenport, angry at having his own views on the subject ignored, refused to go ashore at all. He moped and sulked aboard the ship all the time the expedition was on the island, viewing the operations ashore through his binoculars. Altogether, the *Spindrift* remained at Cocos nine days, that is until December 22nd, and during those nine days Cappie Davenport set foot on the island only once, and then only for the brief space of three hours.

During those three hours, however (as he later confided to us), he checked the original bearings of the Forbes chart with a compass. After several attempts, with due allowance

281

for the annual magnetic variation, he located the exact spot where the treasure was buried. And right over that spot, so he said, there was an enormous, square boulder.

However, the rest of the party figured that they also had located the exact spot some distance away, and although their digging failed to produce the slightest sign of the treasure, when the *Spindrift* eventually returned to Puntarenas on Christmas Day, it was proudly announced to the press and the public that they had found the exact spot beneath which the treasure lay buried. (We were present at that press conference.)

"Then, why," we asked, "didn't you dig it up?"

"Because we didn't have the right tools and equipment," was their answer. "We are going back to California and very soon we shall return with a bigger and better expedition. In fact, it will be the best equipped expedition that has ever been to Cocos. Money is no object, for we know now that the treasure put there in 1821 by James Alexander Forbes is still there and we are coming back to get it."

They kept their word. They did come back, and, just as they said they would, they came back with a bigger and better expedition—possibly the best equipped that ever went to Cocos Island. Size, we learned, determines neither merit nor honor, and certainly not success. Indeed, it only increases the Cocos hocus-pocus.

C
O
C
O
S

I
S
L
A
N
D

26.

WE are aware, of course, that this is not the last chapter on Cocos Island. We know, too, that we won't write it. The treasures on Cocos are going to remain hard to find, and even if one is found it will only spur the search for the others, multiply the number of expeditions, create more discord between men, and cost a few more lives. It's been going on for a long time and it will continue long after we are gone. Even the number of treasure hunting expeditions that have gone to Cocos, authorized and unauthorized, within the past quarter century would fill a chapter just to list them and a whole shelf of books to describe them and the antics of their members. We could do it, given the time, the space and the vitamins, but it would cause a lot of embarrassment and make a few enemies and we are too fond of Cocos Island, Costa Rica and its *ticos* to make that mistake.

Of the 25 years that preceded the evanescence of Treasure Recovery Limited, the Panama *Star & Herald* once printed a little item that summed it up nicely. It appeared in the edition of March 13, 1936:

Cristóbal, March 13. The recent acknowledgment by past and present promoters of Treasure Recovery Ltd. that their £75,000 investment to unearth Spanish gold from Cocos Island has failed, has led old residents here to indulge in reminiscences of the legions of adventurers who have crossed the isthmus, treasure-bent, in the vain hope of wresting whatever secrets Cocos Island has to guard.

For the past twenty-five years they have been coming. They arrive with high hopes and return crestfallen and weary from the isle which has impelled them to spend money, energy and time in the search for a will o' the wisp which apparently does not exist; the isle which has made enemies out of friends; the isle of disillusionment and bitterness, where men have starved, suffered and fought each other, and which stands as remote and silent today as it was when the treasure myth was first broadcast to a wondering world.

They have come in dude yachts and schooners, broken-down launches and rowboats. Some have sworn that they found treasure, though none has displayed the luster of Spanish gems, or the glint of Spanish gold. The man who tells the biggest story gets the biggest audience, even as did those recent explorers who declared that the British Admiralty was in possession of conclusive proof that treasure lay buried in the caves of Cocos and had lent its official approval to their quest.

Then there were the two who came in a life-boat from New York. For equipment they carried a spade and a motorcycle. The latter occupied more space on their craft than they could afford, but as they had little else except themselves aboard, and expected the machine to prove useful in scouring the jungle-covered island, they carried it along. Their fate was never known.

A couple of Hearst men once found their way to Cocos, their launch being wrecked on the beach in a storm. They lived on coconuts and came close to killing each other before a United States destroyer finally rescued them and sent them home.

Then there was the lad with the divining rod with which he hoped to detect the hidden treasure. His fate was also a mystery.

And then came Arthur! Charles Arthur, one of the original promoters of Treasure Recovery Ltd., and with him Commanders Worsley and Stenhouse of the Royal Naval Reserve. They came on the Drexel yacht, *Queen of Scots,* with scientists and electrical detectors, camping equipment and supplies. . . .

After that, the first authorized expedition of importance was that of Captain Charles M. Wilkins, of Long Beach, California, on his 150-ton auxiliary schooner, *San Pedro,* in February and March, 1938.

Back in California, Wilkins had been approached by a young fellow, a man in his early thirties, by the name of Milton Canham. Mr. Canham had a story to tell comparable only with that of Mr. Bergmans of unhappy memory.

Canham's story was that a few years previously, while he had been visiting Cocos Island with some friends from California, on a small yacht, he had accidentally stumbled on the treasure cache. He had, so he told Wilkins, carried away with him a part of the treasure when he eventually left the island, and he was now looking for someone to bear the expense of an expedition to go to Cocos to recover the rest of the treasure.

Wilkins, a tough sea captain, if ever we saw one, had been roaming up and down the coasts of California and Mexico for more years than he could remember. But he was interested in Canham's tale. He checked it as far as he could, and he discovered that round about the time indicated, Canham had actually disposed of a substantial quantity of pure gold.

Wilkins then formed a private syndicate with some friends to pool the expenses of the expedition and Canham was given several hundred dollars in cash as an advance on his share of the treasure everyone was sure they would find.

They sailed from California on February 20th and in due course arrived at Puntarenas where Wilkins obtained the formal permission to visit Cocos to search for treasure.

Less than two weeks after leaving Puntarenas, Wilkins &

Co. were back again in Puntarenas. His first action on reaching port was to have young Canham locked up in the local jail on a charge of obtaining money under false pretences. Then he came up to San José and told his story to the U.S. consul, and, over a cocktail, to us.

Canham, he said, was a fraud. He had brought Wilkins and his friends all the way from California on a fool's errand. "Why, the very moment we stepped ashore on Cocos," fumed the captain, "we knew that Canham had never even seen the island before. He was completely lost and didn't know which way to turn. His story about having been there before and finding the treasure was a lot of bunk. And then he had the nerve to laugh it off as a good joke."

The next important expedition to visit Cocos also came from California (is there something in the California climate that inspires them?), and it came in November of 1936. It was lead by Mr. Marino Bello, stepfather of the late Jean Harlow, on board his 350-ton yacht the *Metha Nelson*.

But this expedition could hardly be called a serious treasure hunting enterprise, since the participants did not seem to care whether they found the treasure or not. There were other treasures, most of them other pleasures, on the yacht. It was a holiday jaunt and the visit to Cocos and the halfhearted search for the treasure were planned merely with the idea of providing the guests on board with a momentary thrill.

The "expeditionaries" on the *Metha Nelson* were hardly the type one would expect to find engaged in a serious treasure hunt, for included were Mr. Bello's beautiful young wife, an Italian countess, an English writer, two California millionaires, a doctor, and a couple of "secretaries" from Hollywood. And, naturally, the party would have been incomplete without a mysterious "one" who knew exactly where the treasure was buried. By now you must be familiar with his type: Keating, Bergmans, Bellamy, Canham—and this time the gentleman's name was Bill Bowbier. And how or where Mr. Marino Bello had picked up Bill Bowbier must remain a secret between the two of them. But he was there, armed with his own private charts of Cocos Island, and ready and willing to show his patrons where the treasure lay buried.

The yacht had set out gaily from Los Angeles, but before she got as far as Puntarenas, trouble set in. While she was in port in Guatemala, two members of the crew deserted. They were Jews, they said, and they jumped ship because the German captain of the vessel had been treating them on recognizably Nazi lines. The men refused to return to the *Metha Nelson* and there was a lot of argument with the Guatemalan authorities before the ship was allowed to proceed without them. The incident received considerable attention in the United States newspapers at the time.

The expedition remained on the island just two weeks, and a good time was had by all except Mr. Bowbier.

The first day on the island, this worthy, with his bundle of maps and charts under his arm, led various members of the expedition along first one jungle trail and then another, up this hill and down that, back along the beach, into shallow caverns, and around rocks and boulders. Mr. Bowbier's methods were very much akin to those of Mr. Bergmans. At the end of the day, he admitted having made slight errors in his calculations, but he was ready to tackle the job again on the following morning.

When the morning came, the treasure hunters again meekly followed Mr. Bowbier as he led them from one end of the beach to the other and back again. Finally, perhaps realizing that his employers were beginning to get a bit fed up with his indecision, he stamped his foot on the ground at a spot halfway along the beach (where have we seen this scene before?) and said: "Here's the spot. All you have to do is dig!"

Everybody dug, even the beautiful Mrs. Bello, the aristocratic (American) Italian Countess, and the sedate English writer dug a few grains of Cocos sand so that later they could say truthfully that they had been legitimate parties to the discovery of the treasure.

The digging continued apace throughout the day, but no treasure came to light, not even a little, bitty, teeny, weeny old gold coin. Finally the rueful Mr. Bowbier admitted that his maps and plans were apparently valueless, but it was not his fault, etc., etc.

Well, there was the party on the island, they were all rich and did not need the treasure anyhow, so why spoil a nice vacation? The fishing was good, the swimming was good, and the sunbathing was good; there was plenty of good food and drink at hand so "Let's enjoy ourselves," they said—which is what everybody proceeded to do for the rest of their stay on the island.

That is, everybody except poor Bill Bowbier. He automatically became an outcast, ostracized by all. He moped around the camp and brooded upon his failure. "There must be a mistake somewhere," he said, over and over. It was probably the only honest thing he ever said.

And how about the return of Jimmy Forbes? James Alexander Forbes the First had handed down an authentic document. With that a man ought to be able to promote a pretty fancy expedition to Cocos. Jimmy did—several of them.

After the first one, which we have reported, came one of the best equipped and probably the best financed we ever saw. Its principal backer was California millionaire Fred Lewis, whose magnificent 250-ton yacht *Stranger* brought the expedition to Cocos.

With the failure of the *Spindrift* expedition and its return to Puntarenas on Christmas Day, 1939, Jimmy and Charlie Forbes, Douglas Narron and "Doc" Johnston returned to

California. Captain Davenport and the rest of the expedition hung around port for a few days and then left for Panama, supposedly to obtain tools and equipment for the "bigger and better expedition."

What was not reported at the time was the fact that Captain Davenport and the Forbes syndicate had parted company in disagreement over the interpretation of great-grandpa's charts. Each side was determined to organize a new expedition and get to the island before the other. When we heard this, we said "Here we go again!"

Early in February, both Davenport and Forbes were back in San José waiting for the government to decide which outfit should get the nod. But money talks and Jimmy, apparently, was able to prove that he had a well-financed company behind him. He got the concession, and on March 5, 1940, the expedition to end all expeditions arrived at Puntarenas.

This, briefly, was its complement: the yacht *Stranger* was a beautiful double-ender of 15 knots, fitted with every modern convenience, and worth even in those days around half a million dollars. On board, in addition to the professional crew of some 17 men and owner-captain Lewis, there were the captain's beautiful young wife, Lyne (about 30 years younger than her husband); Mr. V. Britton, engineer with the Mojave Engineering Company; Alden Bryan, the general factotum of the expedition, combining the talents of movie man, photographer, painter, publicity man and errand boy; our old acquaintance, Doc Johnston, the archeologist and bug collector; and an elderly man named Seaman, a guest of the captain. In equipment they had on board about everything that money could buy, from hand shovels to power lifting machinery, electrical detecting devices and plenty of food supplies.

This looked like the successful approach and wanting to

be in on the kill, so to speak, we asked Lewis for permission to tag along. But the captain was of another mind. We could go along and write the story, he said, if we'd give him 50 per cent of our royalties.

Several words and several days were involved in this argument, but in the end we told Captain Lewis we'd write the story from information we got on our own somehow and we wouldn't split with him. Anyway, we thought, if that's the kind of expedition this one is we shall probably be able to tell its story in a few paragraphs. And we did, in the words of one of his own party:

We arrived at Chatham Bay about dawn, the second morning out from Puntarenas, and started unloading the men and the equipment for our camp about 8 A.M. We spent the greater part of the first two days in clearing the spot and erecting our camp. Under the supervision of Jimmy Forbes, Doc Johnston and others, we succeeded in getting up eight tents, a cooking department and a screened 14 x 20 foot building to serve as a mess hall. The Costa Rican soldiers were very willing workers and the job was completed in lots less time than anticipated.

Then Captain Lewis and the mate of the *Stranger* took up the finding of the bearings which they found to be about 50 feet to the south of where we had excavated on our first trip to the island on the *Spindrift*. The so-called "Doodle-bug" was brought into play and that, too, signified that we were on the right spot according to the chart. So there was nothing else to do but dig. So we dug. The going was pretty tough on account of the many huge boulders and some water which seeped in.

A boom, with a hand winch, was erected and handled the boulder situation very well. After working for about two days, we uncovered a boulder with an arrow and a large "K" inscribed on one side, and a pair of boots on the other. Everyone was convinced that this was the mark left by John Keating, but we were unable to derive any benefit from the find. We continued on with the hole, to the extent of about 60 feet long, 20 feet wide and 16 feet deep. At the same time, having more manpower than we really needed, we picked out several likely spots in the same locality and had some of the men dig there. There were no results, of course.

I will say, however, that there was a very systematic, honest effort made to uncover something. We found the rock filled with some kind of ore, which caused the "Doodle-bug" to function at that particular spot.

After ten days of continual digging without any encouraging signs, everyone became quite disheartened and from then on it was just a question of staying longer or going home. On the sixteenth day, going home won. It was the opinion of everyone there that there must be some more information other than the chart, which the Forbes family have overlooked, and which we should try to dig out.

And that was the end of the Forbes-Lewis expedition on the *Stranger*. Captain Lewis wasted no time in Puntarenas, but pushed off for California the very same day that he returned from Cocos. Only Jimmy Forbes remained in San José for a few days to square up expenses with the government and then he, too, returned to California, by plane.

Before he left, Jimmy said he would be back again one day to have another shot at finding the treasure. And he did, or, rather, perhaps we should say he is, for James Alexander Forbes IV has promoted so many expeditions to Cocos Island that we have sort of lost track. If we are not mistaken, he is, at the moment, working on his seventh—or is it his eighth?

With the general prosperity of the 1950's came an increase in the number of expeditions to Cocos, for no matter how much money a man has, the hunt for treasure never loses its appeal. With more people with more money and leisure time, Cocos in recent years has become the lodestone of treasure hunters everywhere.

One of the most persistent of the Cocos treasure hunters was a pale, handsome, deep-drinking British adventurer named Victor Frederick Cochrane Hervey (Earl Jermyn), nephew and prospective heir to the wealthy Marquis of Bristol

In his thirty-odd years, Hervey had done a two-year stretch for a Mayfair jewel robbery, tossed a few 1,000-bottle champagne parties, twice gone through bankruptcy, and helped sell arms to Franco and the Arabs. One day, while rummaging among papers belonging to his ancestor, Admiral Lord Cochrane,* Hervey found what looked like Captain Thompson's directions for locating the Cocos treasure. As soon as he could, he sailed for Jamaica and there organized an expedition.

But young Hervey had trouble. This first came over the electronic device he had counted on to spot the gold amid Cocos' hematite sands; its inventor quarreled with Hervey, wrecked the instrument, and flew home to England. Then the captain of the special landing craft Hervey had hired got tired of waiting and sailed off on another job. But at the Kingston yacht club, Hervey found a friend in need—blonde, fortyish Lillian Lowell Sorensen, travel-loving daughter of an adopted member of Boston's Lowell clan. She was accompanied by a grizzled Dane whom she had acquired in Copenhagen as her fourth husband and skipper of her yacht, the *Langesund III*.

Mrs. Sorensen was impressed by Victor Hervey. She agreed to supply capital for the expedition and give Hervey a lift to Cocos.

From the very start of the trip Mrs. Sorensen's husband proved difficult. In Costa Rica, while Hervey and Mrs. Sorensen sat in the bar of Puntarenas' tumbledown Imperial Hotel drinking Scotch and making plans, the old skipper studied them jealously through his spyglass from the *Langesund's* deck. Presently he roared ashore and knocked Hervey down; then he rushed back to the ship, wrote "Goodbye, Lil, good-

* For our story on Admiral Cochrane and his connection with the Lima treasure, see Chapter One and Appendix No. 1.

bye *Langesund*" in the ship's log, came back to port, and took a plane for Denmark.

Undismayed, Hervey continued his expedition aboard the 70-foot ketch *Culver,* taking along his heavy digging gear and a labor gang of *tico* beachcombers. Mrs. Sorensen was to follow with food and other supplies as soon as she could get repairs made on the *Langesund.*

At Cocos Hervey's party got down to business in Wafer Bay. Hervey was betting on Wafer Bay on the theory that in December, when his papers said Captain Thompson had put in, only Wafer Bay would have provided adequate shelter. But he never got a chance to test his theory, for when the *Langesund* failed to arrive with food, his Costa Rican laborers mutinied. Hervey and his party returned to Puntarenas. The *Langesund,* it turned out, had been stuck with engine trouble.

As though that were not enough, Hervey's pretty English wife, Countess Jermyn, arrived on the scene. Mrs. Sorensen became moody, and the two women quarreled. When Hervey sided with his wife, Mrs. Sorensen threw herself off her yacht into the harbor—and swam around strongly. Fished out, she announced that she was through with Hervey and the treasure hunt.

But Hervey would not give up. He tried to pawn his wife's diamond earrings to raise more money for the expedition, and he also talked a Los Angeles tuna-boat operator named Erwin Katzer into letting him have a boat on credit.

The last we heard, Hervey, Earl Jermyn, and his wife, the Countess, were living in luxury on their yacht in the Thames, but we don't think he was paying the bills with Cocos gold.

Then there were the several expeditions headed by one Charles W. Williams of Manhattan Beach, California; and another one from Canada (some of the members of which were from as far away as Baffin Island, near the Arctic Circle); and a modest one from England called Ocean Enterprises Ltd.

Obviously, the Costa Rican newspapers never lack for local news, for it is a rare day now that there isn't at least one expedition on the island, one on the way, half a dozen being planned, or several limping home broke, fruitless and tired. But none without hope, may we repeat. And again, as August Gissler, most persistent and most famous Cocos hunter of them all said shortly before he died, "The treasure is on the island, but it will take money and a good deal of effort to unearth it. . . . I have gone through many hardships and dangers and perhaps shall have to do so again, but this will not keep me away. . . ."

So, as we said, this is not the last chapter on Cocos Island, but it is, for the moment.

APPENDIX I

IN THE *Biblioteca Nacional de Costa Rica* (the National Library of Costa Rica) in San José, we found by chance *A View of South America and Mexico,* a rare edition in two volumes, by "A Citizen of the United States," published by H. Huntingdon, Jr., in New York in 1826. It contains a remarkably detailed account of the events at Callao, doubtless taken from the newspapers of that time, or from other contemporary records.

According to this account of those stirring times, the combined military and naval expeditions of General San Martín and Admiral Cochrane, consisting of three large warships of 60, 50 and 40 guns, respectively, four smaller warships and twenty transports, with 4,900 men in all, sailed from Valparaiso, Chile, on August 20th, 1820, and reached Pisco, Peru, 100 miles south of Lima, on September 7th. Here, the disembarkation of San Martín's army was completed on the 11th, and Cochrane's squadron continued on up the coast.

At first the rebel army encountered little resistance, and by October 26th, after a temporary armistice, moved northwards to Ancon. Meanwhile, Cochrane had anchored in the outer roads of Callao. In the inner harbor, under the protection of the batteries of the fort, lay a 40-gun Spanish frigate and two sloops, guarded by 14 smaller gunboats. On the night of November 5th, 1820, Cochrane with 240 volunteers in 14 small boats, boarded and captured the enemy frigate with a loss of 41 killed and wounded, while the Spaniards lost 120 men. This rebel success was the

295

turning point in naval warfare. From this moment on Spain's naval power in the Pacific was crippled.

After resting for six months at Huara, 75 miles north of Lima, meanwhile extensively recruiting and spreading the doctrine of independence, San Martín began his advance on the capital on July 5th, 1821. The Viceroy, alarmed for the city's security, at once issued a proclamation announcing his intention of abandoning the capital, and pointing out Callao as an asylum for those who felt insecure in Lima. "This was a signal for immediate flight . . . and the road to Callao was crowded with fugitives carrying their most valuable effects."

The government left Lima on July 9th, and San Martín victoriously entered the capital on July 12th, proclaiming that he came, not as a conqueror, but as a liberator. Peru's independence was formally proclaimed on July 28th.

The old history goes on to say (Vol. 1, page 153) that on September 10th, 1821, the main Spanish army returned from the interior and, marching right past Lima, entered Callao. As the royalist army passed by the capital, San Martín drew up his own army ready for battle, but did not attack the enemy because he wisely foresaw that this increase of the garrison at Callao would rapidly diminish the enemy's provisions there and thus hasten the surrender of the fortress.

"The Spanish army, after a short stay at Callao, retired, carrying off the treasures deposited in the fort, which shortly afterwards surrendered to the rebels."

The date when the treasures were taken from the fort, according to this account, is given as sometime soon after September 10th, 1821. Obviously the historian did not have access to Admiral Cochrane's diary which, as in the text of Chapter 1, gives the date as occurring in August. Thus, in all probability, the two different accounts concern two entirely different accumulations of treasure. The first, mentioned by Cochrane, was the King's treasure and that from the churches in Lima; the other was mostly the personal fortunes and possessions of the *limeños*. The latter was never included in the hoard put aboard the *Mary Dear*, and in all likelihood it was never lost.

APPENDIX II

THE following news item appeared in the San Francisco *Call,*
Tuesday, February 2, 1909:

CAPTAIN JAMES BROWN'S STORY
OF BURIED TREASURE

The following account of the famous treasure supposed to
have been buried on Cocos Island, and the object of so many
adventurous expeditions, was dictated last night and signed by
Captain James Brown, who leaves today for the South Seas to
recover the treasure trove.

"In the year 1850 I shipped on board a vessel in New York as
second mate for the West Indies. Arriving at Kingston, Jamaica,
I became acquainted with Captain Henry Smith of the schooner
Sea Foam, 400 tons register, who was there fitting out for pearl
fishing, and I joined his vessel as chief mate. After being at sea
for some time the captain told me what his real business consisted
of, which was that we were to go to Cocos Island after treasure
which had been buried there by his father.

"Then he told me about his father, Captain Smith, of the
schooner *Black Witch* of Salem, Mass. He was on the coast of
Peru when the Spaniards were fighting that country in 1820,
and came in contact with their vessels from which he took all
their treasure, amounting to about $60,000,000, and consisting
of silver, silver dollars, gold bars, bullion and gold and silver
jewels from the churches, also diamonds and other precious
stones, all of which were taken to Cocos Island and buried.

"Before Captain Smith died he imparted the secret to his son,
with whom I was now connected. We arrived at Cocos Island

297

and found the treasure and moved it to another island in the South Pacific, where we again buried it. Here all of the crew died except the captain, the steward and myself. We had a fine ship's longboat, which we fitted out as the schooner had all broken up, and on board her we put $1,000,000 and started for Australia. On the passage the captain and steward died. I arrived at Cochin Bay, West Australia, and am sure that I am the only living man who knows where the treasure was buried. It has been proven that it cannot be found on Cocos Island, and the reason is that we removed it."

(Signed) *Captain James Brown.*

This story by Captain Brown is typical of the many fantastic and improbable ones that have been published. It is the basis for another news item that appeared in the San Francisco *Call* on Sunday, February 7, 1909:

LOS ANGELES MAN ASSERTS KNOWLEDGE OF $17,000,000 BURIED ON COCOS ISLAND. TELLS WEIRD TALE OF HIDDEN GOLD AND WILL MAKE SEARCH FOR FORTUNE

Los Angeles, Feb. 6. Convinced that he can locate and recover treasure to the amount of $17,000,000, supposed to have been buried on Cocos Island, 350 miles off the Costa Rica coast, W. A. Desborough of Los Angeles is about to embark for the tropic seas in search of the vast fortune.

Desborough says he knows nothing of the proposed expedition of Captain Brown, who wrote the statement printed in the *Call*, Feb. 2nd, and does not think they are after the same treasure. Desborough says he was on the island eleven years ago, but did little more than to locate the cache where the money was hidden. He declares it is buried by a landslide and lies beneath a quantity of earth forty feet deep, and as large as a city block. It is his purpose to raise enough money to take hydraulic machinery to uncover the treasure.

Desborough's story of how the treasure came to be buried there sounds like a tale of some weird writer of sea yarns. In speaking of it today, he said: "In the war between Chile and Peru in the middle of the last century, the people of Callao became alarmed by rumors of an attack on the city. They took all their treasure aboard the bark *Mary Deane* [sic] of Boston. The captain's cupidity was aroused and he sailed away with the

treasure, which he cached on Cocos Island. The bark was over-
taken by a Peruvian man-of-war and all the crew, excepting the
captain and the mate, were slain. These men escaped after awful
torture; they swam to an American whaler and were at sea
eighteen months. The mate died and the captain returned to
Boston.

"I obtained possession of the chart from a daughter of the
captain, whom I had befriended. Eleven years ago I visited the
place with an expedition but for private reasons did not disclose
the correct hiding place. While the men were working at the
wrong place I located the treasure and we left the island."

APPENDIX III

THE following ships' (or personal) names and the dates when they visited Cocos Island were copied from those engraved on stones in Chatham and Wafer Bays and are here arranged in chronological order (with most of the punctuation ours). The list is incomplete, for many of the engravings are so old and weathered one can decipher only an occasional letter or figure.

His Brit. Maj. Schr. LES DEUX AMIS—1797
WASHINGTON GARDNER—1807
JORUVE—Nov. 1813
G. TODD—1813
Bark MARRIPO—1814
Ship ATALA. Boston—1817
CRETAN—July 3, 1819
Brig ADEON. Wm. Low—Nov. 20, 1830
Bark OCTAVIA. C. Mantor. Cuban.—April 18, 1831
Ship KINGSTON—August, 1931
Ship UNCAS. H. C. Bunker, Falmouth—Sept. 23, 1833
Ship ALEXDR. COFFIN. D. Baker, Nantucket—Oct. 12, 1833
Ship KINGSTON. W. E. Sherman—1833
Ship MYP. E. SMITH—1833
WEST—1834
DAVIS—1835
Ship ATALA. G. Winship, Boston—1837
MARTHA. Newport—March 2, 1839
JOSHUA—March, 1839
P. F. LIEN. Granville—1840
S. H. HARRIS. New Bedford—Apr. 15, 1842
R. C. FAY—May 21, 1842
Ship G. W. MORGAN—July 14, 1843
GEO. HOWLAND—Aug. 24, 1843

G. DUFFY—Oct. 30, 1843

BRICK DES MTE LE GENIE. Comm. P.M.L. Cte. de Gueydan—Nov. 1, 1846

BALAENA—1846

H. B. M. Steam Frigate SAMPSON. Sir C. Seymour. Capn. Henderson—1847

Ship INDIENCHIEF of New London. Cpt. Baley—March 28, 1848

L. LEVRETT—May, 1849

Ship ROYAL B.—Oct., 1849

Ship EVA—1849

BOYCOTT—1849

LUCY ANN—1849

THO SIMPSON—Sept. 18, 1850

P. H.—1851

WINSDO. Tomas Cass, Lima. B. S. Clarke—May 11, 1851

Ship SUSAN P. HOWLAND—August 26, 1851

Ship OCEAN—1852

Ship BLO. A. A. Campau—1852

Bark CORNELIA. P. B. Rolufs, Mst.—April 14, 1852

G. N. MACY—1853

FROST—1855

CHADWICK—1855

S. ENTERPRISE. N. T.—Dec., 1855

Bark JAVA—Nov. 14, 1856

Bark TYBEE—Feb., 1858

ADDISON—1861

BX. HYDSPE—1862

H. R. VIGILANT—Sept. 3, 1862

B. COLCOND—1863

TRIDENT—May, 1863

E. H. FISHER, JR.—May 7, 1863

P. CLEVELAND—1864

Ship ISAAC FOOD. A. M. Morrison—1865

ARAUJO—1865

S. LEONIDAS. N. B. 17 M.—1870

Sch. ROSCOE—Mar. 7, 1870

MARIPOSA—Oct. 17, 1870 (or 1878?)

FRANCIS L. STEELE—Mar. 28, 1871

C. MARKS—1871

VIRGINIA MARKS—April 11, 1873

DEXTER—16 June on D. 2 Nov., 1873

Bk. VIRGINIA MARKS. A. Savvely—1875

J. Maria ZELDON—Julio 22, 1879

Ship BRAND—Feb. 7, 1881

ADOLFO MESSEN—October, 1889

Those marks easily identified as having been made since the turn of the twentieth century we consider too numerous and of too little historic value to mention. The following names, without dates, apparently are all of ancient vintage.

Bk. ANARORA J. M. E.
ANDERSON
Bark BEN
Ship BLO
J. BOND, Marblehead
CRETAN
D. DACK
W. U. Davidson McH. CAHU. PAUOA H. U. M. 25
C. H. DUNN
FERNANDO
O. FISHER
FURY
JOS. GRANT, Nantucket
The GREENW-LEONID, Boston
HENRY HALL of LONDON
GRANDw HAMMOND
JOHN HOWLAND
CAP. HENDERSON
Ship JOHN ANDERSON
S. JOHN
F. A. KEMPTON, N.B.
J. G. LEA
N. P.–J. R. LAWRENCE
LOUISE
LYS
H. OSBORN
PETREL
SCHR. GEN. PIERCE
SAAIL SHREW
VAPOR

APPENDIX IV

THE following interview with August Gissler was published in the *New York Times* in 1907:

COCOS ISLAND AND ITS KING LIABLE TO AGAIN COME INTO PROMINENCE

Captain August Gissler, Governor of Cocos Island, left New York hurriedly on Wednesday to meet a party of Englishmen at Panama, with whom he will sail on the steam yacht *Rosa Marie* for his possessions in the Pacific. The trip requires fourteen days from New York. The yacht is said to be the property of Harold C. Grey, a millionaire Britisher, and the journey is undertaken to head off an alleged filibustering expedition.

Cocos Island has figured in many a strange romance of lost treasures. Montezuma's billions are said to be buried there, instead of in Southern Mexico, or Guatemala, and numerous expeditions have been fitted out with a view to finding the gold. In olden times there was a heavy trade between Central America and the Philippines, and ships following the equatorial "counter current" had to pass Cocos. Tradition says vessels laden with precious metals were wrecked on the island and adventurers from many lands have undertaken in vain to find the buried cargoes.

Governor Gissler's pet theory just now is that England wants to obtain possession of Cocos Island for a coaling station. It is situated in latitude 5 degrees 33 minutes north, longitude 87 degrees west, 350 miles from Puntarenas, or Punta Arenas, Costa Rica, and 450 from the mouth of the Panama Canal. Vessels passing through the canal for Australia, or points in Polynesia, will find it directly in their path. Germany has her eye on it, and England, aware of the fact, is probably trying to anticipate Teutonic occupation. If the United States government has any intentions regarding the island they have not yet been revealed even to Gov. Gissler.

Early in the last century Cocos Island, which is twenty square miles in area, was a penal colony of Costa Rica, and before the discovery of petroleum in Pennsylvania was the headquarters and general post office of the great Pacific sperm oil fleet.

When Captain Gissler, who had sailed the Pacific for years, discovered it, in 1888, absolutely uninhabited, and with only a few ruins to mark the sites of prisons and a residence, he claimed possession in the name of Costa Rica, the nearest land, and raised the flag of that country.

Cost Rica granted him a concession in perpetuity, with a salary of $100 a month, equivalent to $50 in gold, and has taken good care of him ever since.

Captain Gissler is a man of 47 years, and a breathing replica of Michael Angelo's heroic statue of Moses. His reddish beard reaches to his waist, his hair is luxuriant on a splendidly poised head, his eyes are as clear and searching as an eagle's, his nose is classic, his voice is profoundly mellow, fitting the man to perfection. His height is 6 feet 3 inches. He is built like a wedge, as a man should be, with massive shoulders, firm hips, and an almost imperceptible embonpoint. His hand is as big as the hand of Providence, and so hard that his clenched fist is used as a spike maul.

"Cocos," said Gov. Gissler, on the eve of his departure, "is unquestionably of volcanic origin. Our highest mountain is 2,500 feet. We have seven rivers. On one is a grand waterfall of 600 feet, and on another a cataract of 500 feet. Within 100 feet of my residence I can get a force of 2,000 horse power."

"What is the character of the soil?"

"We have sand, clay, and chocolate loam. The soil is very rich. Vegetation is abundant. The forests are magnificent. Our cedar, the white or yellow species, is plentiful and apparently grainless. It should make fine pencils."

"What of the climate?"

"The temperature ranges between 62 and 90 degrees. We never need a fire or an overcoat, and the heat does not trouble us at all. I wear a suit of overalls the year round and am comfortable. It rains ten months in the year, and occasionally we have showers in the other two. The water is the purest in the world. I never had it analyzed."

304

"Any game?"

"There are many kinds of birds, but none that you would eat. They are only pretty to look at, and are mostly of the parrot and cockatoo order. The woods are full of wild pigs, and when I want fresh meat I kill them. The waters are alive with fish, but tropical fish, you know, are not very edible."

"You raise domestic animals, I suppose?"

"I did have some cattle, a few horses, sheep, and chickens, but when I came to America the time before this trip an expedition from Vancouver went down there and killed every living thing."

"Why did your people permit that?"

"My people? I haven't any."

"I mean your—your subjects."

"Oh, there are no subjects. Only I and my wife live on the island."

"And when you go away?"

"She goes with me. We leave the cattle, horses, and so forth to take care of themselves. There is enough to eat all the time."

"No children?"

"Not one. What would be the good of a parcel of children on Cocos Island? Only trouble. They would always want to go to the mainland."

"Isn't your wife lonely?"

"Not where I am. She likes it down there. Besides, there is plenty to do. We both work."

"What do you find to do?"

"Lately I have been growing tobacco. I raise 1,000 pounds to the acre on the chocolate loam, and then I have a return crop in six weeks which gives 800 pounds more. If I care to do so I can raise several crops in a year, one right after the other, up to a total of 3,000 pounds to the acre."

"That sounds incredible, Governor."

"But it is true. I sell my crop in Costa Rica at $1 a pound."

"One man cannot cultivate many acres. Why don't you import some labor?"

"I took out eighteen Germans once, with their families, and thought they would raise great crops and all get rich, but in a short time they raised an insurrection instead."

"What became of the insurrection?"

"I quelled it."

"Tell me how?"

"I declared martial law, as Governor of the island, and with my big pistols pointed in the faces of the Germans scared them

305

into submission. They laid down what arms they had and peace was restored. But the incident induced me to ship the whole caboodle away."

"You are Governor, General, Colonel, and the whole army, as well as lord high executioner, judge, jury, and undertaker?"

"Everything, I suppose. I have to be. When a filibustering expedition came to Cocos from San Francisco—you read about it, of course—they landed and told me they had come to search the island and intended to kill all the game on it. I called the captain of the ship into my room and, showing him my credentials as Governor, told him that if he dared touch a piece of my property I would regard him as a pirate and treat him and his crew as such. I showed him the flag of Costa Rica flying above our heads and said he would be called to account for any violation of my rights. He was no fool, that fellow. I had my pistols on at the time, ready to use them. He had the good sense to apologize and sail away with his crew of adventurers."

"Any minerals on the island?"

"Yes. I knew absolutely nothing about geology, having been on the ocean all my life; but after appropriating Cocos I got some books on minerals and made a careful study of the subject. I gathered a great quantity of specimens and had them lying around my house trying from time to time to determine their character. One day a yachting party arrived—the same party I am going back with tomorrow on the yacht *Rosa Marie,* belonging to Harold C. Grey—and after spending a few days with me they departed promising to return some time. After they had been gone a week I discovered that most of my specimens had mysteriously disappeared. Well, they did come back, and in the meantime had had the specimens analyzed. They found gold, silver, and copper, and were much excited. I shall know more, much more, when I return to Cocos."

"As to coal, is there any on the island?"

"I have found one vein of hard coal, but cannot say whether it is anthracite or bituminous."

"What is the character of the harbors?"

"There are two magnificent harbors, one on the northeast corner of the island, the other on the northwest. The former is called Chatham Bay, the latter Wafer Bay. The water is from 14 to 80 fathoms deep. Three of the largest men-of-war could coal at the same time, lying end to end along the dock that would be built. The shore is very steep, and coal chutes could be arranged so that the bunkers could be filled in an incredibly short time."

306

"Where would England obtain her coal if she takes the island and there is not sufficient on it to be mined?"

"From Australia, of course. She would ship it over in barges. The distance is about 8,300 miles."

"What of the Monroe Doctrine?"

"I do not think it would be operative in the case of Cocos Island, but I may be mistaken. I do not think the Monroe Doctrine would cover an island over 300 miles from the mainland and in the Pacific Ocean. Speaking strategically, I do not see how England can afford to lose the opportunity to get Cocos. I cannot sell, however, without the consent of my government, Costa Rica."

"What are your immediate intentions, Governor?"

"I am going to take out a cargo of peons to Cocos and with them shall plant 50,000 rubber trees. I am looking to my material interests. If there are filibusters I shall fix them. I am not afraid. I once stopped a mutiny by striking the leader between the eyes with my fist, and he fell so hard and so far that his partners all ran away. Rubber should be very profitable on Cocos. It is a climate in which everything grows to perfection. After a rubber plantation is once established you have no more trouble with it."

"You will not grow tobacco any more?"

"I shall grow great quantities of it with my peons. The tobacco of Cocos is as fine as the product of Cuba, and I can raise ten times as much to the acre. There is another crop in which I am interested, and that is ginseng. What is ginseng, anyway? What is it used for? I hear it can be grown to enormous profit, as much as $50,000 an acre. I shall take along some roots and try what I can do. I take one sweet potato vine, plant it, and in a few weeks have yams bigger than my head. They are very fine flavored."

"What are your native fruits?"

"Cocoanuts and bananas, principally. We have three kinds of bananas, so many that we do not know what to do with them. They rot by the thousand."

307

APPENDIX V

THE following is a copy of a letter delivered to Admiral Palliser in Lima and, presumably, stimulated that British officer's interest in Cocos Island. The date of the letter is unknown. A copy of it was sent by August Gissler in 1927 to Lieutenant George Williams, who was planning to visit Cocos, with the explanation that Gissler had obtained it from Admiral Palliser during the latter's visit to the island in 1897. The writer, Patrick Fitzgerald, is doubtless the same Fitzgerald (despite the variation in name) whose clues subsequently came into the possession of Sir Malcolm Campbell. There are a few flaws in Fitzgerald's story as he recounts it here, and this prompted Gissler's suspicion that Fitzgerald was working a profitable "Spanish Prisoner" swindle. We do not suffer from that doubt.

Dear Sir:

My name is Patrick Fitzgerald. I come from Kildare. I am imprisoned in this city *incommunicado*. The jailer, who is my friend, will deliver this letter to you. I believe you will help me when you know the following facts:

Many years ago, when I was captain of a fishing boat, I was shipwrecked on the coast of Newfoundland. My crew and I managed to get ashore, and we made camp in a shack whose occupants were living in the utmost misery, having been snowbound for several months. I was glad to share with them the provisions we had salvaged from the boat.

One of the men of the family was sick and at death's door. His wife was also sick. This man's name was Keating. He had

308

evidently been a world wanderer and he had once had plenty of money.

One night, feeling that death was not far away, Keating told me an interesting story. He told me that he had once received from a certain pirate, by name Thompson, the secret of a great treasure buried on Cocos Island, 500 miles from Peru, in 1820.

He declared that he knew exactly where this treasure was because he had already obtained a part of it. I remained several days with him and learned his secret. Then I came to Peru to satisfy my curiosity as to whether such a treasure had really existed, and if it had been taken out of Peru and buried, as Keating had claimed.

I found, after careful investigation, that a complete record is in the official archives, including the trial and escape of Thompson, the only survivor, who knew where the treasure was buried.

In the course of my investigations, I had occasion to deal with the officers of the Bank of Peru. I was presented to the director of the bank when they learned what my mission was, and they seemed very interested when I said that I knew where the treasure was buried. They gave me access to the files of the bank, and there I found proof of the removal of the treasure, and a note that "said funds had been lost at sea."

When I had finished my examination of the archives, the director sent for me, and invited me to a family reunion at his house. I accepted, of course, and spent an enjoyable afternoon with his family. He tried to get from me the information about the treasure but I refused to say anything definite, seeing that the secret belonged to Keating, with whom I was in partnership, as he had recovered his health before I left Newfoundland.

I observed that the director was upset at my refusal. Therefore, I hastened to leave the house but scarcely had I gone 200 yards when, in a dark and narrow street, I was attacked by a gang of men who tied me up and carried me away with them in a carriage.

When I was freed of my bonds, I found myself in prison and one of the men told me that I would not be released until I had told the director of the bank what he wanted to know. I have been a prisoner ever since. I refuse to betray Keating's confidence.

Can you find a way to help me, a brother Irishman? I am a British subject. I have tried unsuccessfully to communicate with the British consul.

Patrick Fitzgerald.

APPENDIX VI

THE following news story appeared in a London paper under date of July 2, 1939. It concerns the death of Captain C. W. A. Arthur and his connection with the famous blackmail case of the 1920's.

DEATH OF FORMER A.D.C. RECALLS
"MR. A" CASE PLOT TO BLACKMAIL
EASTERN PRINCE

The death last week in the West Indies of Captain Charles Arthur recalls the famous "Mr. A" case of 15 years ago in which Captain Arthur was one of the central figures.

"Mr. A" was the pseudonym used in the High Court to hide the identity of Sir Hari Singh, nephew and heir-presumptive of the Maharajah of Kashmir—to which title he has since succeeded—who was the victim of a gigantic blackmail plot.

His name was kept secret at the express wish of the India Office, and it was not until the last day of the hearing of a case concerning certain of the prince's cheques that a barrister, in cross-examination, accidentally let the name slip out, and so disclosed the true identity of "Mr. A" to the world.

Captain Arthur, an Irishman, acting in the capacity of aide-de-camp and adviser to the fabulously wealthy Sir Hari, was alleged to have played a part in the conspiracy to blackmail his employer.

The cause célèbre first burst upon the world when a Mr. Charles Robinson brought suit in the King's Bench Division against the Midland Bank to recover £125,000, the balance of the proceeds of a cheque for £150,000 drawn by Sir Hari Singh in favor of "C. Robinson."

Some years earlier, Sir Hari Singh, while on a visit to this country, had attended a costume ball at the Albert Hall, where he was introduced to a Mrs. Charles Robinson, wife of a bookmaker.

From this meeting developed a series of incidents which eventually led to the action.

Within a week or two of their meeting, Sir Hari Singh and Mrs. Robinson were living in a Paris hotel.

One morning, in the early hours, a man named Montague Noel Newton walked unannounced into the bedroom which Sir Hari and Mrs. Robinson were sharing, with the result that shortly afterwards two cheques—one the subject of the action four years later—were drawn by Sir Hari in favor of Mr. Robinson.

Mr. Robinson's claim against the bank was based on the contention that, through their negligence, the money was paid, not to him, but to Newton and another man, a solicitor's clerk, William Cooper Hobbs.

It was alleged that Newton, aware that a liaison existed between Sir Hari and Robinson's wife, conspired with Captain Arthur to persuade the Prince that her husband knew of their illicit association and intended to take proceedings for divorce, and that two cheques for £150,000 each, drawn by Sir Hari, were paid over to avoid a scandal.

It was also alleged that Newton incited Robinson to threaten divorce proceedings, and then persuaded him to abandon these in consideration of a payment of £25,000. Robinson, who admitted that he had received this amount of £25,000, stated that for a long time he had been under the impression that this was Sir Hari's full settlement.

The bank, in defense of the action against itself, denied liability on the grounds that the £150,000 cheque it had paid had been extorted by blackmail, and that, therefore, as it had been obtained illegally, Mr. Robinson was not entitled to recover any part of the proceeds. It also alleged that the Robinsons were in the conspiracy with the others, and that it was at Mrs. Robinson's suggestion that Newton posed as her husband.

But the jury would not accept this, and, although the bank won its case, it was decided that neither Mr. nor Mrs. Robinson was a party to the plot to blackmail Sir Hari.

One of the most sensational features of the case was the appearance of Newton in court to give evidence on behalf of the Midland Bank in consideration of a payment of £3,000. He confessed that he and the others, including Captain Arthur, had engaged in a conspiracy to frighten Sir Hari Singh into paying over £300,000 to avoid the scandal of divorce proceedings after he had been found in compromising circumstances with Mrs. Robinson.

He even admitted that he had not been satisfied with his share from Sir Hari Singh's first cheque for £150,000, and had visited the prince at his palace in India in the hope of obtaining from him the second cheque for £150,000, payment of which, after a somewhat belated consultation with his solicitor, Sir Hari had stopped.

William Cooper Hobbs, the solicitor's clerk, who had been named by Newton as one of the conspirators, was arrested as he was about to board a boat at Gravesend, and a month or two later at the Old Bailey he was sentenced to two years' hard labour, having been found guilty of conspiring to obtain money from Sir Hari Singh.

No proceedings were taken against Newton. A warrant was issued for the arrest of Captain Arthur, the remaining conspirator, who, when divorce proceedings were threatened, is said to have told Sir Hari that the only thing to do was to pay up, and whose share of the first cheque for £150,000, cashed by Newton, is said to have been £40,000.

The charge was that of participating, as an accessory before the fact, in the receiving of cheques, knowing them to have been stolen. He was arrested in Paris, but proceedings for his extradition were unsuccessful. He was, however, prosecuted in a French court on a charge of receiving part of the proceeds of one of the cheques.

He was sentenced to thirteen months' imprisonment but, as by the time the case against him was finally heard, he had already been in custody awaiting trial for nearly a year, he was released shortly afterwards.

THE prospectus (abridged) with Treasure Recovery, Limited circulated among its prospective subscribers was printed as follows:

ABRIDGED PROSPECTUS

The following is an abridgement of a Prospectus dated 16th March, 1934, a copy whereof has been delivered to the Registrar of Companies for Registration.

Application will be made in due course to the Committee of the Stock Exchange, London, for permission to deal in the shares of the Company. The Subscription List will open today (Saturday) 17th March, 1934, and close on or before Tuesday, 20th March, 1934.

TREASURE RECOVERY LIMITED
Incorporated under the Companies Act, 1929.
SHARE CAPITAL.............. £75,000

Divided into 300,000 shares of five shillings each. These shares must be regarded definitely as speculative. The Directors suggest that no individual applicant should subscribe for more than a reasonable number. It is upon the experience, ability and integrity of the Directors and Executive, coupled with the up-to-date plant and equipment being used, that subscriptions are invited. Thus, these shares can be regarded as a very attractive gamble because, in the event of success, a small holding will secure a very handsome return. ISSUE OF 180,000 SHARES OF FIVE SHILLINGS EACH, AT PAR, PAYABLE IN FULL ON APPLICATION.

OBJECTS: The Company has been formed for the purpose set out in its Memorandum and Articles of Association and, in particular, to arrange for the employment of the latest modern scientific equipment in the search for and recovery of the numerous treasures which have, in the past, been secreted in various parts of the world. The immediate object of the Company is the recovery of treasure from the Island of Cocos. TREASURE ON COCOS ISLAND: The Directors rely upon the following publications, viz., Handbooks Nos. 141 and 142, prepared under the direction of the Historical Section of the Foreign Office and published by H. M. Stationery Office, 1920. These publications state, inter alia, "The existence of treasure concealed on the island is well established." Further reference is made to three distinct treasures, the first "A vast plunder obtained by rifling certain churches in Peru;" the next, "Gold bars and speci, worth ELEVEN MILLION dollars;" and finally, "About TWELVE MILLION dollars worth of stolen gold coin, jewels, and silver ingots." The Handbook further states: "The main stores of treasure are still hidden, in spite of various excavations and blasting operations which have been undertaken from time to time."

Apart from the Foreign Office publications, other records of treasure buried on Cocos Island include 300,000 POUNDS WEIGHT in silver dollars; 733 bars of gold; 7 kegs of gold coin, reputed buried by the pirate Davis. The treasure buried by the notorious Bonito on the Island has been said to comprise THREE HUNDRED AND FIFTY TONS of Bullion.

PRELIMINARY WORK: Most of the Directors and Members of the Executive of this undertaking have studied the Cocos Island problem on the ground; four of them have visited the Island and carried out prolonged, systematic investigations there; and have returned convinced that a search undertaken on scientific lines will be successful.

METHODS FOR RECOVERY: The methods to be employed by the Company are strictly scientific. They have been subjected to many rigorous tests in the field. The geo-electric and electro-magnetic methods which the Company will employ in the search for Cocos Island treasures are today extensively and successfully employed in important surveys.

It is proposed that the Expedition will leave St. Katherine Dock, London, during the month of April. Four weeks after sailing, the Expedition should arrive at Cocos Island, when operations for the location of the treasure will start forthwith.

The Company has in view a highly suitable vessel, fully equipped, which will constitute the Headquarters of the Expedition.

WHY SUCH METHODS HAVE NOT BEEN PREVIOUSLY EMPLOYED IN THE SEARCH FOR TREASURE: This is explained by the fact that geo-electric methods are not generally known. They have been operated exclusively by Corporations interested in prospecting, who are not concerned with any other aspect. This expedition, owing to the specialized knowledge of the Directorate, will be the first to employ scientific methods of search.

THE FIELD EXECUTIVE: The Directors are convinced that never before has an expedition sailed under such excellent chances of success as the present one.

The task on Cocos Island is a formidable one, but the personnel composing the Field Executive which is handling it is unique. This Executive has a fund of highly valuable knowledge and experience which will be pooled and scientifically applied in the present enterprise. The Executive includes the following: Colonel J. E. Leckie, C.M.G., C.B.E., D.S.O., F.R.G.S., mining engineer, Pacific Treasure Expedition, M.Y. *Silver Wave*, 1932–33; Dr. J. W. Harris, B.Sc., Ph.D., geologist; and Commander Worsley, Commander Stenhouse, Mr. Stratford Jolly, and Captain Polkinghorne, directors of the Company.

The portion of the Island in which treasure is likely to have been concealed is not more than 350 acres. Well-authenticated clues to the hiding place of the main treasures are all in agreement as to general locality. When the presence of metal is detected, by electrical means, a sample will be obtained by means of a mining drill, and thus unproductive excavation will be avoided. Modern science having provided such highly efficient apparatus for the locating of buried metals and minerals, clues form no part of the Company's programme.

OWNERSHIP: Since all of the treasure buried on the Island of Cocos dates back to the period of the great American Colonial Empire of Spain, which Empire no longer exists, there is little risk of an individual claimant putting forward any claims to the Cocos treasures.

WORKING CAPITAL: In order that more ample funds may be available for other expenses of the Expedition, the several members of the Field Executive are giving their services under contract, in return for very modest remuneration. The average rate of pay of the Executive will be under Twenty Pounds per month. This may be taken as a striking expression of their confidence in the success of the Expedition.

The minimum amount which, in the opinion of the Directors, must be raised by this issue is £20,000, but as 80,000 shares of the present issue have been underwritten, the Directors will proceed to allotment upon the closing of this list.

The above sum of £20,000 is required: (a) for the purchase of the Ship and the equipment of the Expedition, £6,800; (b) for the preliminary expenses of the Company, including cost of registration, £6,000; and (c) for Working Capital, £7,200.

Spanish Main Exploration Limited, whose Registered Offices are situate at 40 Broadway, Westminster, London, S.W.I., has agreed to transfer to this Company the benefit of all the agreements with the members of the Executive, thereby ensuring to this Company a valuable fund of knowledge and experience of the actual task ahead; the consideration payable in this respect is the issue to Spanish Main Exploration Limited of 120,000 shares in the Company of five shillings each, credited as fully paid.

Copies of the full Prospectus and Application Forms, on the basis of which alone applications will be considered, can be obtained from the Registered Office of the Company, and from the Company's Solicitors, Bankers or Brokers, as above; also from Union Founders' Trust Limited, 55/61 Moorgate, E.C.2.

APPENDIX VIII

THE complete text of the letter signed and circulated by Richard H. Studdert to members of the first Cocos Island Expedition of Treasure Recovery, Ltd.:

TREASURE RECOVERY LIMITED
Circular Letter to all Members
of the Company's Expedition.
August 15th, 1934.

With reference to the Expedition to Cocos Island which is now about to sail, I have to inform you, as one of the Members of same, that the following arrangements have been made by the Board.

(1) From the time of sailing from London, all members of the Expedition will come under the instructions of Commander J. R. Stenhouse until S. Y. *Queen of Scots* arrives at Cocos Island.

(2) After arrival at Cocos Island, all members will come under Mr. C. W. A. Arthur, who is in sole charge of operations.

(3) You will be invited to sign an Allotment Form for the purpose of having a proportion of your pay remitted direct from this office to your dependents. Allotments will be paid monthly, first payment 30 days after sailing.

(4) The balance of your pay will be credited to you monthly in the books of Commander Stenhouse who is acting as Paymaster to the Expedition.

(5) The Company will use its own currency. Books of "chits" to the value of £1 may be obtained from the Paymaster who will debit your account with same. Purchases of wines, tobacco and cigarettes, etc. from the Company while the yacht is at sea,

and at a Cocos Island will be by chit. Those requiring small sums in cash for going ashore at any Port of Call, may draw on the Paymaster, within the amount of their existing credit.

(6) Members are reminded that S. Y. *Queen of Scots* has only been lent to the Company and that all damage to the yacht must be made good before handing her back to the Owner. You are therefore asked to co-operate in keeping your own quarters and the general accommodation clean and tidy, paying particular attention to cigarette ends.

(7) By a resolution of the Board on August 2nd, 1934, it was decided that six per cent of the recovered value of all treasure found should be set aside for equal division amongst the several Members of the Expedition. The yacht's officers and crew are not included in this pool. Estimating the total personnel at 24 men, this would be equivalent to £2,500 per member per million recovered.

(8) In the interests of the success of the Expedition, you are asked to agree to censorship of your outgoing mail and it is hoped that the Controller of Operations can rely on your consent. This will only apply after arrival at Cocos.

(9) The Board feel confident that all Members can be relied upon to carry out any work they may be called upon to perform, in a cheerful spirit, putting the welfare of the expedition before personal considerations.

(10) Members of the Expedition will eventually be landed back in England at the Company's expense, but the Company can not be responsible for the passage of Members who wish to leave before the work on Cocos or elsewhere is concluded, or whose services have to be dispensed with for dereliction of duty.

APPENDIX IX

THE following Associated Press cable was filed in Balboa, Canal Zone, October 27, 1931, and appeared in several U. S. West Coast papers on the 28th:

Three American castaways, wearing nothing but loin cloths, were found on a beach of the lonely Pacific island of Cocos today by the United States gunboat *Sacramento* after they had lived a Robinson Crusoe existence for six months.

The refugees are Paul Stachwick of Huron, S. D.; Gordon Brawner of Springfield, Ill., and Elmer J. Palliser of San Diego, Calif.

They were shipwrecked April 15, the rescue ship reported by radio. Tonight they are on their way to Balboa.

Until they were first found by a searching party from the yacht *Camargo* of Julius Fleischmann of Cincinnati, Ohio, who happened upon traces of them while cruising in that vicinity, they had lived on coconuts, fish and wild pig, they said.

The three men were sighted this afternoon by the *Sacramento,* which had been sent out from Balboa to search for them.

INDEX

321

323

Date Due

DEMCO NO. 295

NOV 29				
MAY 12				
MAR 18 '63				
JAN 3 '69 CANISIUS				
FEB 27 '74 CANISIUS				